The Rise of Advertising in the United States

A History of Innovation to 1960

Edd Applegate

THE SCARECROW PRESS, INC.
Lanham • Toronto • Plymouth, UK
2012

Published by Scarecrow Press, Inc.
A wholly owned subsidiary of The Rowman & Littlefield Publishing Group, Inc.
4501 Forbes Boulevard, Suite 200, Lanham, Maryland 20706
www.rowman.com

10 Thornbury Road, Plymouth PL6 7PP, United Kingdom

British Library Cataloguing in Publication Information Available

Library of Congress Cataloging-in-Publication Data

Applegate, Edd.
The rise of advertising in the United States : a history of innovation to 1960 / Edd Applegate.
p. cm.
Includes bibliographical references and index.
ISBN 978-0-8108-8406-9 (cloth) — ISBN 978-0-8108-8407-6 (ebook)
1. Advertising—United States—History. I. Title.
HF5813.U6A733 2012
659.10973—dc23
2012018903

ISBN 978-1-4422-4438-2

This book is for Eva, Judy, and Carolyn.

Contents

Acknowledgments

Numerous individuals at colleges and universities, advertising agencies, corporations, and organizations provided valuable resources while I was researching and writing this book.

I wish to thank the librarians at the James E. Walker Library, Middle Tennessee State University, for their assistance in obtaining specific articles and books. I wish to thank the librarians at the following libraries for their help: Felix G. Woodward Library at Austin Peay State University, Lila D. Bunch Library at Belmont University, Stephens-Burnett Memorial Library at Carson-Newman College, Charles C. Sherrod Library at East Tennessee State University, Hartzler Library at Eastern Mennonite University, Eli M. Oboler Library at Idaho State University, University Library at the University of Illinois Urbana-Champaign, The Kansas City Public Library, Library of Congress, A. R. Wentz Library at the Lutheran Theological Seminary at Gettysburg, Murray Library at Messiah College, Nashville Public Library, Pius XII Memorial Library at Saint Louis University, St. Louis Public Library, Martha M. Brown and Lois H. Daniel Memorial Library at Tennessee State University, Angelo and Jennette Volpe Library at Tennessee Technological University, Waggoner Library at Trevecca Nazarene University, Burke Theological Library at Union Theological Seminary, J. D. Williams Library at the University of Mississippi, Bizzell Memorial Library at the University of Oklahoma, Thomas Cooper Library at the University of South Carolina, Lupton Library at the University of Tennessee at Chattanooga, Health Sciences Library and Biocommunications Center at the University of Tennessee Health Science Center, John C. Hodges Main Library at the University of Tennessee–Knoxville, and the Worcester (Massachusetts) Public Library.

I wish to thank the staff at the Historical Society of Pennsylvania for providing valuable information. I wish to thank the director of the P. T. Barnum Museum, Bridgeport, Connecticut, for information about P. T. Barnum.

I wish to thank the executives of Procter & Gamble (P&G), Cincinnati, Ohio; the executives of Springs Industries, Inc. (Springs Global), Fort Mill, South Carolina; and the executives of the former N. W. Ayer & Partners advertising agency, New York, for their kind responses to my inquiries (N. W. Ayer & Partners advertising agency merged into the Kaplan Thaler Group).

Finally, I wish to thank my editor and the other wonderful people at Scarecrow Press who worked on this book.

Introduction

This book examines several fascinating individuals who were responsible for building or growing businesses, including advertising agencies, from the earliest days in the United States to the second half of the twentieth century. Each chapter focuses on one or more personalities who worked in a particular business and either employed advertising to promote the business and product or produced advertising that helped sell clients' products and services. In some instances, some of these individuals not only earned considerable fortunes but contributed greatly to advertising's development.

The first chapter discusses printers who published newspapers and magazines in the American colonies. The discussion focuses primarily on the differences among the printers, their respective newspapers or magazines, and, of course, the advertisements they accepted for publication. Several examples of these advertisements are included and discussed.

The second chapter examines three of the first advertising agents—including Volney B. Palmer, George P. Rowell, and Francis Wayland Ayer, who founded N. W. Ayer and Son—and focuses on their contributions to the development of advertising as a business.

The third chapter examines P. T. Barnum's professional career, especially the innovative contributions that he made to advertising and marketing. Barnum, a master salesman, employed outdoor advertising and promotion, among other forms, to announce his attractions. In addition, he manipulated publishers and editors of newspapers into running stories about his upcoming shows.

The fourth chapter discusses Lydia E. Pinkham, one of the first women in the United States to establish a successful business as a result of using advertising effectively. Her "Lydia E. Pinkham's Vegetable Compound" was one of the most popular patent medicines of its day. This chapter also discusses the journalistic campaign against patent medicines, including Pinkham's vegetable compound, as well as the problems that the Lydia E. Pinkham Medicine Company experienced under the guidance of Pinkham's heirs in the twentieth century.

The fifth chapter examines John Wanamaker, a retailer who learned about the American consumer a century before Sam Walton, the founder of Wal-Mart. However, few realize that in addition to being an astute businessman, Wanamaker was one of the first major department store owners to understand the power of advertising. Indeed, the advertisements that appeared in newspapers not only informed consumers about articles of clothing but guaranteed their quality. Wanamaker also advertised the policy of "money back." He was the first retailer to place a full-page newspaper advertisement in the United States. In addition to using newspapers, he advertised outdoors and on specialty items, such as pencils and balloons. Before he retired in the early twentieth century, he had built one of the largest department stores in the country.

The sixth chapter focuses on Albert Lasker and the Lord & Thomas Advertising Agency, which Lasker eventually owned. It also discusses the contributions that Lasker and the agency made to advertising.

The seventh chapter examines the first 100 years of Procter & Gamble, as well as the advertising of what eventually became its best-selling product at the time, Ivory Soap. Specifically, this chapter discusses the founding of the company by William Procter and James Gamble, as well as the development and advertising of Ivory Soap from the 1880s to the 1930s. Part of the discussion focuses on Harley Procter, who advertised successfully Ivory Soap, and William Cooper Procter, who introduced several revolutionary concepts into the daily management of the company.

The eighth chapter discusses Elliott White Springs, the owner and president of the Springs Cotton Mills, and the company's advertising campaign of the late 1940s and early 1950s. Springs developed a controversial advertising campaign based on its illustrations of scantily clad young women and the accompanying blocks of copy that contained questionable descriptive terms.

The ninth chapter examines Stanley B. Resor and his influence on the J. Walter Thompson Company (now JWT), which he headed for a half century. Resor created the first research department in an advertising agency. He encouraged his wife, Helen Lansdowne Resor, a copywriter at the agency, to write emotional copy that appealed to women.

The tenth chapter discusses the historical development of advertising as a discipline in colleges and universities from the time that the first courses were offered to the second half of the twentieth century, although emphasis is on the earlier decades. Of course, since several courses were offered by faculty members in psychology and many were offered by schools or colleges of commerce or business administration, this chapter discusses several psychology professors as well as the historical development of marketing as a discipline. In short, advertising as a discipline in institutions of higher education developed primarily in departments or schools of journalism and departments, schools, or colleges of commerce or business administration, especially in the offering marketing.

The purpose of this book is to share some insight into the lives of these individuals as well as some insight into their contributions to advertising.

Chapter One

Colonial America and Advertising

Under Charles II, England occupied the Atlantic coast of North America, from Canada to Georgia. Philadelphia, which had been founded in Pennsylvania in 1682, became the greatest river port in America. Parcels of land in Carolina became plantations farmed by slaves. The chartered colonies became Crown colonies, and governors appointed by the Crown replaced proprietors or managers. The influx of Puritans and Cavaliers increased the colonies' population. Indians eventually lost their land to others.

Boston, Newport, New York, Philadelphia, and Charleston became not only the dominant colonial settlements but marketing centers. Specific days of the week became "market days." Designated marketplaces were established on the village squares for trading activities. As a result, these five colonies controlled the economy, and each colony regulated wholesale and retail trade.[1]

Large quantities of Southern commodities could be processed and exported. Production in the North was on a smaller scale but more diversified. What was produced could be distributed to the various markets in America.[2]

Before 1700, retailing consisted of small shops owned by craftsmen who made and sold specific goods and small stores operated by colonists who would buy goods for resale. Between 1690 and 1720, in Boston, Newport, New York, Philadelphia, and Charleston, specialty shops emerged primarily because of increased urbanization and a higher standard of living. At this time, the so-called Yankee peddler roamed the country, competing against the more established merchants.[3]

Eventually, the older, more established merchants attempted to have legislation enacted that would protect their businesses. They also desired regulations that covered standards, weights, and selling practices. The Yankee peddler was an enemy to the merchant because he went to the customer and used theatrics to sell his wares. Enacted legislation was restrictive, but it actually decreased the abuse in trade practices, which was positive. The economy developed, and new marketing institutions emerged. Retailing continued to grow, and dry goods or general stores appeared in colonies.[4]

Other colonies, such as Georgia, came into existence. However, the French and Indians surrounded the colonists, and England, although it was the mother country, failed to help the colonists in their struggle to survive. Instead, laws were enacted to prohibit colonists from selling anything other than agricultural goods to England. Concurrently, whenever something was purchased, it had to come from England. Tariffs were placed on specific imports to keep the colonists from buying those products, and laws were passed to limit what could be produced, such as iron. Yet, the navigation acts strengthened the shipping industry of the Northern colonies.

To the colonists, one king or queen was as evil as the next; it made little difference whether Charles II, James II, William and Mary, Anne, George I, George II, or George III reigned. The colonists' problems remained the same, yet they had to be pleased when England won the Seven Years' War, for it captured for the British Empire what had belonged to France: Canada. Subsequently, the fear of being invaded by France was eliminated.

Various social and economic groups used and accepted credit as a substitute for exchange, primarily because coins were scarce. Credit had a stimulating effect on the welfare of the colonists because it allowed not only production but consumption on a scale that would otherwise have been impossible. However, as Benjamin Franklin and others pointed out, abuse existed.[5]

When the Crown and Parliament began to restrict American expansion as well as limit American trade, the colonists grew angry. When various acts were imposed, colonists realized that England was trying to tax them for revenue. Although repeated demonstrations forced Parliament to repeal specific acts, other measures were enacted to serve the same function as the acts. Eventually, certain writers convinced the colonists to unite and boycott British goods. In 1770 specific measures were repealed. Three years later, the Tea Act (which fostered the Boston Tea Party of the same year) and, subsequently, the "Intolerable Acts" forced the citizens of Massachusetts to arm themselves for combat. Delegates from twelve colonies attended the First Continental Congress at Philadelphia in 1774 and pledged to defend Massachusetts. The Congress also made demands on England that England would not meet. When Governor Thomas Gage, who was also commander in chief of the British army in America, was ordered to reestablish British rule, his military action initiated the War of Independence, a war that began in 1775 and ended in 1783.

America won its independence, and each colony became a state. But the central government faced many problems, including the ratification of the Constitution.

American society was basically rural and poor. Puritans as well as other colonists lived on farms; few lived in cities, although cities grew rapidly because of the influx of people from other countries. If the farmer or plantation owner visited a city, he would have to travel on roads made of mud; if he made his destination without loss of pocketbook or limb, he would find streets made of cobblestones, gravel, or, in some cases, dirt. But this was merely the beginning of an experience that he would not forget.

According to John M. Blum, Edmund S. Morgan, Willie L. Rose, Arthur M. Schlesinger Jr., Kenneth M. Stampp, and C. Vann Woodward,

> The farmer had been told that the city was a nursery of vice and prodigality. He now saw that it was so. Every shop had wares to catch his eye: exquisite fabrics, delicate chinaware, silver buckles, looking glasses, and other imported luxuries that never reached the crossroads store. Putting up at the tavern, he found himself drinking too much rum. And there were willing girls, he heard, who had lost their virtue and would be glad to help him lose his. Usually he returned to the farm to warn his children as he had been warned. He seldom understood that the vice of the city, if not its prodigality, was mainly for transients like himself. Permanent residents had work to do.[6]

Those who lived in cities were merchants who purchased or traded produce, shipwrights who constructed ships, millers, instrument makers, coopers, schoolmasters, barbers, craftsmen, and a host of others. However, those who lived in cities faced problems such as crime, filth, fires, and poverty that others did not. Many of the jobs in cities depended on overseas trade. Thus, if trade was weak, jobs disappeared. According to Blum and colleagues, "The men and women who lived by them had no place to turn. As cities grew, so did the numbers of the poor and unemployed who had to be cared for."[7]

To tame a harsh wilderness, work had to be done, and the Puritans, among others, performed remarkably well. Though they feared God, they enjoyed the vices of man, including drink and occasionally adulterous relationships. Still, the strict religious views of John Calvin dominated their lives. Predestination instilled in them a spark that ultimately ignited their will to achieve what men had not achieved before: freedom to grow strong both spiritually and economically.

Although witch hunts occurred in the 1690s and differences among Puritan, Anglican, and Quaker philosophies stirred fanatics to commit physical atrocities such as imprisonment or banishment before the eighteenth century, after 1720 religion experienced the "Great Awakening." Revivals, which were more emotional than intellectual, were held throughout the colonies for society's lower classes. From the Dutch Reformed churches of New Jersey to the Scotch-Irish Presbyterian churches of Pennsylvania, revivalism, because it made religion more personal, prospered throughout the eighteenth century.

In his autobiography, Benjamin Franklin discussed Reverend Whitefield, who had arrived from Ireland. Reverend Whitefield journeyed throughout the colonies, preaching to various congregations. Although Franklin was not easily manipulated, he explained what happened to him when he attended one of Reverend Whitefield's sermons:

> I happened soon after to attend one of his Sermons, in the Course of which I perceived he intended to finish with a Collection, and I silently resolved he should get nothing from me. I had in my Pocket a Handful of Copper, Money, three or four silver Dollars, and five Pistoles in Gold. As he proceeded I began to soften, and concluded to give the Coppers. Another Stroke of his Oratory made me asham'd of that, and determin'd me to give the Silver; and he finish'd so admirably, that I empty'd my Pocket wholly into the Collector's Dish, Gold and all.[8]

Preachers affected many colonists.

This period witnessed the founding of social, educational, and political institutions. Colleges prepared students for the ministry and enlightened them in physics, philosophy, and psychology. Literature, too, appeared. From histories and autobiographies to plays and novels, colonists enjoyed entertainment. Perhaps the most important form of entertainment was the newspaper, which was not only read but discussed at the local tavern or coffeehouse.

NEWSPAPER ADVERTISING IN THE COLONIES

The first printing presses in America arrived in the seventeenth century. Advertising appeared in pamphlet and, later, signboard forms. These forms did not appear, however, until settlements had populations to warrant their use.

Pamphlets, which became popular, explained in depth available goods and services. Signboard forms resembled in design those used in England. Generally, these signs contained symbols as well as addresses but not numbers. For example, various symbols represented tobacco shops—from the black boy and the Indian to the Smoking Dutchman. Addresses consisted of brief copy. Although these signs became popular among businesses throughout the colonies, the most colorful appeared in cities such as Philadelphia and Baltimore. Signs for taverns became the most visible.

Printing presses had been in the colonies for more than 50 years before printers used them to print newspapers. Boston had several presses, while Philadelphia and New York had at least one each. These presses printed the *Holy Bible*, the *Freeman's Oath*, almanacs, and other books. One press in

Boston printed tracts. Contrary to popular belief, most authorities in the colonies prohibited operators of printing presses from printing newspapers. In certain colonies, such as Boston, restrictions applied to religious literature.

Advertising appeared in American newspapers in the eighteenth century—from John Campbell's *Boston News-Letter*, which is considered to be America's first newspaper primarily because it continued for more than one issue, to John Dunlap's *Pennsylvania Packet and the General Advertiser*. At first, advertising occupied a few inches of space. As population, trade, and circulation increased, the publishers enlarged these newspapers and accepted more advertising. Several publishers, such as Benjamin Franklin, used white space and headlines to separate advertisements. Then they incorporated small stock cuts or illustrations in advertisements. Later, they used column rules to separate advertisements. Some used different typefaces and type sizes to separate advertisements. They also published display advertisements that filled several columns. By 1800, most, if not all, publishers of newspapers accepted advertising. In fact, some publishers accepted advertising supplements in which advertisements filled separate sections.

Benjamin Harris: *Publick Occurrences, Both Forreign and Domestick*

Benjamin Harris was a printer in London who published religious tracts for the Anabaptists, a group that opposed Roman Catholicism and the Church of England. He also published a newspaper and "supported the Earl of Shaftesbury and the Whig parliament in their opposition to exclude the Duke of York (James II), Charles's Catholic brother, from succession to the throne."[9] Primarily because of his eagerness to publish religious and political tracts as well as articles that were seen as controversial and seditious by those wielding power, Harris was arrested three times. Perhaps realizing that everything he published would be scrutinized by the authorities, he set sail for America in 1686.

Arriving in Boston, he and his son opened a coffeehouse that also sold books. Soon Harris became involved in printing almanacs and *The New-England Primer*, a collection of prayers and verses. However, he realized that Boston was large enough to support a newspaper. On September 25, 1690, he published the first newspaper in the American colonies. Titled *Publick Occurrences, Both Forreign and Domestick*, it was printed by Richard Pierce.

Publick Occurrences, Both Forreign and Domestick differed from its broadside predecessors in the sense that it focused on American, not European, news. Indeed, several brief stories concerned the following: Christianized Indians planning a day of Thanksgiving, two children being abducted by Indians, the suicide of a widower, and the smallpox epidemic in Boston. A longer story concerned a confrontation by the militia of Massachusetts and the lack of cooperation by its Mohawk Indian allies against the French in Canada. The only European story concerned Louis XIV, the King of France, who had seduced his son's wife. According to the story, Louis XIV's son had revolted against him as a result.[10]

Charles E. Clark wrote, "Harris intended primarily to save Bostonians during an exceptionally critical time from rumors and 'False Reports' of the events and affairs, especially the martial affairs, of their own province."[11]

Although the authorities declared the paper a "pamphlet," they prohibited Harris from publishing another issue. Had it not been for the authorities, the newspaper in the New World would have succeeded sooner, and advertising would have found a new medium. Unfortunately, Harris did not have time to improve his newspaper by adding advertising. Although he did not publish another newspaper, he published other material. In fact, in 1692 he became the official printer for Massachusetts. A few years later, he returned to London, where he published newspapers and other material.

John Campbell: *Boston News-Letter*

John Campbell emigrated from Scotland in the 1690s. Settling in Boston, he became friends with several important politicians, including Governor Fitz John Winthrop of Connecticut. Campbell became a constable in the late 1690s, then, after his brother died, was appointed postmaster for Massachusetts. As postmaster, Campbell wrote letters about current affairs, including news that he had obtained from newspapers that had been brought to Boston by sea captains. His newsletters grew in popularity.

In the early eighteenth century, using his position and his friends, Campbell eventually asked the authorities for permission to publish a newspaper. Permission was granted. The *Boston News-Letter*, dated "From Monday April 17 to Monday April 24, 1704," contained the following information:

Advertisement

This News-Letter is to be continued Weekly; and all Persons who have any Houses, Lands, Tenements, Farms, Ships, Vessels, Goods, Wares or Merchandizes, &c. to be Sold, or Let; or Servants Run-away, or Goods Stole or Lost; may have the same inserted at a Reasonable Rate, from *Twelve* Pence to *Five Shillings*, and not to exceed: Who may agree with *John Campbell* Postmaster of *Boston*.

All Persons in Town and Country may have said News-Letter every Week, Yearly, upon reasonable terms, agreeing with *John Campbell*, Post-master for the same.[12]

The *News-Letter*, printed on a sheet of 8 x 12-inch paper, contained two columns of copy on the front and back. Rough in appearance, the *News-Letter* contained news from newspapers published in London, as well as news about Boston. Often, the news was out-of-date. Campbell's writing style, unlike that of Benjamin Harris, was dull and inferior. The advertising received a maximum space of 20 lines by the publisher. The cost per agate line was about 1 1/2 cents.

The third *News-Letter*, dated May 1–8, 1704, contained the first paid advertisements. Although Campbell had published three advertisements, together they occupied only four inches of space in one column. The only headline that separated them from the news was the word "advertisements." Two advertised rewards for the capture of thieves. One read,

> Lost on 10th of April last off Mr. Shippen's Wharf in Boston, Two Iron Anvils, weighing between 120–140 pounds each; Whoever has taken them up, and will bring or give true intelligence of them to John Campbell, Postmaster, shall have a sufficient reward. [13]

The third advertised real estate—the first real estate advertisement to appear in an American newspaper:

> At Oysterbay, on *Long Island* in the Province of *N. York*, There is a very good Fulling-Mill, to be Let or Sold, as also a Plantation, having on it a large new Brick house, and another good house by it for a Kitchen & work house, with a Barn, Stable &c. a young Orchard, and 20 acres clear Land. The Mill is to be Let with or without the Plantation: Enquire of Mr. *William Bradford* Printer in *N. York*, and know further. [14]

As Campbell's *News-Letter* continued, other kinds of advertising appeared. In the May 15–22, 1704, issue, an advertisement targeted men who desired to sail:

> CAPTAIN Peter Lawrence is going a Privateering from Rhode Island in a good Sloop, about 60 Tons, six Guns, and 90 men for Canada, and any Gentlemen or Sailors that are disposed to go shall be kindly entertained. [15]

Advertisements for slaves appeared frequently, as the following example illustrates: "A NEGRO Woman about 16 years Old, to be sold by John Campbell, Postmaster, to be seen at his House, next door to the Anchor Tavern." [16]

The first advertisement for a store appeared in the August 21, 1704, issue: "AT Mr. *John Miro* Merchant, his Warehouse upon the Dock in Boston, There is to be Sold good Cordage of all sizes, from a Spurn-yarn to Cables of 13 inches, by whole-sail or Retail." [17]

Campbell restricted the amount of advertising in his paper; even after three years, five inches devoted to advertising was rare. Some issues contained no advertising whatsoever. As a result, Campbell earned very little from the paper. Indeed, he wrote occasional articles that pleaded with subscribers to pay for their subscriptions.

Campbell lost his postmaster's position when William Brooker became postmaster. Brooker assumed that the paper was part of the postmaster's job, but Campbell refused to surrender it to him. Brooker refused to allow Campbell use of the mail to send the paper to subscribers. The two bickered until Brooker decided to start another paper. The *Boston Gazette* appeared on December 21, 1719.[18] The next day, in Philadelphia, Andrew Bradford published the *American Weekly Mercury*. Both newspapers were similar to the *News-Letter* in size and typography. Even the advertisements were similar, except that Brooker employed brief headlines that actually identified what the various advertisements concerned.

Campbell kept the *Boston News-Letter*, although he could not use the mail to send it to subscribers. In 1722 he sold the paper to Bartholomew Green, a printer. The paper changed hands in 1733, when John Draper became the publisher. Draper turned it over to his son Richard in 1762. When Richard died in 1774, Margaret Draper, his widow, in partnership with others, published the paper for another two years.

The *Boston News-Letter*'s circulation increased over the years. As a result, John Draper increased the paper's content—from two pages to four. He also accepted more advertisements. As Sidney Kobre wrote, "By 1750, a column of advertising appeared regularly, two columns frequently. Occasionally, three columns of advertisements were published. The *News-Letter* had become a more stable business enterprise by the mid-century. It had advanced far from the puny sheet with two pages which Campbell first issued in 1704."[19]

Benjamin Franklin: *Pennsylvania Gazette*

Benjamin Franklin was born in 1706 in Boston. His father, Josiah Franklin, had seven children with his first wife and ten, including Benjamin, with his second wife. Although Benjamin was sent to school, he failed arithmetic. He was persuaded by his father to work with him boiling soap. Desiring more from life, Benjamin grew bored. He became an avid reader and learned about the world, which he eventually desired to see. However, his father persuaded him to become an apprentice in his older brother James's printing business.

In 1721 James Franklin published the *New England Courant* in Boston. However, he was too much like Benjamin Harris in the sense that he questioned authority. When he published controversial political essays, he was sent to jail. Benjamin, a mere teenager, had contributed numerous articles signed by "Silence Dogood" to the paper. Now, he served as editor in his brother's absence. Benjamin Franklin wrote,

During my Brother's Confinement, which I resented a good deal, notwithstanding our private Differences, I had the Management of the Paper, and I made bold to give our Rulers some Rubs in it, which my Brother took very kindly, while others began to consider me in an unfavourable Light, as a young Genius that had a Turn for Libelling & Satyr. [20]

Franklin printed the word "advertisements" in bold capital letters and separated it from the copy. The word undoubtedly attracted attention. Franklin's editorship ended two years later, however, and he sailed to New York, where he met William Bradford, a printer, who informed him that his son Andrew, who owned a print shop in Philadelphia, may have a position. Franklin traveled to Philadelphia. Unfortunately, Andrew Bradford did not have a position.

Franklin met Samuel Keimer, another printer in Philadelphia, and Keimer hired him. Within a few months, however, he returned to Boston, then sailed to London in 1724, where he found a job in a print shop. Within two years, he returned to Philadelphia and, eventually, to Keimer's print shop. His relationship with Keimer deteriorated, and he left in 1728.

He and Hugh Meredith, a friend, eventually opened a print shop. Franklin desired to publish a newspaper that would compete against Andrew Bradford's *American Weekly Mercury*. Keimer learned about this and published the *Universal Instructor in All the Arts and Sciences and Pennsylvania Gazette*, a newspaper that was not necessarily successful. Within a few months, Franklin, with the help of Hugh Meredith, purchased the paper. Immediately, Franklin shortened the name to *Pennsylvania Gazette* and improved the writing and typography. Within several months, most readers considered the *Gazette* the most attractive newspaper in the colonies.

Franklin considered advertising important for the *Gazette*. In the September 25–October 2, 1729, issue, he printed the word "Advertisements" in bold letters, then left about a half inch of white space. The issue contained nine advertisements. The first letter of the first word of each advertisement was capitalized. In addition, each advertisement had at least a half inch of white space above and below it. One of the advertisements was for soap: "To be Sold by *Edward Shippen*, choice Hard Soap, very Reasonable." [21]

In the same issue, Franklin advertised that he printed the following:

BIBLES, Testaments, Psalters, Psalm-Books, Accompt-Books, Bills of Lading Bound and unbound, Common Blank Bonds for Money, Bonds with Judgment, Counterbonds, Arbitration Bonds, Arbitration Bonds with Umpirage, Bail Bonds, Counterbonds to save Bail harmless, Bills of Sale, Powers of Attorney, Writs, Summons, Apprentices Indentures, Servants Indentures, Penal Bills, Promisory Notes, &c, all the Blanks in the most authentick Forms, and correctly printed; may be had at the Publishers of this Paper; who perform all other Sorts of Printing at reasonable Rates. [22]

Franklin increased the number of pages from two to four so that he could handle more advertisements and news stories. He separated each advertisement with white space. He used at least a fourteen–point heading for each advertisement. Later, he incorporated small stock cuts or illustrations. In the May 23–30, 1734, issue, for instance, he employed a stock cut of a ship for the *Three Batchelors*, which had docked. The advertisement informed merchants that the ship accepted freight. Franklin realized that illustrations could enhance an advertisement, so he used half-column and column cuts made especially for specific advertisers. By merely the illustration, readers could determine for whom or what the advertisement was. For instance, a cut of a clock face was employed to identify a watchmaker's advertisement. Retailers who normally stayed away from advertising in newspapers realized they could increase sales by advertising in Franklin's newspaper. As a result, Franklin had to enlarge his newspaper again. Instead of two short columns, he put in three deep columns, which made the newspaper about the size of a modern tabloid.

In the *Pennsylvania Gazette*'s August 14–21, 1735, issue, Franklin advertised the following product, which he sold: "VERY good COFFEE Sold by the Printer hereof."[23]

Franklin, like other printers of newspapers, published advertisements for sale of slaves. In the June 23–30, 1737, issue, for instance, the following advertisement appeared. It attracted attention not because of what was being sold but because Franklin italicized most of the copy:

A Fine young Negro Fellow Speaks English, us'd to Labour, and is fit for either Town or Country, to be Sold by James Efdaile *at Mr.* Dering's *in* Front-Street, *or at his Store on* Carpenter's *Wharff, where is also to be sold, good* St. Kitts *Mellasses, Ginger & Indigo.*[24]

In the same issue, Franklin advertised that his wife's prayer book had been stolen from the church. The advertisement is typical in the sense that almost every printer who published a newspaper included advertisements about personal items lost or stolen: "TAKEN out of a Pew in the Church some Months since, a Common Prayer Book, bound in Red, gilt, and letter'd DF on each Corner. The Person who took it, is desir'd to open it and read the *Eighth* Commandment, and afterwards return it into the same Pew again; upon which no further Notice will be taken."[25]

In the same issue, Franklin advertised that he was selling a black woman:

TO BE SOLD

A LIKELY young breeding Negroe Woman, speaks good English, understands her Needle and any sort of Household Work, and has had the Small-Pox. Enquire of the Printer.[26]

In the January 18–25, 1738–1739, issue, Franklin advertised *Poor Richard's Almanac*, which he wrote and published:

Just Published,

POOR RICHARD's ALMANACKS, for the Year 1739. Wherein is contained the Lunations, Eclipses, Judgments of the Weather, Spring-Tides, Planets Motions, and mutual Aspects, Sun and Moon's Rising and Setting, Length of Days, Time of High Water, Fairs, Courts and observable Days. Together with many witty Hints, Sayings, Verses, and Observations, as usual, viz. The Art of Foretelling the Weather. Why he continues to call himself *Poor Richard*. Teague's Criticism on the First of *Genesis*. Giles Jolt's Syllogism. John's Wife. Kings and Bears. Miss Cloe's Café. Squire Edward's Kindness. The Knave in Grain. Codrus and Caesar. Bright Florella. The ninth Beatitude. On his late Deafness. An infallible Cure for the Toothach. George's fine Fruit-bearing Tree. Lower County Teeth. The Emblem of a Friend. Modern Faith, Pinchall's Temperance, A———'s Wit. Life a Journey. Homer's Fate. Sam's Lawsuit, &c, &c, &c.

To which is added,

A most true and unerring PROGNOSTICATION for the Year 1739, relating to the Condition of these Northern Colonies, The Diseases the People will be subject to, and the Quantity of the Fruits of the Earth.
    Sold by *B. Franklin*, Price 3 s. 6 d. per Dozen.[27]

It should be mentioned that Franklin was not the only printer who published an almanac. Several printers who published newspapers also published almanacs.

In the February 15–22, 1738–1739 issue, the following advertisement, which was typical of small merchants, appeared:

TO BE SOLD

By PETER DELAGE, *over-against* Mr. James Steele's, *in* Second-Street, Philadelphia:
    CHOICE Double-and Single-refin'd Loaf-Sugar, Muſcovado Sugar fit for Shop or Family Use, Sugar-Candy, Mollasses, Bohen and Imperial TEAS, all at the cheapest Rates.[28]

In the June 17, 1742, issue, another small merchant advertised the following:

Lately imported from London, And to be SOLD by Joseph Saunders, At his House next to Joe Goodson's, in Chesnut-Street, Philadelphia, the following GOODS, viz.
    FINE London Shalloons, Horse Hair and fine mohair Buttons, silk and hair Twist, fine Durettees, sewing Silk and Threads, figured Dimities and Fuſtians, Mens and Womens worsted and thread Hose, shammery and sundry other sorts

of Gloves, Hat Linings, scotch Handkerchiefs, Womens Clogs and Childrens Shoes, sundry sorts of Shoemaker's Tools, cutlery and hard Ware, Weston's Snuff, fine writing Paper, with sundry other Goods.
Also good West-India RUM.[29]

Franklin's newspaper contained advertisements about numerous products and services, including glasses, wine, cheese, chocolate, mathematical instruments, codfish, tea, coffee, and stoves. No other printer of that time did more for advertising. Without question, advertising in America owes a great debt to Franklin.[30]

In addition to publishing a newspaper and selling various products, including books, Franklin trained others, such as Thomas Whitemarsh, in his print shop, then sent these individuals into various colonies to establish newspapers. Whitemarsh, for instance, went to South Carolina and established the *South Carolina Gazette* in 1732. Franklin provided financial assistance to these printers and in turn received part of their profits. In his advice to younger Americans who desired to become successful, Franklin wrote:

Remember that Money is of a prolific generating Nature. Money can beget Money, and its Offspring can beget more, and so on. Five Shillings turn'd, is *Six*: Turn'd again, 'tis Seven and Three Pence; and so on 'til it becomes an Hundred Pound. The more there is of it, the more it produces every Turning, so that the Profits rise quicker and quicker. He that kills a breeding Sow, destroys all her Offspring to the thousandth Generation. He that murders a Crown, destroys all it might have produc'd, even Scores of Pounds.[31]

This excerpt exemplified Franklin's philosophy toward business and money. Like other successful entrepreneurs of his day, Franklin was richly rewarded for his untiring labors. In 1748 he sold his printing business to David Hall, his associate, primarily because he now had other interests, including science.

William Bradford: *New-York Gazette*

Bradford was born in England in 1663 and became an apprentice in Andrew Sowle's print shop. A Quaker, Sowle taught Bradford well. Bradford married Sowle's daughter Elizabeth and, having met George Fox, who founded the Quakers, sailed to the colonies. He settled in Pennsylvania, which was governed by William Penn.

Bradford established the first print shop in Philadelphia in 1685. His first publication was an almanac by Samuel Atkins, which received criticism from the governor because it referred to him as "Lord Penn." The Provincial Council informed Bradford that he was not to print anything unless he had a license from the council. A year or two later, he clashed with the authorities again and was ordered not to print anything about Quakers unless he had their permission. Two years later, he angered John Blackwell, the new governor of Pennsylvania, when he printed William Penn's charter for Pennsylvania. He acknowledged that he had not necessarily obtained permission to print the document; however, the document had been printed in England. Bradford clashed with the authorities several years later when he printed a pamphlet by George Keith, which the Quaker authorities found objectionable and even seditious. Bradford was arrested and jailed. The authorities seized his printing press. Bradford defended himself during the trial, and the jury grew divided. Eventually, Bradford was released and his printing press restored. However, he had grown tired of being harassed by the authorities.[32]

He left Philadelphia in 1693, when he was offered the position of official printer for New York. Bradford brought his son Andrew into his print shop and taught the craft to him. Then he helped Andrew become established as a printer in Philadelphia in 1712. Bradford printed books, religious tracts, and government documents for New York. He printed documents for other colonies as well.

He started the *New York Gazette* in 1725, which contained factual accounts about the colonies and information borrowed from newspapers published in London. Occasionally, he would include an essay and a letter to the editor.

In 1728 Bradford purchased a paper mill in Elizabethtown, New Jersey. Earlier, in 1690, he had purchased interest in a paper mill in Pennsylvania. As a result, no longer was he or his son dependent on paper from England.

In 1736 Bradford attacked John Peter Zenger, a former apprentice who had started the *New York Weekly Journal*, a rival newspaper, and who had printed opposing points of view toward the authorities. Zenger had accused Bradford's newspaper of being nothing more than a mouthpiece for the governor. Basically, Bradford claimed that Zenger had been incorrect in his accusations. Indeed, Bradford claimed that he had never submitted his newspaper to the governor prior to printing. Yet, Bradford's paper had never included an article that had been so controversial as to anger the authorities.[33]

In the October 3–10, 1737, issue, Bradford published the following advertisement, which concerned a stay maker who had arrived from London:

> *Moses Slaughter*, Stay-Maker, from *London*, has brought with him a Parcel of extraordinary good and Fashionable Stays, of his own making, of several Sizes and Prices. The Work of them he will warrant to be good, and for Shape, inferiour to none that are made.
>
> He lodges at present at the House of *William Bradford*, next Door but one to the Treasurer's, near the Fly-Market, where he is ready to suit those that want, with extraordinary good Stays. Or he is ready to wait upon any Ladys or Gentlewomen that please to send for him to their Houses. If any desire to be

informed of the Work he has done, let them equire of Mrs. *Elliston* in the
Broad-Street, or of Mrs. *Nichols* in the *broadway*, who have had of his
Work. [34]

Whether Moses Slaughter paid for the advertisement is unknown. Whether
he paid for his room at William Bradford's residence or was his indentured
servant is also unknown.

Bradford also published advertisements for wine, tea, nails, steel, and a
host of other products. For instance, in the September 26–October 3, 1737,
issue, the following advertisement appeared: "Choice Good Canary Wine to
be Sold at *Three Shillings and six Pence per Gallon*, by the Five Gallons, at
the Widow *Desbrosses* in Hannover-Square." [35]

Bradford, like Franklin and other printers, sold various products, includ-
ing almanacs, as the following advertisement illustrates: "TITAN LEED's
Almanacks, and W. BIRKET's Almanacks for the year 1738, are now
Printed & Sold by *W. Bradford*." [36]

Bradford continued to print his newspaper until 1743, when he sold it to
James Parker. Bradford's paper was similar to the pattern set by Campbell's
Boston News-Letter. He failed to add anything new as far as layout or overall
design. Like Campbell, he pleaded with subscribers to pay for their subscriptions.

John Peter Zenger: *New-York Weekly Journal*

Born in the Rhenish Palatinate in 1697, John Peter Zenger immigrated to the
colonies with his family in 1710. Settling in New York, he became an apprentice in William Bradford's print shop. Marrying Mary White in 1719, he
left Bradford and moved to Maryland. Within two years, his wife died,
leaving him with a son to support. He returned to New York, where he
married Anna Maulin in 1722.

Zenger worked briefly for Bradford before he opened a print shop in
1726. Although he published books, religious tracts, and a few government
treatises, he earned very little. However, he learned about the struggle between Lewis Morris and Stephen De Lancey, both of whom were embroiled
in politics. Later, he learned about the clash between Rip Van Dam, the
president of the Provincial Council, and William Cosby, the new governor.
Although Van Dam had been acting as governor until Cosby arrived, Cosby
demanded that Van Dam return the salary he had been given. Van Dam
refused. Cosby decided to sue in the Provincial Supreme Court. However,
Lewis Morris, the Chief Justice of the Supreme Court, refused the case.
Cosby removed Morris from the Supreme Court and appointed James De
Lancey, Stephen De Lancey's son.

Those who opposed Cosby realized that Bradford, the official printer for New York, would not necessarily print their views. Consequently, they chose Zenger, a struggling printer who needed their business. Zenger published the first issue of the *New York Weekly Journal* on November 5, 1733. Primarily because of its editorial content, the newspaper became popular. Cosby's administration was criticized and ridiculed. In addition, Zenger printed a pamphlet that listed thirty-four charges against Cosby. The war of words between the two sides continued in print. Although Cosby did not know who the writers were, because they employed pseudonyms, he tried several times to have the printer charged with libel. He was not successful. However, the Provincial Council brought action against Zenger, and he was arrested. A trial by jury was scheduled, and contrary to the authorities, Zenger was found innocent. His lawyer, Andrew Hamilton, orchestrated a masterful defense, and Zenger's verdict triggered the dawn of liberty that "revolutionized America."[37]

Zenger's newspaper was superior to Bradford's. The *Journal* contained eight to ten advertisements, while the *Gazette* contained two. In addition, Zenger used column rules to separate advertisements, and he did not restrict advertising to a particular amount of space. One advertisement, for instance, was more than a half-page deep. Like Franklin, Zenger realized the importance of illustrations and used various cuts to improve the appearance of certain advertisements.

In the March 29, 1736, issue, Zenger published an advertisement about a cosmetic:

> At Mrs. Edwards next door to Mr. Jamison, opposite the Fort Garden, an admirable Beautifying Wash for Hands, Face and Neck, it makes the Skin soft, smooth and plump, it likewise takes away Redness, Freckles, Sun-Burning, or Pimples, and cures Postules, Itchings, Ring Worms, Tetters, Scurf, Morphew and other like Deformities of the Face and Skin (Intirely free from any Corroding Quality) and brings out an exquisite Beauty, with lip Salve and Tooth Powder, all sold very cheap.[38]

Zenger charged three shillings for the first insertion of an advertisement and one shilling for each insertion thereafter. Although a few printers such as Zenger published rates for advertisements, most did not, because they engaged in bartering. Often, individuals could not afford to pay for the advertisements they placed with printers; thus, they bartered with products and services.

Zenger became the official printer for New York in 1737 and the official printer for New Jersey a year later. He continued printing the paper until his death in 1746, after which his wife published it.

James Parker: *New-York Post-Boy*

James Parker was born in Woodbridge, New Jersey, in 1714. After his father, Samuel Parker, died, he became an apprentice in William Bradford's print shop in New York. Parker learned the craft and eventually left New York for Philadelphia, where he met Benjamin Franklin. Franklin hired Parker. Later, in 1742, he helped him become established as a printer in New York.

Almost a year later, Parker became the official printer for New York and started the *New-York Weekly Post-Boy*, a newspaper. When Bradford tired of printing his *New-York Gazette*, Parker renamed his paper the *New-York Gazette, Revived in the Weekly Post-Boy*. Parker's newspaper was conservative in size. However, within several years, it had become one of the most innovative papers in the colonies. The paper's size grew over time, and Parker changed the name to the *New-York Gazette; or, The Weekly Post-Boy*. The newspaper lived until 1773.

Advertisements in Parker's paper occupied as many as six columns, or half the paper. Advertisements concerned real estate, slaves, runaway apprentices, books, wines, medicines, and lotteries. Headlines appeared in all capital letters of ten-point, sometimes fourteen- or eighteen-point type.

By 1760, type sizes and typefaces varied within most advertisements. Headlines were at least eighteen-point. Display advertisements filled the columns. The newspaper became so successful among advertisers that advertisements filled three of the four pages. The October 30, 1760, issue's front page contained fifteen advertisements in its three columns. Franklin's paper had come close, but Parker's paper was probably the first in the American colonies to devote the entire front page to advertising.

Parker expanded by opening a print shop in New Jersey. He hired apprentices and, like his mentor, Benjamin Franklin, formed partnerships with printers. In addition to printing a newspaper in New York, his print shops printed books, religious tracts, and government documents. He opened a print shop in Connecticut and printed material for Yale College (Yale University). In 1755 he and John Holt, a partner, started the *Connecticut Gazette*, the first newspaper in New Haven. Like the paper in New York, the *Connecticut Gazette* contained news about the colonies, shipping, and numerous advertisements about foreign goods.

Parker also printed several magazines in the 1750s that ceased publication after several issues. Although Parker's businesses were successful, he was arrested in 1756 for printing an article that was indirectly critical of the authorities in New York. He was released after paying a fine.

Within two years, he became the official printer for New Jersey. His print shop printed religious tracts, government documents, almanacs, and numerous books of fiction and nonfiction. Eventually, he and his partners dissolved their business relationships primarily because the partners, like Holt, desired to have their own businesses. For instance, Holt became the sole printer of the *New-York Gazette; or, The Weekly Post-Boy*.

In 1765 Parker printed the *Constitutional Courant*, which protested the Stamp Act. Parker used a pseudonym so that the authorities could not necessarily identify him as the publisher. Although he had been appointed to several political posts over the years, he resented government interference and government taxation. In 1769 he printed a political tract that the authorities claimed was seditious. The authorities charged Parker with libel. He died before the trial, however, and his life was celebrated by fellow patriots.[39]

John Dunlap: *Pennsylvania Packet, or the General Advertiser*

Born in Ireland in 1747, John Dunlap arrived in Philadelphia in 1757 primarily to serve as an apprentice in William Dunlap's print shop. William, John's uncle, had become the postmaster in Philadelphia. However, William desired to study to become an Anglican priest, so in 1766, he left his print shop in his nephew's hands.

Like the overall population, the number of printers had increased. As a result, John Dunlap struggled. Printing religious tracts, political pamphlets, and books, among other material, allowed him to purchase the shop from his uncle. In 1771 he started the *Pennsylvania Packet, or the General Advertiser*, a newspaper. Initially, Dunlap was conservative in the sense that he printed few controversial articles in the newspaper. However, as more newspapers were founded for political causes in Philadelphia, he realized that to compete he had to print more controversial articles. He also became well known to members of Philadelphia's prominent families.

During the Revolutionary War, he served as a soldier at the battles of Princeton and Trenton. In addition, he served the government by printing the first copy of the Declaration of Independence. However, when the British army approached Philadelphia in 1777, he had to move his printing press to Lancaster, Pennsylvania, to publish his newspaper. When the British left Philadelphia a year later, he returned with his printing press to Philadelphia.

In addition to printing his paper, he printed journals for Congress until it claimed that Dunlap's charges were excessive. Although Congress found another printer, Dunlap continued to print government documents for Pennsylvania. He also purchased thousands of acres of land. He financially supported James Hayes Jr., who started the *Virginia Gazette, or the American Advertiser* in Richmond in 1781. He partnered with David Chambers Claypoole in publishing the *Pennsylvania Packet, or the General Advertiser* during this time as well. In 1784 the newspaper became a daily. The publishers changed the name to the *Pennsylvania Packet and Daily Advertiser*. The newspaper printed the U.S. Constitution in 1787. When Dunlap died in 1812, he had earned a fortune from his print shops and his investments in land.

The *Pennsylvania Packet, or the General Advertiser* illustrated how advertising could help sell newspapers. It is obvious that Dunlap learned from Franklin. He realized the importance of how an advertisement should look. As a result, the advertisements in his paper were easier to read and attracted reader interest. Dunlap's newspaper featured commercial news, too, rather than political stories. Commercial news attracted merchants. Thus, he was able to attract those who needed to advertise. He revived the illustration, and special cuts were created for specific advertisers. Of course, that the word "advertiser" was part of the newspaper's name helped. Within two years, Dunlap's newspaper was so successful that he had to enlarge its size and increase its columns. At the time, advertising accounted for two-thirds of the paper's content. In 1784 the newspaper, which had started as a weekly, became the first successful daily to be published in America. The reason was not readers' hunger for news; rather, it was the amount of advertising Dunlap received.[40]

Francis Childs: *New-York Daily Advertiser*

Another daily appeared a year later, in 1785. Published in New York by Francis Childs, the *New-York Daily Advertiser* contributed to advertising by employing headlines as large as thirty-six points. These headlines, usually one word, appeared in bold print to attract attention.

Born in 1763 to impoverished parents in Philadelphia, Childs had served as an apprentice in John Dunlap's print shop. He had become friends with John Jay, who had known several prominent people, including Benjamin Franklin. Encouraged by Jay, Childs had corresponded with Franklin about becoming a partner in a print shop. Eventually, by providing a press and equipment, Franklin had helped Childs become an established printer in New York.

Starting in 1785, Childs published the *New-York Daily Advertiser*, a newspaper that focused primarily on news about business, which appealed to advertisers. News items included travel schedules for ships and stagecoaches as well as prices for various commodities. In addition, Childs included news stories about politics that he borrowed from papers in Boston and other cities. He published articles that criticized government and included attacks made by politicians toward their enemies. These attacks were paid for by the politicians. Franklin was appalled when he learned about this practice. He even addressed the controversial issue in his autobiography.[41] The paper was filled with advertisements. Indeed, advertisements often filled the entire front page as well as another page or two and contained illustrations and other elements of persuasion.

The relationship between Childs and Franklin became strained when Childs would not pay Franklin what he owed. Unfortunately, Franklin died before Childs could pay anything toward the debt.

In 1789 Childs formed another partnership with John Swaine, a printer. However, this partnership did not last. In 1796 he turned the newspaper over to John Morton. Childs became a politician.[42]

General Comments

Certain publishers in the late eighteenth century filled the front pages of their newspapers with advertisements in an attempt to attract merchants. According to Sidney Kobre,

> The press . . . helped to promote the commerce and prosperity of the new Americans. Through its news columns, its lists of ships clearing and entering, its notes about the West Indies, the colonial newspaper acquainted merchants, shippers and others with facts and information pertinent and valuable to their business.[43]

Kobre noted that colonial printers of newspapers catered to the merchants, farmers, shippers, and fishermen because they depended on them for advertising and subscriptions. Kobre wrote that "the colonial newspaper kept pace with the prosperity of these groups."[44]

According to Ronald Hoffman, "The merchant employed the newspaper as a retailing agent. Advertising was needed by certain merchants because it served as a means of communication between the seller and the buyer."[45]

Other publishers included advertising supplements in which advertisements filled separate sections. Also, numerous publishers accepted countless advertisements of lotteries. In most instances, these lotteries were conducted to raise money to improve towns or cities. Other lotteries benefited college libraries or churches.[46]

Although most newspapers at this time depended on advertising revenue and street sales, some newspapers were privately supported by political figures for the purpose of spreading political propaganda.

In 1765, primarily because there was a shortage of paper in the colonies, display advertising was cut from several newspapers. For instance, instead of large type and illustrations, small type and thumbnail-size art filled the advertising columns in the *Pennsylvania Gazette*.

According to Isaiah Thomas, there were thirty-seven newspapers in America when the Revolutionary War started in 1775.[47] William A. Dill, however, claimed that there were forty-eight newspapers being published in

1775.[48] It does not necessarily matter whether Thomas or Dill is correct. What matters is that both indicated that the number of printers, like the population, increased. The number of advertisements appearing in newspapers also increased. Indeed, advertisements filled more than a page in specific newspapers before 1775.

By 1800, the number of newspapers published in the United States was about three hundred. Most publishers were satisfied with their advertising. Few actually worried about how advertisements appeared. Thus, advertising remained constant in appearance for numerous years. In most cases, no more than one cut illustrated each advertisement. The copy was dull and usually small in size. The reason that advertising remained popular among businesses is simple: populations of cities increased. Consequently, proprietors realized that prospective customers were moving close to their enterprises every day; thus, these prospective customers had to be informed.

The early newspaper advertisements reflected early American culture. Painters of portraits and houses advertised their services in practically every newspaper that was published along the Atlantic coast. Booksellers, too, advertised, especially those in Boston, which had more booksellers than any other city at the time. Entertaining shows and unusual artists traveled from one colony to another and advertised in various newspapers. Artisans and craftsmen advertised their wares, including various pieces of furniture, such as the "Hadley" chest and the popular "Windsor" chair, which they carved. Theaters, the first of which had been built before 1720, became somewhat popular before 1750, and colonists enjoyed watching plays and other forms of theatrical entertainment. Such, of course, was advertised in newspapers.[49]

As James Playsted Wood wrote,

> Colonial newspaper advertising was informed by briskness and vitality. It spoke not only of the busyness of small enterprise, the practical considerations of merchants and the purveyors of services, but also of the feelings, beliefs, and prejudices of people in New England and the Middle Colonies. The devious ways of free publicity had not yet been perfected. Men announced their attitudes and opinions in paid advertising. Public relations had not yet taught the importance of moving softly. These advertisers said what they meant and meant what they said.[50]

COLONIAL MAGAZINE ADVERTISING

Magazines lived briefly in the eighteenth century. Numerous advertisers refused to place advertisements with this medium. No merchant wished to advertise in a magazine that had financial problems, and most magazines had financial problems because advertisers had this attitude. Thus, advertising in magazines was sporadic. Or, if a printer did not solicit advertisements for a magazine, he soon suffered financially because of expenses. Nonetheless, Benjamin Franklin, Andrew Bradford, and others thought that such periodicals were needed and proceeded to publish several titles.

Benjamin Franklin Versus Andrew Bradford

Andrew Bradford was born in Philadelphia, the oldest son of William Bradford. He moved with his father to New York, where he learned about printing in his father's shop. In 1712, with his father's encouragement, he returned to Philadelphia to become a successful printer. Bradford printed religious tracts for the Quakers as well as documents for the government. In addition, he printed almanacs, books, and pamphlets on various subjects. He sold merchandise, like other printers, in his print shop and invested in other businesses, including real estate. In 1719 he started the *American Weekly Mercury*, a newspaper that enjoyed a large circulation and numerous advertisers. Bradford served as the postmaster in Philadelphia for years.

Benjamin Franklin was one of the first printers to plan a magazine for the colonies. He inserted an advertisement about his magazine in the November 13, 1740, issue of the *Pennsylvania Gazette:*

In January *next will be published,*
(To be continued Monthly)
The General Magazine,
AND
Historical Chronicle,
For all the *British* Plantations in *America:*
CONTAINING,
I. Extracts from the Votes, and Debates of the Parliament of *Great Britain.*
II. The Proclamations and Speeches of Governors; Addresses, Votes, Resolutions, &c. of Assemblies, in each Colony.
III. Accounts of, and Extracts from, all new Books, Pamphlets, &c. published in the Plantations.
IV. Essays, controversial, humorous, philosophical, religious, moral or political.
V. Select Pieces of Poetry.
VI. A concise CHRONICLE of the most remarkable Transactions, as well as in *Europe* as *America.*
VII. Births, Marriages, Deaths, and Promotions, of eminent Persons in the several Colonies.
VIII. Course of Exchange between the several Colonies, and *London*; Prices of Goods, &c.
This MAGAZINE, in Imitation of those in *England*, was long since projected; a Correspondence is settled with Intelligent Men in most of the Colonies, and small Types are procured, for carrying it on in the best Manner. It would not, indeed, have been published quite so soon, were it not that a

Person, to whom the Scheme was communicated *in Confidence*, has thought
fit to advertise it in the last *Mercury*, without our Participation; and, probably,
with a View, by Starting before us, to discourage us from prosecuting our first
Design, and reap the Advantage of it wholly to himself. We shall endeavour,
however, by executing our Plan with Care, Diligence and Impartiality, and by
Printing the Work neatly and correctly, to deserve a Share of the Publick
Favour: But we desire no Subscriptions. We shall publish the Books at our
own Expence, and risqué the Sale of them; which Method, we suppose, will be
most agreeable to our Readers, as they will then be at Liberty to buy only what
they like; and we shall be under a constant Necessity of endeavouring to make
every particular Pamphlet worth their Money. Each Magazine shall contain
four Sheets, of common sized Paper, in a small Character: Price *Six Pence*
Sterling, or *Nine Pence Pennsylvania* Money; with considerable Allowance to
Chapmen who take Quantities. To be printed and Sold by B. Franklin in
Philadelphia.[51]

Bradford learned about Franklin's concept for a magazine from John
Webbe. Although Franklin offered the position of editor to Webbe, Webbe
apparently was dissatisfied with Franklin's proposition because he went to
see Bradford. Bradford offered Webbe a more lucrative proposition, and
Webbe accepted.

This advertisement apparently offended Webbe, because he wrote three
articles that explained Franklin's proposition and his perspective toward it.
The articles appeared in Bradford's newspaper, the *American Weekly Mercury*. Franklin ignored the first and second articles, then responded to the third,
which concerned Franklin's refusal as postmaster to have Bradford's newspaper delivered by the post office. Franklin included the former postmaster
general's letter of instruction to him to not forward Bradford's newspaper,
because Bradford had been negligent in filing reports. Webbe responded to
Franklin's rebuttal in a lengthy, two-page diatribe. The confrontation ended
after Webbe's article, except for a humorous essay by Franklin that ridiculed
Bradford's advertisement about his proposed magazine.[52]

Three days before *The General Magazine, and Historical Chronicle, for
All the British Plantations in America* was printed in February 1741, Frank-
lin's rival, Andrew Bradford, printed *The American Magazine, or a Monthly
View of the Political State of the British Colonies*.

Bradford's magazine lasted three issues. Franklin's magazine, which contained approximately seventy-five pages, lasted six issues. In the January
1741 issue, Franklin inserted the following advertisement:

Advertisement

THIS *Magazine* will be published Monthly, the Paper and Page will be continued of the same Size, that so the Twelve Months may be bound in one Volume
at the Year's End, with a compleat Index or Table, which we shall add to the
Month of *December*.

No Care shall be wanting, or Expence spared, to procure the best Materials for the Work, and make it as entertaining and useful as possible. The Character will generally be small, for the sake of comprising much in little Room, but it shall be good, and fairly printed. [53]

Franklin's magazine was the first of its kind to run an advertisement. Dated May 10, 1741, it appeared with the heading "ADVERTISEMENT," followed by

Maryland, Charles County, May 10, 1741.
THere is a FERRY kept over Potomack, (by the Subscriber) being the Post Road, and much the nighest Way from Annapolis to Williamsburg, where all Gentlemen may depend upon a ready Passage in a good new Boat and able Hands. By Richard Brett, Deputy-Post-Master at Potomack. [54]

Franklin's magazine, like Bradford's, contained only one or two advertisements in any given issue, and these advertisements generally concerned announcements or notices about books or other magazines. Some advertisements, in a simplistic manner, informed readers about certain products such as inexpensive coffins, shoes, and cure-all compounds. The advertisements were brief and seldom contained ornaments or engravings. The purpose of Franklin's magazine was not to attract advertisers. According to James Playsted Wood, the purpose was "to present political information, knowledge of which he felt should be widespread among the thirteen colonies. To this end he devoted about a third of the space in his magazine to the reprinting of state papers." [55]

Other Magazines

The first issue of the *American Magazine and Historical Chronicle, for all the British Plantations* appeared in October 1743. Printed by Gamaliel Rogers and Daniel Fowle in Boston, the magazine's first few issues were supported by Samuel Eliot and Joshua Blanchard, both of whom sold books. Rogers and Fowle had formed a partnership in 1740 and had printed several religious tracts as well as other material, including books. They had printed another magazine, but it had ceased publication after two or three issues. The *American Magazine and Historical Chronicle, for all the British Plantations*, which was edited by Jeremiah Gridley, contained 50 pages and imitated *The London Magazine* in its appearance. It contained a cut of Boston on the title page. *The London Magazine* contained a cut of London on its title page. The magazine contained advertisements, most notably about books "just published." The word "advertisement" was occasionally used. Beginning with the January 1746 issue, the word "advertisement" was printed in bold and preceded the advertisements, which for the most part concerned books.[56] The editorial content included political articles, especially about Europe. The magazine lasted for more than three years.

Rogers and Fowle printed *The Independent Advertiser*, a newspaper, in 1748. Two years later, the printers dissolved their partnership. Rogers opened a print shop that eventually burned. Fowle opened a print shop and printed books and pamphlets, including *The Monster of Monsters*, which ridiculed the authorities. Fowle claimed that he had not printed the pamphlet; rather, he had merely stocked and sold it in his establishment. Nonetheless, the authorities arrested him; he was held for several days, then released. He moved to New Hampshire, where in 1756 he started the *New-Hampshire Gazette*, a successful newspaper that he renamed years later.

In October 1757 in Philadelphia, William Bradford III—who had been born in New York but was reared by his uncle Andrew Bradford in Philadelphia—published *The American Magazine, or Monthly Chronicle for the British Colonies*. The purpose of the magazine was to support England, especially in its war against France, and to enlighten the colonies. The magazine's content reflected Bradford's patriotic beliefs and values, as well as Philadelphia's culture. The magazine lasted about a year. Prior to publishing the magazine, Bradford had founded and published the *Weekly Advertiser, or Philadelphia Journal*, a newspaper that he renamed the *Pennsylvania Journal, or Weekly Advertiser*.

Robert Aitkin published the *Pennsylvania Magazine, or American Monthly Museum*, which began in early 1775 and ended in mid-1776. Thomas Paine edited several issues. Aitkin had been born in Scotland and had served as an apprentice to a bookbinder. In 1771 he had moved his family to Philadelphia, where he had opened a successful bookstore and had become a successful publisher.

The magazine focused primarily on the Revolutionary War but contained material from American and British writers and political advocates. Contributions by Paine, for instance, appeared. Aitkin included the Declaration of Independence in the last issue. The magazine was popular among readers; it had more than fifteen hundred subscribers.

Albert H. Smyth wrote, "Bradford's magazine had failed because of the imperfect communication between the colonies. Aitken's magazine, throughout its life of eighteen months, is overshadowed by the war, and the grave news successively reported from both sides of the ocean."[57]

Aitkin continued to publish other material, including the first complete Bible in English in America.

A group of men, including Mathew Carey, John Trenchard, Charles Cist, and William Spotswood, published *The Columbian Magazine, or Monthly Miscellany* in October 1786. The magazine's contents included articles about agriculture, business, fashion, manners, morals, politics, and science—subjects that were popular among readers. Carey left the publication after a few issues. Cist and Spotswood left in 1788. Trenchard published the magazine until the end of 1792.

Carey started *The American Museum* in 1787. The magazine published writing that was worth preserving, including Thomas Paine's *Common Sense*. In addition, it published articles about agriculture, business, education, and slavery, which Carey opposed. Carey had been born in Ireland and had learned about selling and publishing by serving as an apprentice. He had written essays that had appeared in pamphlets. He had published a newspaper in Ireland. However, he had published a controversial cartoon and had been arrested for sedition.

Carey had arrived in Philadelphia in 1784. He had started a newspaper before he had founded *The American Museum*. The magazine ceased publication in 1792, when the postmaster in Philadelphia increased rates. Carey had other interests, however, after the magazine died. He wrote essays, published pamphlets and books, including the Bible. His publishing company, Carey and Lea, became one of the leaders in the industry.[58]

In 1774 Isaiah Thomas published the *Royal American Magazine, or Universal Repository of Instruction and Amusement*. The magazine featured illustrations as well as material that had been borrowed from other magazines and books. The magazine contained original articles such as essays about various topics, including politics, and fiction. The magazine ceased publication in 1775.

Thomas had been born in Boston in 1750 and had served as an apprentice in Zechariah Fowle's print shop. However, he had learned more about the craft of printing from Fowle's partner, Samuel Draper, than he had from Fowle. Thomas had left Fowle and had worked for various printers in other colonies. Later, he had returned to Boston and had purchased Fowle's print shop. He had founded the patriotic newspaper *Massachusetts Spy* in 1770.

In 1775 he moved his family and his business to Worcester, where he continued publishing the newspaper until the Massachusetts legislature enacted a tax on newspapers. In 1786 Thomas started publishing the *Worcester Magazine; Containing Politicks, Miscellanies, Poetry, and News*, which was a smaller version of the newspaper. The magazine contained articles that had started in the newspaper as well as advertisements. Many articles concerned politics. Other articles focused on agriculture and medicine, among other topics. The magazine ceased publication in 1788, when Thomas continued publishing the newspaper.

In 1789 he started the *Massachusetts Magazine, or Monthly Museum of Knowledge and Rational Entertainment*. The magazine was a miscellany in the sense that it contained material that any reader would find interesting. Essays, fiction, musical compositions, and articles about politics, among other subjects, filled the pages. Thomas sold the magazine to other printers before 1794. The magazine was sold to still other printers before it finally ceased publication in 1796.

Thomas, who had formed partnerships with other printers over the years, continued as a printer. In addition to his newspaper, he published numerous books about arithmetic, grammar, law, medicine, music, and spelling, among other subjects. He published the Bible. He published biographies. He published fiction for children and adults.

By the time he retired from printing, he had become a wealthy man.[59]

General Comments

Although printers founded other magazines, most lasted a few months. Advertisements were few, and they appeared on the last page or in supplements. Many issues of magazines carried no advertisements whatsoever. Therefore, publishers of magazines relied on subscribers to cover most, if not all, of their expenses. Unfortunately, some subscribers could not afford to pay; others paid periodically. As if this was not bad enough, certain publishers of magazines were handicapped by discriminating postal regulations. For instance, certain postmasters who published magazines refused to have other printers' publications delivered. This practice, which was common, applied to newspapers, too.

NOTES

1. Carl A. Bridenbaugh, *Cities in the Wilderness* (New York: Ronald Press, 1938), 26–54.

2. Emory R. Johnson, T. W. Van Metre, Grover G. Huebner, David Scott Hanchett, and Henry W. Farnam, *History of Domestic and Foreign Commerce of the United States* (Washington, DC: Carnegie Institution, 1915), 1:162–74.

3. Bridenbaugh, *Cities in the Wilderness*, 175–205.

4. Bridenbaugh, *Cities in the Wilderness*, 330–63.

5. Wilbur C. Plummer, "Consumer Credit in Colonial Philadelphia," *Pennsylvania Magazine of History and Biography* 67 (1942): 389–409.

6. John M. Blum, Edmund S. Morgan, Willie L. Rose, Arthur M. Schlesinger Jr., Kenneth M. Stampp, and C. Vann Woodward, *The National Experience: A History of the United States* (New York: Harcourt Brace Jovanovich, 1981), 64.

7. Blum and colleagues, *The National Experience*, 65.

8. J. A. Leo Lemay and P. M. Zall, eds., *The Autobiography of Benjamin Franklin: A Genetic Text* (Knoxville: University of Tennessee Press, 1981), 105.

9. William David Sloan and Julie Hedgepeth Williams, *The Early American Press, 1690–1782*, History of American Journalism Series (Westport, CT: Greenwood Press, 1994), 1:2.

10. *Publick Occurrences, Both Forreign and Domestick*, September 25, 1690.

11. Charles E. Clark, "The Newspapers of Provincial America," *Proceedings of the American Antiquarian Society* (Worcester, MA: American Antiquarian Society, 1990), 100: 373–74.

12. *Boston News-Letter*, April 17–24, 1704.

13. *Boston News-Letter*, May 1–8, 1704.
14. *Boston News-Letter*, May 1–8, 1704.
15. *Boston News-Letter*, May 15–22, 1704.
16. *Boston News-Letter*, June 5–11, 1704.
17. *Boston News-Letter*, August 21, 1704.
18. Sidney Kobre, *The Development of the Colonial Newspaper* (Gloucester, MA: Smith, 1960), 27; also, Sloan and Williams, *The Early American Press*, 22.
19. Kobre, *The Development of the Colonial Newspaper*, 45.
20. Leonard W. Labaree, Ralph L. Ketcham, Helen C. Boatfield, and Helene H. Fineman, eds., *The Autobiography of Benjamin Franklin*, by Benjamin Franklin (New Haven, CT: Yale University Press, 1964), 69.
21. *Pennsylvania Gazette*, September 25–October 2, 1729.
22. *Pennsylvania Gazette*, September 25–October 2, 1729.
23. *Pennsylvania Gazette*, August 14–21, 1735.
24. *Pennsylvania Gazette*, June 23–30, 1737.
25. *Pennsylvania Gazette*, June 23–30, 1737.
26. *Pennsylvania Gazette*, June 23–30, 1737.
27. *Pennsylvania Gazette*, January 18–25, 1738, 9.
28. *Pennsylvania Gazette*, February 15–22, 1738, 9.
29. *Pennsylvania Gazette*, June 17, 1742.
30. In 1950, the American Advertising Federation inducted Benjamin Franklin into the Advertising Hall of Fame.
31. Benjamin Franklin, "Advice to a Young Tradesman, Written by an Old One. To My Friend A. B.," *The Instructor: Or Young Man's Best Companion*, 9th ed., revised and corrected, ed. George Fisher (Philadelphia: B. Franklin and D. Hall, 1748), 375; also, Leonard W. Labaree, ed., and Whitfield J. Bell Jr., associate ed., *The Papers of Benjamin Franklin, Vol. 3: January 1, 1745, through June 30, 1750* (New Haven, CT: Yale University Press, 1961), 306.
32. George Henry Payne, *History of Journalism in the United States* (Westport, CT: Greenwood Press, 1970; originally, D. Appleton, 1920), 37–38.
33. Payne, *History of Journalism in the United States*, 57.
34. *New-York Gazette*, October 3–10, 1737.
35. *New-York Gazette*, September 26–October 3, 1737.
36. *New-York Gazette*, November 14–21, 1737.
37. Stanley Nider Katz, ed., *A Brief Narrative of the Case and Trial of John Peter Zenger, Printer of the New-York Weekly Journal*, by James Alexander (Cambridge, MA: Belknap Press of Harvard University Press, 1972); also Frank Luther Mott, *American Journalism: A History: 1690–1960*, 3rd ed. (New York: Macmillan, 1962), 31–38.
38. *New-York Weekly Journal*, March 29, 1736.
39. Merrill Jensen, ed., *Tracts of the American Revolution* (Indianapolis, IN: Bobbs-Merrill, 1967), 80–93; also, Jeffery A. Smith, *Printers and Press Freedom: The Ideology of Early American Journalism* (New York: Oxford University Press, 1988), 136–38; also Charles R. Hildeburn, *Sketches of Printers and Printing in Colonial New York* (New York: Dodd, Mead, 1895), 34–54.
40. Dwight L. Teeter Jr., "John Dunlap: The Political Economy of a Printer's Success," *Journalism Quarterly* 52 (1975): 3–8, 55; also Kobre, *The Development of the Colonial Newspaper*, 154.
41. Ralph Frasca, *Benjamin Franklin's Printing Network: Disseminating Virtue in Early America* (Columbia: University of Missouri Press, 2006), 184.
42. Frasca, *Benjamin Franklin's Printing Network*, 177–85, 189–91.
43. Sidney Kobre, "The Revolutionary Colonial Press—A Social Interpretation," *Journalism Quarterly* 20, no. 3 (1943): 198–99.
44. Kobre, "The Revolutionary Colonial Press," 196.
45. Ronald Hoffman, "The Press in Mercantile Maryland: A Question of Utility," *Journalism Quarterly* 46, no. 3 (1969): 536–37.
46. James M. Lee, *History of American Journalism* (Garden City, NY: Garden City, 1917), 94.

47. Isaiah Thomas, *The History of Printing in America, with a Biography of Printers in Two Volumes* (New York: Burt Franklin, n.d.; originally, 1874), 2:8–9.

48. William A. Dill, *Growth of Newspapers in the United States* (Lawrence: University of Kansas, Department of Journalism, 1928), 11.

49. Louis B. Wright, *The Cultural Life of the American Colonies, 1607–1763* (New York: Harper and Brothers, 1957).

50. James Playsted Wood, *The Story of Advertising* (New York: Ronald Press, 1958), 65.

51. *Pennsylvania Gazette*, November 13, 1740.

52. Lyon N. Richardson, *A History of Early American Magazines 1741–1789* (New York: Octagon Books, 1966; originally, Thomas Nelson and Sons, 1931), 17–25.

53. *The General Magazine, and Historical Chronicle, for All the British Plantations in America* (January 1741).

54. *The General Magazine, and Historical Chronicle, for All the British Plantations in America* (May 1741).

55. James Playsted Wood, *Magazines in the United States*, 3rd ed. (New York: Ronald Press, 1971), 13.

56. Frank Luther Mott, *A History of American Magazines: 1741–1850* (New York: D. Appleton, 1930), 78–79.

57. Albert H. Smyth, *The Philadelphia Magazines and Their Contributors, 1741–1850* (Freeport, NY: Books for Libraries Press, 1970; originally, 1892), 52–53.

58. Earl L. Bradsher, *Mathew Carey: Editor, Author and Publisher—A Study in American Literary Development* (New York: AMS Press, 1966; originally, Columbia University Press, 1912).

59. Thomas, *The History of Printing in America*, 1:155–70, 1:181–83, 2:61–65.

Chapter Two

The First Advertising Agents in the United States

During the nineteenth century, the United States progressed at a remarkable rate. In 1800 the principal forms of retailing included general stores, markets, and peddlers. General stores were prevalent, and the majority of merchants sold at wholesale and retail. Eventually, retailing leaned toward specialization by merchandise lines or by function. Advertising by merchants stressed the availability of products rather than products' attributes. The source of the merchandise was given, as was the amount on hand. However, retail advertising, at least in its early days, rarely contained prices. [1]

The selling agent appeared before 1860 and provided a broad range of services to manufacturers, including sales assistance, market information, and advice regarding which means of transportation should be employed. Many selling agents owned stock in manufacturing firms and consequently had considerable influence on managerial decisions. [2]

Commerce gave rise to regional specialization and contributed to the growth of cities. By 1860 the nation had prospered to the extent that it no longer depended on Europe to purchase its goods. Innovations in technology helped increase production, especially in textiles. Industrial workers formed unions because of exploitation. Banks increased in number. Transportation projects such as canals, steamboats, and turnpikes advanced and helped reduce costs of specific products. According to George Rogers Taylor, the rapid development of a national transportation system made interregional trade economically feasible. [3] In the South, cotton became the chief asset. In the North, factories supported employees who lived in cities. For most of the nation's citizenry, agriculture was the primary means of livelihood.

Immigrants from the Old World, including England, Ireland, and Germany, arrived daily. Immigrants from Germany fared well, while those from Ireland fared poorly. Germans, who had money or access to financial aid, purchased farms. For the most part, the Irish congregated in cities, where they worked at low-paying jobs. Generally, because of their low wages, they had to live in slums filled with pestilence and disease. African Americans were worse off, for they had to take jobs that whites refused. In addition, most faced hostility from whites almost every day. Freedom for many of them was merely a word.

To survive and expand their obligations to the citizenry, city governments were forced to tax. Police forces came into existence, garbage was removed, streets were undeniably improved, and education progressed.

Religion witnessed a rise in interdenominational revivalism before 1840, which was similar to what occurred in Europe. City after city received scores of ministers who believed that cities were the dens where Satan dwelled.

As the country progressed, so did its citizenry. Wealth was obtained by a select few, however. Various movements affected more people. These movements were created by specific groups for specific issues, such as women's rights, capital punishment, workers' rights, education, mental health, temperance, and pacifism. Abolitionism was the most controversial. These movements swept across the country. Other movements, which included communistic communities such as Brook Farm, were not as popular as their promoters hoped.

The nation's population increased, and when nine million immigrants entered the nation in the late nineteenth century, citizens of the United States grew concerned. The western territory was settled and eventually gained statehood. Silver and gold were discovered. Cattle became an industry not only in Texas but in the Dakotas. Railroads branched from the East and the West; in 1869 one complete line crossed the American landscape. Unfortunately, owners of railroads realized their power; consequently, they fixed prices, they monopolized transportation, they discriminated against certain customers, and they used their power to influence local and state legislators and subsequent legislation.

The Native American was pushed aside until federal legislation intervened.

Industry, which had grown from the beginning of the century, more than doubled in production between the late 1870s and the 1890s. Production of iron and steel in the United States, unlike that of the rest of the world, increased. The telephone, phonograph, electric light bulb, and typewriter, among other inventions, spawned new industries. Petroleum used for engines as well as heating and lighting created another major industry.

Industries led to the creation of trusts, which were monopolies, by John D. Rockefeller and others. Company mergers also appeared. Tensions between management and employees ensued; subsequently, laborers formed more unions, a few of which became national in size. Through strikes and boycotts, labor tried to obtain higher wages, better working conditions, and fewer hours. Before the turn of the century, primarily as a result of several incidents in which people were either injured or killed, labor unions received severe criticism from the press and the public.

The advocacy and muckraking journalists reported vividly the opening of the West, the wars between the United States and its adversaries, and the unscrupulous practices by managers and owners of large companies, especially monopolies.

In this climate of change, the first advertising agents appeared. Ralph M. Hower reported that advertising agencies passed through four stages before N. W. Ayer and Son was founded. The first stage was the newspaper agency, which was inaugurated by Volney B. Palmer, who represented newspaper publishers. The second stage occurred in the 1850s, when agents became independent. Space-jobbing, as this stage was called, became popular as agents realized they could earn more by selling space to advertisers. This stage caused many agents to question their role. After all, they did not work for publishers, and they did not work for advertisers. Yet, they referred to themselves as agents. The third stage developed out of the second when George P. Rowell purchased large amounts of space in newspapers, then resold them in small amounts to advertisers. This stage, which has been called space-wholesaling, began in 1865. The fourth stage was based on Rowell's idea and appeared in the late 1860s. Called the advertising concession agency, this stage occurred when Carlton and Smith (later, the J. Walter Thompson Company) purchased most, if not all, of the advertising space in specific publications for a specified period of time. Consequently, the agency, not the publisher, was responsible for securing advertisers for the entire publication. This practice actually closed the gap between agent and publisher, but the agent worked as an independent middleman nonetheless.[4]

VOLNEY B. PALMER

Volney B. Palmer was a pioneer in the sense that he was the first advertising agent in the United States. Eventually, he had offices in Boston, New York, Baltimore, and Philadelphia. He represented more newspapers than other agents of his day. In addition, he promoted advertising as an integral part of marketing and produced as well as delivered advertisements to publishers.

Palmer was born to Nathan and Jerusha Palmer in Wilkes-Barre, Pennsylvania, in 1799. His father, a lawyer who held several political positions in Wilkes-Barre, moved his wife and six children to Mount Holly, New Jersey, in 1818, where he published *The Burlington Mirror*, a newspaper on which every member of the family worked. He changed the name of the newspaper to *The New Jersey Mirror and Burlington County Advertiser* about a year later. The newspaper continued to be popular among readers and advertisers, even after Nathan's death in 1842, when it was published by his widow, then his daughter Eliza.

Palmer and one of his four brothers moved to Pottsville, Pennsylvania, in 1830, where he invested and worked in real estate. In 1841, after he married, Palmer moved his family to Philadelphia, where he attempted to sell real estate in an economically depressed city. By 1842 he had added a coal office as well as an advertising business to his real estate venture, as the following advertisement illustrates:

V. B. Palmer's
Philadelphia

Agency for the Purchase and Sale of Houses and Lots, Farms, Farming, Timber and Coal Lands, Bonds and Mortgages, Ground Rents, Anthracite Coal, & c.

ADVERTISEMENTS and Subscriptions received from some of the best and most widely circulated newspapers in Pennsylvania and New Jersey, and in many of the principal cities and towns throughout the United States, for which he has the agency, affording an excellent opportunity for Merchants, Mechanics, Professional Men, Hotel and Boarding House Keepers, Railroad, Insurance and Transportation Companies, and the enterprising portion of the community generally, to publish extensively abroad their respective pursuits—to learn the terms of subscription and advertising, and accomplish their object here without the trouble of perplexing and fruitless inquiries, the expense and labor of letter writing; the risk of making enclosures of money &c, &c.[5]

Palmer remained in real estate for the next several years, even though his advertising business was fruitful. In 1849 he used "Advertising Agency" in an advertisement for the first time. He claimed to be the sole representative of thirteen hundred newspapers. This, Palmer realized, allowed advertisers to be selective. In addition, Palmer created speculative presentations for these prospective advertisers. The advertiser was informed of the total cost, not just the space rates for each newspaper selected. Palmer received a 25 percent commission from the publisher upon payment. The commission system was used by advertising agencies for one hundred years, except that agencies usually received from 12.5 percent to 15 percent, not 25 percent. Today, some agencies offer clients contracts based on the commission system; however, most agencies offer clients contracts that are based on something other than the commission system.

According to *V. B. Palmer's Business-Men's Almanac* of 1849, Palmer's advertising agency provided the following advantages:

1. The most widely circulated journals in America are on file for the convenient examination and selection, and the terms for each recorded for the inspection of subscribers and advertisers.
2. The publishers have appointed and authorized him to make contracts for subscriptions and advertising. His receipts are regarded as payments, and therefore valid and sufficient.
3. Advertisements are inserted in any one paper or (from a single copy) in any number, at the lowest cash price, without extra charge, at the earliest practical time, and a copy of each paper furnished to the advertiser, that he may be sure that his order was complied with.
4. Editorial and Business Notices inserted on the most favorable terms, calling attention to advertisements.
5. Reliable explanatory information of places, character and circulation of papers, adaptation of various business pursuits and comparative rates of advertising in different papers cheerfully given with every reasonable facility, for adopting at once a safe, judicious, efficient system of advertising.
6. Advertisers save the postage and avoid the labor of correspondence with publishers, risk of remittances, unseasonable and repeated calls of strangers with separate bills, the various deceptions of journals of dubious character, and losses from contracting with incompetent and irresponsible persons.
7. To avoid unnecessary expense, concise forms of advertising are written without charge, and valuable practical suggestions made for improvement in style and force such as are written by unpracticed hands.[6]

In the *V. B. Palmer's Business-Men's Almanac* of 1850, he listed similar advantages for his agency; however, he did not use numerals:

- he is Agent for the best papers of every section of the whole country.
- he is empowered by the proprietors to make contracts and give receipts.
- his long experience and practical knowledge qualify him to give valuable information.
- the same prices only are charged to advertisers as are exacted by his principals, the publishers.
- a selection can be made suitably adapted to the various pursuits of advertisers.
- a complete system of advertising can be adapted upon either a large or small scale.
- the papers are on file at the Agency, where advertisers can examine them, see the terms, and obtain all requisite information to enable them to advertise judiciously, effectively and safely.[7]

From the preceding, it is easy to ascertain that Palmer's agency did more for advertisers than most agencies at the time. Palmer promoted his services by using endorsements from publishers. According to Donald R. Holland, Palmer "urged business men to use advertising on a regular basis, to use it to develop new markets, to take advantage of the flexibility of advertising to specific regions or in specific seasons."[8]

By the mid-1850s, Palmer was considered by numerous clients as a god-send, and his agency grew. He opened four offices in four major cities. He maintained the office in Philadelphia and hired others to manage the other three. He visited the other offices at various times throughout each year.

In the late 1850s, John E. Joy, W. W. Sharpe, and J. E. Coe became partners. When Palmer retired in either 1862 or 1863, Joy and Coe operated the Philadelphia and the New York offices, respectively. Eventually, the latter office was purchased by W. W. Sharpe. The office in Boston was controlled by S. R. Niles.

Palmer died in 1864; he was sixty-five. Palmer helped advertisers and newspaper publishers. He sold the idea of advertising to advertisers and consequently made hundreds of proprietors realize how important advertising was in a capitalistic society.

S. M. Pettengill, who had worked for Palmer, described him as "a short, thick-set gentleman of good address, genial and pleasant in manner, and had a good command of language, full of wise saws and modern instances. He was a capital story-teller, wore gold spectacles and carried a gold-headed cane, and was a first-rate canvasser. He had more self-possession and assurance than any man I ever knew."[9]

GEORGE P. ROWELL

George P. Rowell was born in 1838 in Concord, Vermont, to Samuel and Caroline Rowell. When he was a teenager, he moved with his parents to a farm outside Lancaster, New Hampshire. Rowell, who was studious, attended Lancaster Academy. At seventeen, he left home to pursue employment in Boston. He taught school for several years, then worked in a store until the recession of 1857.

Rowell found employment with the *Boston Post*, for which he eventually sold space to advertisers. Rowell was working at the paper when he married Sarah Eastman in 1862. Although Rowell earned enough to support his family, in 1864 he created a theatrical playbill for which he sold space to advertisers. He continued the playbill for several weeks and, as a result of the advertising, netted a comfortable profit.

In 1865 he left the *Post* and opened an advertising agency with his friend Horace Dodd. They devised a "list system" of newspapers for advertisers to consider. Unlike Palmer, they purchased large quantities of column space from these newspapers, then sold the space in small quantities to advertisers. In short, they purchased space at wholesale, then sold it at retail. They persuaded specific publishers to give them a discount based on continued patronage. The agents received an additional 3 percent off the card rate if they paid in cash within a thirty-day period. The agents did not have to pay more than 25 percent of the card rate for most of the newspapers they handled. Rowell was responsible for the cash discount in addition to the commission.

Rowell's "list system" became instantly popular and was adopted by other agencies. Rowell and Dodd started the *Advertisers' Gazette*, a house organ that promoted advertising and the agency.

Rowell sold the agency to Dodd in 1867 and moved his family to New York, which had become the most important commercial city in the nation because of its location. By 1860 New York handled more than 65 percent of the country's imports and more than 30 percent of its exports, and because of its easy access, the city appealed to western markets. [10]

Rowell established the agency George P. Rowell and Company and continued using the "list system," which was criticized by S. M. Pettengill, a competitor, at a New York State Editorial Association meeting:

> Mr. Pettengill . . . berated the publishers for their lack of business methods, and took special exception to the practice, of which many of them were guilty, of selling to Mr. Rowell . . . a column of space at a yearly rate, and allowing him to peddle it out to monthly users of an inch, more or less, at less than half the price the publisher would demand of the advertiser, . . . and much worse than that, at less than half the price the same publisher would demand from him, Pettengill, if he, instead of Rowell, should happen to send the same card of an inch or thereabouts to appear for a single month. [11]

Rowell happened to be in the audience and realized that Pettengill considered him a competitor, even though Pettengill had been in business longer. Rowell and Pettengill became friends primarily as a result of their professional interests.

Rowell made an effort to make sure that circulation figures claimed by publishers were accurate, as he candidly pointed out in an agency flyer:

> In fixing the value of advertising space in any particular journal, the first question to be considered is the number of copies issued; next the character or quality of the circulation.
>
> A well-printed paper is worth more than one badly printed; an influential journal carries more weight than one without reputation.

So also a paper which habitually charges high prices for its advertising thereby makes its columns exclusive, and will have fewer, and as a rule, a better class of advertisements, and is worth something more on that account.

The value of all these considerations is recognized, but exactly *how* much each one is to be considered becomes a question of judgment. [12]

Rowell realized that if his agency could supply the preceding to advertisers, then advertisers would know how much to pay for the space they purchased. As Rowell pointed out, that was one purpose of his agency.

Rowell continued to publish the house organ, *Advertisers' Gazette*, which was mentioned earlier, and in 1869, as a service to prospective advertisers, he published the first volume of *George P. Rowell and Company's American Newspaper Directory*, which listed more than five thousand newspapers in the United States and more than three hundred in Canada that the agency handled and, of course, various advertisements, which defrayed part of the publication cost. Although Rowell had tried to eliminate so-called private lists, he was criticized by other agents for making available at a nominal cost more information than they offered. Rowell had misgivings about the directory because it disclosed information about newspapers that other agencies did not have. Rowell was also criticized by publishers for printing conservative circulation figures of their respective newspapers. Yet, these publishers accepted advertising from his agency. The publication was updated and issued annually. As a result of this publication, publishers of newspapers eventually changed their circulation figures.

Rowell also published the *American Newspaper Reporter*, which was a house organ that preceded *Printer's Ink*. The organ contained insightful features about individuals who worked in the advertising and newspaper businesses, as well as other informative articles. In the November 20, 1871, issue, he wrote about "The Principles of Advertising":

Honesty is by all odds the very strongest point which can be crowded into an advertisement. Come right down with the facts, boldly, firmly, unflinchingly. Say directly what it is, what it has done, what it will do. Leave out all ifs. Do not claim too much, but what you do claim must be claimed without the smallest shadow of weakness. Do not say "we are convinced that," "we believe that" or "ours is among the best" or "equal to any" or "surpassed by none." Say flatly "the best," or say nothing. Do not refer to rivals. Ignore every person, place or thing except yourself, your address and your article. . . . Be serious and dignified, but active and lively. Leave wit, however good it may be, entirely aside. [13]

Rowell realized that advertising copy, which suffered from too many words—that is, overstatement—needed improving. He also realized that every advertisement—even small ones—had to attract attention.

By 1871 Rowell's "list system" had been employed six years and had proved profitable. Rowell himself had accumulated more than $100,000. Yet, the firm continued to add to its various lists of newspapers and clients. Rowell's agency placed numerous advertisements for various questionable remedies, for instance, even though Rowell's opinion toward advertising patent medicine changed dramatically years later.

Rowell's success, which had come at an early age, allowed him to take four months of vacation, which he did almost every year beginning in 1871. The same year, he decided to share the agency's profits with his employees, a practice that he continued but with some regret.

In 1878 Rowell issued a small pamphlet that expressed the principles and conditions that guided the agency. The following paragraph from the booklet summarized the purpose for the George P. Rowell and Company's existence:

> Our Newspaper Advertising Bureau . . . is an establishment intended to facilitate the convenient and systematic placing of advertisements in newspapers. It is conducted upon the principles which we conceive to be the right ones for securing the best results to the advertiser, the publisher, and ourselves. [14]

The same year, Rowell sold the firm's house organ, the *American Newspaper Reporter and Advertisers' Gazette*, to R. H. C. Valentine, who changed the subhead and design. The publication ceased after several issues, however.

In 1880 Rowell purchased "Prospect Farm" in New Hampshire and seldom worked in advertising. The farm did not occupy all of his time, however. In addition to traveling abroad, he fished, unsuccessfully sought public office, and published a small and unprofitable newspaper.

Rowell returned to his office in New York in 1888 and published *Printer's Ink*. Rowell wrote, "I had always an itching to have a mouth-piece through which I could speak to those whose interests were in lines parallel to mine." [15] The purpose of *Printer's Ink*, then, was to discuss the business of advertising. The publication became a journal for advertisers and was so successful commercially that eventually it had at least two hundred imitations.

In 1890 Rowell's marriage ended in divorce; he married Jeannette Hallock several months later in 1891.

In 1892 he sold the agency to several employees. Unfortunately, within several years, the investors owed newspaper publishers more than they had received from advertisers, and Rowell purchased the company for one dollar and assumed all debts.

In 1905 Rowell retired from advertising and wrote fifty-two articles about his life and experiences in advertising. These articles appeared in *Printer's Ink*, then in the book *Forty Years an Advertising Agent: 1865–1905*, which was published in 1906.

Rowell died at Poland Springs, Maine, in 1908. His annual newspaper directory was purchased the same year by the N. W. Ayer and Son advertising agency, which published the *N. W. Ayer and Son's American Newspaper Annual*.

Regarding the operation of an advertising agency, Rowell wrote,

> It is one of the easiest sorts of business in which a man may cheat and defraud a client without danger of discovery; and also note that no agent who was not superior to this temptation has ever been permanently successful. The high reputation for honor and probity uniformly enjoyed by those who have been most conspicuous in the business has been gained by strict integrity—a determination to secure a fair deal for every patron. [16]

N. W. AYER AND SON

Francis Wayland Ayer was born in 1848 in Lee, Massachusetts. He was influenced by the four stages discussed earlier and by his father, Nathan Wheeler Ayer, when he opened his advertising agency in Philadelphia in 1868.

N. W. Ayer, a graduate of Brown University, named his son after Dr. Francis Wayland, one of Brown's presidents. Joanna B. Ayer, his mother, died when Ayer was three. N. W. Ayer, a devout Baptist, married Harriet Post when his son was six. N. W. Ayer practiced law for several years in Massachusetts, taught in Massachusetts and New York, then purchased a seminary in Philadelphia in 1867. He was not successful financially. He earned a modest living until he suffered from ill health.

Francis Wayland Ayer learned from his father the basic principles that helped him throughout his life. He knew what responsibility, integrity, and honesty meant. His value system was never questioned. When he was fourteen, he taught in a country school in New York. A year later, he was offered a position in a village school. For the next several years, one promotion followed another. He desired to go to college, however, and in 1867 he attended the University of Rochester. Within a year, he had spent his savings. Although he asked his father for help, his father was barely earning an income. F. W. Ayer left the university in search of a job. The publisher of *The National Baptist*, a weekly religious newspaper, hired him to solicit advertisements. Ayer earned $1,200 in commissions in less than a year. His employer offered him $2,000 a year to stay with the company. Ayer refused the opportunity. He was certain he could earn more on his own. He persuaded his father to work with him, and on April 1, 1869, he opened the agency N. W. Ayer and Son. He named the agency after his father for several reasons: he admired his father; his father agreed to work with him; and the name sounded more impressive than just F. W. Ayer.

The Ayer agency began with eleven religious newspapers. Like other agents of his day, Ayer solicited advertisements from advertisers, then placed them in the publications listed with his agency. In addition, he purchased the total advertising space in specific publications, then resold it in partials to advertisers. Thus, he acted as manager of advertising departments of some publications. Ayer also placed advertisements in publications that were not on his list. In such instances, he estimated how much the space would cost, then quoted a price that was slightly higher than his estimated cost to advertisers. Ayer earned income the best way he knew how—by selling and bargaining. There was little time for experimenting, especially during the agency's formative years. By the end of its first year, the agency represented more than eleven newspapers. Growth continued, and in 1870 Ayer had to move to a larger office and hire his first employee, George O. Wallace, a bookkeeper.

Within two years, the agency had to move again. It was handling more than three hundred publications located in twenty-seven of the thirty-seven states that made up the nation. In addition, advertisements for clients were placed in other publications through other agents.

In 1873 N. W. Ayer died. Francis purchased his father's interest in the business. His stepmother, Harriet Post, did not have the experience or the inclination to be a partner. Ayer reasoned that absentee ownership would not be beneficial to current and prospective clients. The same year, as a result of growth, Ayer asked Wallace to become a partner; Wallace accepted a one-fourth interest in the agency.

In the mid-1870s, Ayer, like other agencies, placed advertisements for makers of patent medicine. Some of these included Compound Oxygen, Kennedy's Ivory Tooth Cement, Rock and Rye, and Dr. Case's Liver Remedy and Blood Purifier. Other companies were represented, too, including John Wanamaker, Montgomery Ward and Company, Whitman's Chocolates, Blackwell's Durham smoking tobacco, and Singer sewing machines. Ayer also represented manufacturers of farm machinery as well as educational institutions such as Harvard College (Harvard University).

During this time Ayer analyzed Rowell's methods of handling publishers and clients and realized that Rowell had put himself in the middle—that is, he was being paid by the publisher, yet he was representing the advertiser. How could Rowell serve both? Ayer thought about this question and decided to represent the advertiser. Unlike Rowell, he would inform an advertiser as to what the agency received for its services. Instead of being merely a space seller like other agencies, Ayer's agency would become a space buyer and therefore be paid by the client. Ayer believed this plan was fair to the client and actually superior to Rowell's plan.

The Ayer open-contract-plus-commission plan was initiated in late 1875, the year he married Rhandena Gilman. Through trial and error, Ayer learned how to earn a profit from his commission system. This was not as difficult as persuading advertisers to look at advertising from a different perspective. The advertiser had to trust Ayer and vice versa. Ayer would buy space at the lowest possible cost for the advertiser. The advertiser would have access to Ayer's lists of rates. Thus, the advertiser could determine the cost of advertising space in a specific publication and, consequently, the commission to the agency.

This system allowed Ayer to purchase advertising space wisely as well as consider the advertiser's needs, which are hallmarks of modern agencies. The system, although sound, was not adopted by every agency that learned about it, but it forced every agency to recognize that advertisers had interests that needed servicing and, to a certain extent, protecting.

Throughout the 1870s, the Ayer agency grew. By 1876, it could place advertisements in any newspaper published in the United States or Canada because Ayer had created a printing department a year earlier so that the agency could print most of the advertisements in-house. This gave the agency an advantage over other agencies; most agencies hired independent printers to print their clients' advertisements.

In 1877 the agency purchased Coe, Wetherill and Company, another agency in Philadelphia. Coe, Wetherill and Company had succeeded Joy, Coe and Company, which had acquired Volney B. Palmer's agency. In addition, the agency, like George P. Rowell's, published *Ayer and Son's Manual for Advertisers*, primarily to promote its list of publications, and, later, *The Advertiser's Guide*, a quarterly magazine filled with informative features and promotional pieces about advertising.

In 1878 Ayer allowed Henry Nelson McKinney to become a partner. McKinney, an expert in sales, believed in the power of advertising and in the open-contract system. He was extremely important to the growth of the agency.

In 1879 Ayer started another service when it conducted a market survey of the nation to entice Nichols-Shepard Agricultural Implements, a company that manufactured threshing machines. The survey presented the production of grains by counties and states. In addition, the agency included an in-depth advertising plan. This is the first advertising campaign based on a market survey. The company hired Ayer as a result of the survey, and Ayer realized that this particular service could be performed for other advertisers. By 1900, the agency was preparing advertising plans for every client.

In 1880, the agency focused on writing advertising copy in addition to printing advertisements:

The Composition, Illustration and Display of Newspaper Advertisements has so long been a study with us that we have become admittedly expert in preparing the best possible effects.

Having at command the services of an Artist, a Wood Engraver, and a number of Printers who have been for years engaged almost exclusively in this work under our direction, we possess entirely unequaled facilities for serving those who desire to entrust their business to our care.[17]

During the same year, the agency published the *American Newspaper Annual*, which listed every newspaper and magazine published in the United States and Canada. This annual later became the *N. W. Ayer and Son's Directory of Newspapers and Periodicals*. Today, this annual is published under a different title by a different company. Revenue from the annual was from advertising placed by newspaper publishers.

Ayer's business policy changed in the 1880s. For instance, the agency refused advertising that would discredit the agency or disappoint the advertiser. In 1887 Ayer presented his agency's philosophy in a circular:

We do not wish any advertising which cannot reasonably be expected *to pay the advertiser.*

We do not wish any advertiser to deal with us unless it is to *his interest to do so.*

We always say just what we believe, even though we have to advise a man not to spend any money in newspaper advertising.

We aim to give as conscientious consideration to little as to larger matters. Small orders entrusted to us receive just as careful attention as the largest ones get.

We thoroughly believe in newspaper advertising, and that there is more value in it than most people think. We therefore contend that the subject deserves an intelligent and unprejudiced consideration, to which should be applied as good business sense as any other matter of business commands.

We are not anxious for any order with which there does not come the reasonable expectation, *first*, that the advertising will pay our customer; and *again*, that we can so handle the business as to convince him that his interests will be best served by entrusting to us all his future advertising orders.[18]

Most of the advertising handled by the agency in the 1880s came from small businesses, such as retail stores, and from schools and colleges. The agency handled large accounts, too, such as Hires' root beer, J. I. Case threshing machines, and Procter & Gamble soaps. As early as 1891, the agency added the N. K. Fairbanks Company, which produced soaps, and Mellin's Baby Food. In 1892 Jarvis A. Wood became the manager of the agency's newly established copy department. A year later, the agency placed the first colored advertisement in a magazine; it was for Mellin's Baby Food.

From 1894 to 1898, the agency's clients were affected by the recession. When businesses expanded in the late 1890s, so did Ayer. For instance, it handled advertising for Standard Oil and several of its subsidiaries. In 1899 it handled the major campaign that introduced the Uneeda Biscuit, which was sold in individual, airtight packages. The campaign, which was for the National Biscuit Company (Nabisco) and was the largest up to that time, included newspaper, magazine, and outdoor advertisements. The campaign was an overwhelming success.

Because the agency now had large clients, it no longer needed beer and whiskey accounts. In addition, it could curtail patent medicine accounts. In 1896 beer advertising was dropped. Three years later whiskey advertising was halted. Patent medicine advertising was stopped in the early twentieth century.

In 1898 Ayer promoted Jarvis A. Wood and Albert G. Bradford to partners. Wood had supervised employees in the copy department, and Bradford had supervised employees in the space-buying department. Ayer realized that he and McKinney could not manage the growth of the agency by themselves.

Ayer realized before 1900 that advertising specific brands was just as important as advertising new products. He made certain that businesses were aware of this as well in 1900, when he conducted a massive campaign for the agency.

By 1900 Ayer saw his agency grow into the largest in the country, with more than 160 employees and profits exceeding $58,000. In 1902 the agency moved because of much-needed space. Ayer opened branch offices in New York in 1903, Boston in 1905, Chicago in 1910, and Cleveland in 1911. [19]

Ayer realized that the agency had become too large to manage, even for him and the partners. None of the partners knew enough about every aspect of the agency to manage it properly, and he was tired of managing it on an everyday basis. He hired one manager, then another, but neither handled the agency and its varied personalities properly. Ayer hired his son-in-law Wilfred W. Fry in 1909. Fry had married Ayer's oldest daughter, Anna Gilman Ayer, in 1904. Fry, a hard worker, was made a partner two years later. Ayer gave the responsibility of managing the agency to Fry when the second manager resigned.

During World War I, the agency participated in war-work activities, and Ayer himself donated his energy to the Young Men's Christian Association (YMCA), which provided funding to Europe in its time of need. Rhandena, his wife, had died in 1914; Ayer, alone, needed something other than the agency to occupy his time.

After the war, businesses spent millions of dollars on advertising, and the agency's profits soared to $500,000-plus in 1919, the year the agency celebrated its fiftieth anniversary. Francis Wayland Ayer was congratulated for his untiring, ethical approach to advertising by such dignitaries as William Howard Taft, the former president of the United States. The same year Ayer married Martha Lawson.

Four years later, Ayer died; he was seventy-five.

In describing F. W. Ayer, George P. Rowell wrote, "He is an indomitable worker; thinks of work all the time, eats little, drinks nothing but water; has no vices, small or large, unless overwork is a vice; is the picture of health; and I sometimes think a good deal such a man as Oliver Cromwell would have been had Oliver been permitted to become an advertising agent."[20]

Although the agency continued after Ayer's death, it experienced economic problems in the late twentieth century. Several investors, including W. Y. Choi from Korea and Richard Humphreys from England, primarily through a holding company, purchased a major share of the company in 1993. Immediately, senior executives were let go and replaced. However, the agency lost major clients, including DeBeers. In 1996 the agency became part of the MacManus Group. Three years later the MacManus Group, the Leo Group, and Dentsu formed Bcom3, a major holding company that had advertising agencies and other kinds of marketing companies throughout the world. The Ayer agency continued to exist. Unfortunately, in 2002 the agency was merged into the Kaplan Thaler Group and closed.

NOTES

1. Lewis E. Atherton, "The Pioneer Merchant in Mid-America," *University of Missouri Studies* 14 (1939): 121–25.

2. Evelyn H. Knowlton, *Pepperell's Progress* (Cambridge, MA: Harvard University Press, 1948), 73–77.

3. George Rogers Taylor, *The Transportation Revolution, 1815–1860* (New York: Holt, Rinehart and Winston, 1951), 174–75.

4. Ralph M. Hower, *The History of an Advertising Agency: N. W. Ayer and Son at Work, 1869–1949* (Cambridge, MA: Harvard University Press, 1949), 13–19.

5. *M'Elroy's Philadelphia Directory* (1842), 1.

6. *V. B. Palmer's Business-Men's Almanac* (New York: V. B. Palmer, 1849).

7. *V. B. Palmer's Business-Men's Almanac* (New York: V. B. Palmer, 1850).

8. Donald R. Holland, "The Adman Nobody Knows: The Story of Volney Palmer, the Nation's First Agency Man," *Advertising Age* (April 23, 1973): 108.

9. S. M. Pettengill, "Reminiscences of the Advertising Business," *Printers' Ink* (December 24, 1890): 687.

10. Robert G. Albion, *The Rise of New York Port* (New York: Charles Scribner's Sons, 1939), 386.

11. George P. Rowell, *Forty Years an Advertising Agent: 1865–1905* (New York: Printers' Ink, 1906), 148.

12. Rowell, *Forty Years an Advertising Agent*, 245.

13. *American Newspaper Reporter* (November 20, 1871).

14. Rowell, *Forty Years an Advertising Agent*, 240.

15. Rowell, *Forty Years an Advertising Agent*, 355.

16. Rowell, *Forty Years an Advertising Agent*, 454.

17. Folder (advertisement) for N. W. Ayer and Son (April 1880).
18. "Our Creed," folder (advertisement) for N. W. Ayer and Son (1887).
19. N. W. Ayer and Son announcements (1903, 1905, 1910, 1911).
20. Rowell, *Forty Years an Advertising Agent*, 443.

Chapter Three

P. T. Barnum and His Influence on Advertising

In 1910 some celebrated the one hundredth anniversary of P. T. Barnum. The same year a writer for *Printers' Ink* mentioned this celebration and proceeded to dismiss Barnum and his contributions to advertising. According to the writer,

> it is entirely misleading to celebrate the "advertising ability" of a man like Barnum without making some very sharp distinctions. It is as if medical men should celebrate a hoodoo medicine man of long ago—it is interesting as a starting point of a profession, but lamentably gross and misrepresentative of the modern development of it. [1]

However, Frank Rowsome Jr. claimed that Phineas Taylor Barnum was "one of a little group of men whose ideas and enterprise permanently shaped the art" of advertising before his death in 1891. [2]

EARLY YEARS

Phineas Taylor Barnum was born in 1810 in Bethel, Connecticut; he was named for his maternal grandfather. Barnum learned the value of money early in life. For instance, when he was twelve, he sold lottery tickets for his grandfather. At fifteen, he clerked in his father's store. Two years later, he opened a porterhouse in Brooklyn. One year later, he worked as a bartender in a porterhouse in New York. From the money he earned, he opened a store in Bethel, Connecticut. As Barnum wrote in his autobiography, he learned quickly about consumer behavior. "It was 'dog eat dog'—'tit for tat.'"

Our cottons were sold for wool, our wool and cotton for silk and linen; in fact nearly everything was different from what it was represented. The customers cheated us in their fabrics: we cheated the customers with our goods. Each party expected to be cheated, if it was possible. Our eyes, and not our ears, had to be our masters. We must believe little that we saw, and less that we heard. [3]

One of the first items he advertised was the best-selling lottery ticket. These advertisements consisted of handbills, circulars, gold signs, and colored posters. The language was extravagant, and many of the advertisements rhymed. [4]

When he was twenty-one, he wrote, edited, and published *The Herald of Freedom*, a democratic weekly newspaper, in Danbury, Connecticut, and libeled a deacon of a church, for which he was jailed. Barnum claimed that the deacon had "been guilty of taking usury of an orphan boy." Barnum used the occasion to his advantage, however. When he was released, he rode in a parade that was preceded by a brass band and forty horsemen and followed by carriages filled with friends and supporters. This event was reported by the press, including his newspaper:

P. T. Barnum and the band of music took their seats in a coach drawn by six horses, which had been prepared for the occasion. The coach was preceded by forty horsemen, and a marshal, bearing the national standard. Immediately in the rear of the coach was the carriage of the Orator and the President of the day, followed by the Committee of Arrangements and sixty carriages of citizens, which joined in escorting the editor to his home in Bethel.

When the procession commenced its march amidst the roar of cannon, three cheers were given by several hundred citizens who did not join in the procession. The band of music continued to play a variety of national airs until their arrival in Bethel (a distance of three miles), when they struck up the beautiful and appropriate tune of "Home, Sweet Home." After giving three hearty cheers, the procession returned to Danbury. The utmost harmony and unanimity of feeling prevailed throughout the day, and we are happy to add that no accident occurred to mar the festivities of the occasion. [5]

Three years later he and his wife, Charity Hallett, moved to New York, where he purchased an interest in a grocery. Barnum and Hallett had married in 1829. Barnum learned about Joice Heth, an African American who had been the slave of George Washington's father. She was reportedly 161 years of age. Barnum purchased Heth for $1,000 from her promoters. Through handbills, posters, and advertisements in newspapers, the public learned that she was the first to clothe George Washington. For Heth's appearance at Niblo's in New York, Barnum arranged for the hanging of lighted transparencies—a new technology at the time—bearing the simple message

JOICE HETH

161
YEARS OLD.

In addition, he commissioned a woodcut with Heth's likeness, showing a woman with a deeply wrinkled face and nearly closed eyes wearing a lacy bonnet and a modest dress.[6]

Within the first week of her appearance, Barnum earned a profit. After New York, he brought Heth to other cities.

To sell Heth's appearances, he placed informative advertisements in newspapers and mailed anonymous letters to editors denouncing her credibility. She is "a humbug, a deception cleverly made of India rubber, whalebone, and hidden springs," he wrote.[7] Receipts and, consequently, profits increased until her death five or six months later. In response to the public's curiosity about Heth's age and to earn more money, Barnum arranged for an autopsy before the public. Each person had to pay to be admitted. Barnum learned that Heth had been about eighty years of age. He, like the public, had been deceived.

For the next several years, Barnum earned a meager living. In 1841 he tried to support a family of four by writing advertisements for the Bowry Amphitheater for four dollars a week. According to M. R. Werner, "Barnum was one of the first men in the United States to realize the power of the paid adjective in advertising theatrical attractions."[8]

Later the same year, Barnum acquired Scudder's American Museum, which was filled with natural and unnatural curiosities. The museum brought Barnum fame and fortune. He entertained the public with educated dogs, industrious fleas, jugglers, ventriloquists, Gypsies, albinos, giants, dwarfs, ropedancers, mechanical figures, glassblowers, and American Indians. More important, he knew how to advertise the museum. He placed newspaper advertisements to announce acts; sometimes these advertisements had qualities of incantations:

VISION OF THE HOURIS
VISION OF THE HOURIS
VISION OF THE HOURIS
A Tableau of 850 Men
Women and Children
CLAD IN SUITS OF SILVER ARMOUR
CLAD IN SUITS OF SILVER ARMOUR
CLAD IN SUITS OF SILVER ARMOUR[9]

Other advertisements appeared but in other forms. A brass band, which could be heard for several city blocks, played harmoniously on the balcony of the museum. Gaslights, which had the effect of modern electronic spectaculars, illuminated lower Broadway from the top of the museum. Panels placed on the outside of the museum featured large paintings of rare animals. Banners strung across streets announced a rare find. Handbills were used, as well as the reliable news column, which Barnum had perfected. As he wrote,

> I thoroughly understood the art of advertising, not merely by means of print-ers' ink, which I have always used freely, and to which I confess myself so much indebted for my success, but by turning every possible circumstance to my account. It was my monomania to make the Museum the town wonder and town talk. I often seized upon an opportunity by instinct, even before I had a very definite conception as to how it should be used, and it seemed, somehow, to mature itself and serve my purpose. [10]

When ordinary forms of advertising failed, Barnum improvised. For in-stance, he instructed a man to place bricks on the corners of several streets. He then instructed the man to carry at least one brick to each corner and exchange it for the other. The man was not to comment to anyone. On the hour, the man was to go to the museum and present a ticket, then enter. Within the first hour, approximately five hundred men and women stood and watched, trying to solve the mystery. When the man went to the museum, they followed and purchased tickets, hoping to learn the answer inside. Bar-num's walking advertisement attracted so many people that after a few days the police asked Barnum to withdraw the man from the street. Reporters wrote about the event for several weeks. Harvey W. Root wrote, "This was his aim in advertising, the goal for which he strove in all his publicity, to make people 'talk,' to make them wonder 'what Barnum would do next,' and to have the papers repeat and spread it." [11]

Another example of improvisation was his invention of "Dr. Griffin" and his preserved Feejee Mermaid. "Dr. Griffin" was actually Levi Lyman, an associate of Barnum. To sell the mermaid to the public, Barnum placed stories in numerous newspapers. These stories informed readers that Dr. Griffin had purchased the mermaid in China for the Lyceum of Natural History in London but that he would be exhibiting the specimen at Concert Hall for one week. A week later Barnum announced that he had secured the rare specimen for the American Museum. According to Frank Presbrey, "Barnum told the public that the 'Wonder of Creation' had been viewed at Concert Hall by 'hundreds of naturalists and other scientific gentlemen' who 'beheld it with real wonder and amusement.'" [12] Because of the advanced publicity, the exhibition was a success; the museum's receipts more than tripled the first week—from slightly more than $1,000 to slightly more than $3,000. According to James W. Cook, "The Feejee Mermaid made Barnum the most famous trickster of the nineteenth century." [13]

Another example of improvisation occurred when he hired a man to ac-cuse the American Museum of swindling him out of twenty-five cents. The man had paid twenty-five cents to see the "bearded woman" at the museum.

The man believed that the woman was actually a man garbed in a dress "to deceive and defraud" the public. The man asked that Barnum be punished. Of course, the press covered the trial, which Barnum had desired. Barnum protested his innocence. For additional publicity, he recruited witnesses who testified to the gender of the "Bearded Lady." These witnesses included her father, her husband, and several physicians who had examined her. An editor of a Connecticut newspaper observed, "Being a case of so novel a character, the newsmongers caught it up and reported it at great length, giving our friend Barnum the advantage not only of a most extensive free advertisement of the Bearded Lady still on exhibition at the Museum, but in a form which his money could not well have purchased." [14]

The publicity was so arranged "that the newspaper accounts of the trial and the sworn evidence of the Bearded Lady's genuineness would appear just at the right time to attract business to the museum on a national holiday." [15]

In addition to these uncommon forms of publicity, Barnum implemented baby shows, baby contests, and beauty contests to arouse the public's curiosity. Undoubtedly, he was the first in the United States to use these shows and contests to attract attention. He was responsible for implementing the first successful advertising campaigns. He realized that campaigns increased sales. According to Frank Rowsome Jr.,

> in Barnum's time advertising was simply a series of announcements, a process but not a progression. His acute sense of timing told him that this was wrong, that any promotion should have a carefully timed sequence, leading up to a crescendo of interlocked advertising and publicity. [16]

He applied this belief in advertising Tom Thumb.

MIDDLE YEARS

Tom Thumb

Charles Stratton, a midget, was born in Connecticut. In 1842 his parents signed an agreement with Barnum that allowed Barnum to exploit the child; the parents could accompany their son and would get paid. However, for the first year, the family earned only a few dollars a week, plus food and lodging. When the receipts increased after the first year, Barnum raised their income to $25 a week. To sell "Tom Thumb," Barnum had him tour the United States. Barnum advertised the age of Tom Thumb as eleven instead of five. He advertised his place of birth as England instead of Connecticut. He had Tom Thumb introduced to prominent families, which was mentioned in advertisements. Biographies as well as lithographs were printed and distributed wherever he toured. Newspaper editors published stories about him, which sparked additional interest. When he appeared at the American Museum, most of the public had read about him and desired to see him. Barnum introduced him as "General Tom Thumb freshly arrived from England," and the crowds laughed. In the thirteen months that he was at the American Museum, almost one hundred thousand persons paid to see him.

Barnum, who had grown to enjoy the General, brought him to Europe, where they entertained royalty, including the Duke of Wellington and Queen Victoria. Dressed like Napoleon, Tom Thumb made an unforgettable impression on the noble class. He and Barnum were invited to rambling palaces and plush estates and chateaus. News stories featured these exploits primarily because readers desired to learn about society's elite.

Barnum had a miniature carriage built for the General:

> It was a four-wheeler, with a body eleven inches wide and twenty high, painted red, white and blue. The door handles, hub caps and lamp brackets were silver. The plate-glass windows had Venetian blinds. The cushions were covered with yellow silk. The panels of the doors displayed Britannia and the Goddess of Liberty, supported by the British lion and the American eagle, with the motto, "Go Ahead!"[17]

The carriage cost Barnum $1,500. Barnum purchased four Shetland ponies to pull the carriage, and he hired an eight-year-old as the coachman and a seven-year-old as the footman. Both were garbed in tailored attire. Wherever the carriage with Tom appeared, crowds cheered.

In Paris the General was so popular that a café was named Tom Ponce. Artists begged him to sit for them. Composers wrote songs about him. Shop windows displayed statuettes of him.

After Paris, they toured southern France, Spain, Belgium, and other European countries. General Tom Thumb was greeted with the same enthusiasm wherever he toured. Barnum applied reverse psychology in his advertising. Before the General appeared anywhere, Barnum had an announcement posted. He directed the public not to get excited but to keep quiet. He wrote, "Strange as it may seem, people who were told to keep quiet would get terribly excited, and when the General arrived excitement would be at fever heat . . . and the treasury filled!"[18] The tour lasted three years. Approximately five million persons paid to see Tom Thumb. He had been kissed by four queens and thousands of other women. The tour's profits were more than $1 million; Tom Thumb's share was half. Barnum was not greedy, and Tom Thumb toured in one of Barnum's shows for several years. They remained friends for life.

In 1846 Barnum employed carpenters and other laborers to construct a Chinese- and Turkish-style lavish mansion along the sea in Fairfield, Connecticut. Two years later he moved his family to Iranistan, his new home.

During the 1840s, Barnum expanded a small lecture hall into the Moral Lecture Room in the American Museum. The Moral Lecture Room was actually a large theater in which patrons saw moral dramas played out by actors and actresses. Such plays included *The Drunkard; or, The Fallen Saved.*

Jenny Lind

Jenny Lind was the most famous performer in Europe. According to Ruth Hume, "She had everything: a thrilling voice, dramatic talent, and a reputation for piety, modesty, and good works."[19] Barnum had read about her when he was touring Europe with General Tom Thumb, and he desired that she tour America. In 1850 he hired an Englishman to offer her $1,000 per concert, plus expenses. Jenny accepted with stipulations. Barnum had to assure her that he would hire her conductor, composer, and pianist, as well as a sixty-member orchestra. He also had to deposit $187,500 in a London bank before she left Europe.

Barnum soon realized that most Americans had not heard of Jenny Lind. Therefore, he had to enlighten them. An excerpt from his first press release set the tone:

> Miss Lind has numerous better offers than the one she has accepted from me; but she has great anxiety to visit America. She speaks of this country and its institutions in the highest terms of praise, and as money is by no means the greatest inducement that can be laid before her, she is determined to visit us.
>
> In her engagement with me (which includes Havana as well as the United States), she expressly reserves for herself the right to sing for and give charitable concerts whenever she may think proper.
>
> Since her debut in England, she has given to the poor from her own private purse more than the whole amount which I engaged to give her, and the proceeds of concerts for charitable purposes in Great Britain, where she has sung gratuitously, have realized more than ten times that amount. During her last eight months she has been singing entirely for charitable purposes, and is now founding a benevolent institution in Stockholm, her native city, at a cost of $350,000.
>
> A visit from such a woman, who regards her high artistic powers as a gift from heaven, for the melioration of affliction and distress, and whose every thought and deed is philanthropy, I feel persuaded, will prove a blessing to America, as it has to every country she has visited, and I feel every confidence that my countrymen and women will join me heartily in saying, "God Bless Her!"[20]

Barnum then distributed an authorized biographical pamphlet and photograph that informed the reader of her inimitable talent.

Before Jenny left for the United States, she gave two concerts in Liverpool, at Barnum's request. Both sold out. A critic in London covered the concerts, then wrote a review that praised her performances. When the review appeared in one of the newspapers hours later, several copies were sent to Barnum. The review, which detailed "the unbridled enthusiasm of the Liverpool audience and its grief at Jenny's imminent departure,"[21] was published in newspapers throughout the United States before she arrived.

Barnum then wrote a letter addressed to himself. The letter, which was supposed to be from Julius Benedict, her composer, appeared in the *New York Daily Tribune*:

> I have just heard Mlle. Jenny Lind, whose voice has acquired—*if that were possible*—even additional powers and effect by a timely and well-chosen repose. You may depend on it, that such a performance as hers—in the finest pieces of her *repertoire*—must warrant an unprecedented excitement. . . . Mlle. Lind is very anxious to give a Welcome to America in a kind of national song, which, if I can obtain the poetry of one of your first-rate literary men, I shall set to music, and which she will sing in addition to the pieces originally fixed upon.[22]

The letter was followed by an announcement about a song-writing contest. To enter, one had to write a poem that could be set to music. Barnum received more than seven hundred entries. The winner, poet Bayard Taylor, received $200.

When the ship entered New York harbor, Barnum greeted it with a reporter from the *New York Tribune*. When the ship docked on Sunday, September 1, 1850, about forty thousand persons were present. They followed Jenny and her entourage as they traveled in Barnum's carriage to the Irving House Hotel. Barnum, surveying the crowd, realized that his promotional efforts had paid off. Merchants in New York immediately advertised "hastily renamed Jenny Lind products: everything from Jenny Lind cigars to Jenny Lind sewing stands, gloves, scarves, riding hats, and perfume."[23]

Barnum then promoted the Great Jenny Lind Opening Concert Ticket Auction. He persuaded his friend John Genin to be the first person in the United States to purchase a ticket to hear Jenny sing. Barnum then visited Dr. Brandreth, who was known for his patent medicines, and persuaded him to purchase the first ticket at auction. Barnum assured him that it would be an excellent opportunity for him to advertise his medicines. When the auction occurred, several thousand were present to bid against one another, including Genin's bookkeeper and Dr. Brandreth's cashier. The cashier's bid of $25 was the first. Genin's bookkeeper bid $50. Others announced various bids. However, everyone, except Genin's bookkeeper, stopped bidding at $225.[24]

The publicity was so encouraging that Barnum repeated the auction in several cities. The reviews of Jenny's performances were filled with superlatives; some critics claimed that she was the greatest singer they had heard. Barnum, of course, was ecstatic. Although wealthy, he realized that such publicity would help sell tickets and consequently add to his fortune.

The tour covered more than fifteen cities in the United States and Canada, as well as Havana, Cuba. Jenny gave more than 90 concerts, not the 150 that had been planned. Barnum claimed that he renegotiated Jenny's contract after her successful performances at Castle Garden in New York. The renegotiation benefited Jenny, not Barnum, as she was provided a percentage of profits in addition to her fee. Barnum claimed that the renegotiation was his idea, not Jenny's.[25]

On June 9, 1851, Jenny informed Barnum she was ending the tour. Barnum and Jenny parted friends. The tour he had managed earned more than $700,000. Others in her entourage encouraged her to leave Barnum and tour alone. Jenny tried, but she was not very successful. Organizing the advertising was too difficult. Her affection for Otto Goldschmidt, her pianist, was blossoming; they were married in Boston on February 5, 1852. On May 24, 1852, she performed her last concert in the United States in Castle Garden, the concert hall where she had performed her first.

The campaign for Jenny Lind reflected Barnum's brilliance. "It converted her, in the months before her arrival in this country, from a relatively unknown soprano to the toast of America, greeted by ecstatic thousands who vied to draw her carriage."[26]

Barnum wrote and published *The Life of P. T. Barnum, Written by Himself* in 1854. The book, which was edited and published under different titles over the years, became a best seller.

Barnum invested in the Jerome Clock Company, which ultimately went bankrupt, forcing him and his family to leave Iranistan in 1856. They retreated to a rented house in New York, and Iranistan was closed.

In 1857, desiring to return to Iranistan until it was sold or auctioned, Barnum hired carpenters and painters to repair it. Apparently, a worker's pipe was carelessly misplaced; it set fire to the mansion, causing it to burn to the ground. In New York, Barnum received a telegram about the fire from his brother Philo. Although the home was worth $150,000, it was insured for only $28,000.

In 1865 Barnum became a Republican representative of the legislature of Connecticut. On July 13, while he addressed the legislature, a telegram from his son-in-law Samuel H. Hurd arrived. It informed Barnum that his famous American Museum in New York had burned. Barnum continued his oratory. The following morning he went to New York to see what remained of his museum. Later, he wrote,

Here were destroyed, almost in a breath, the accumulated results of many years of incessant toil, my own and my predecessors', in gathering from every quarter of the globe myriads of curious productions of nature and art—an assemblage of rarities which a half million of dollars could not restore, and a quarter of a century could not collect. [27]

A reporter for the *New York Times* wrote that the fire "originated in a defective furnace in the collar under Groor's restaurant, beneath the office of the Museum." [28] The following day, a reporter for the same newspaper wrote, "Some of the employees of the Museum were notified a day or two ago that threats of burning the establishment had been made, but little attention was paid to this information." [29] H. O. Tiffany, an employee at the museum, claimed that he discovered flames on the second, third, and top floors. Had the fire "originated in a defective furnace"? Or had fires been started on the second, third, and top floors? Several Confederate soldiers had set fires to several hotels and Barnum's American Museum in 1864. [30] However, the fire department had responded immediately. Had another Confederate soldier or an enemy of Barnum's repeated the act?

Undeterred by his loss, which he estimated to be $400,000, Barnum opened Barnum's New American Museum on November 13, 1865. However, it, too, burned on March 3, 1868. Barnum was asleep at his home in New York; he learned about the fire the next morning when he read the newspaper. Barnum claimed he lost more than $250,000 as a result of the fire.

Although he thought about retiring after his beloved New American Museum burned, he promoted other acts and tours, including General Tom Thumb. In 1870 he and a partner created the P. T. Barnum's Grand Traveling Museum, Menagerie, Caravan and Circus, the largest of its kind in the United States.

In 1872 the Hippotheatron—a multisided wood-and-iron building in New York that Barnum purchased for part of his Grand Traveling Museum, Menagerie, Caravan and Circus—burned, killing most of the animals. As if this was not bad enough, Charity, his wife, died a year later. Several weeks later, in 1874, he married Nancy Fish, a much younger woman.

Barnum dissolved his partnership and disposed of some of his enterprises in 1876. With others, he created the Greatest Show on Earth, which included a circus and a museum. He had rail cars built for his show, which traveled across the country. He employed large-scale colored posters. He had a rail car—"Advertising Coach"—that preceded the show by at least two weeks. Opened to the public, this rail car displayed posters and other media of Barnum, his circus, and his animals.

LATER YEARS: JUMBO

In 1881 Barnum propositioned his leading competitors, James Bailey and James Hutchinson, and together they merged the Greatest Show on Earth and the London Circus. Barnum knew that the circus needed a major attraction. Jumbo, perhaps the largest elephant ever, was on display in the London Zoo. Barnum offered $10,000 for the animal. Eventually, the superintendent agreed. Reporters in London learned of the agreement and interviewed statesmen and others, who urged that the sale be canceled. The following excerpt appeared in the *London Daily Telegraph* and reflects the sentiment of the British press at the time:

> Our amiable monster must dwell in a tent, take part in the routine of a circus, and, instead of his by-gone friendly trots with British girls and boys, and perpetual luncheon on buns and oranges, must amuse a Yankee mob, and put up with peanuts and waffles.[31]

Yet, the press in the United States encouraged Barnum to purchase the animal.

Barnum watched the ship that carried Jumbo ease into New York harbor. Thousands of spectators waited patiently for the large elephant to be brought ashore. Thousands more lined the streets as Jumbo passed on the way to Madison Square Garden. Public interest was widespread. Although Barnum had paid $10,000 for Jumbo and $20,000 for the elephant's transportation to the United States, he grossed more than $30,000 the first week that the elephant was on display.[32]

Newspapers carried stories about Jumbo, and readers sent hundreds of gifts. Some consumer products carried Jumbo's name; others were compared to the elephant's strength or size. When the Brooklyn Bridge was completed, Jumbo tested its strength. Thousands lined the shores to watch.

On September 15, 1885, after the Greatest Show on Earth had performed in St. Thomas, Ontario, Jumbo and a smaller elephant were led to a train car. The trainer saw an unexpected freight train approaching and tried to get both elephants off the track; the engineer saw the elephants and applied the brakes. Jumbo was hit and killed; the smaller elephant was injured. Barnum informed the press that Jumbo had pushed the smaller elephant to safety, and the news was cabled all over the world. Like Barnum, millions experienced grief. Never missing an opportunity, Barnum the showman arranged for Henry Ward, the nation's leading taxidermist, to prepare Jumbo for exhibition. Eventually, Jumbo was given to Tufts University.

Two years later, Barnum offered Bailey an equal partnership in the new Barnum and Bailey circus, which Bailey accepted. The same year, their winter quarters in Bridgeport, Connecticut, which contained several buildings that housed numerous animals, burned. The fire started around 10 pm in the main building but spread to the other buildings, killing most of the animals. A reporter for the *New York Times* wrote, "The watchman making his rounds discovered the fire and started to give the alarm, when some unknown person hit him on the head with a blunt instrument, felling him to the ground and cutting a number of severe gashes on his head. He staggered to his feet and gave the alarm, enabling the other watchmen in the building, who were preparing for bed, to escape."[33]

In the November 22, 1887, issue of the *New York Times*, a reporter wrote,

> George W. Myers, the watchman who discovered the fire and sounded the first alarm, had an experience that seems to prove the fire to have been of incendiary origin. He found the door of the stable in which the ponies were housed open when it ought to have been closed. The stable was already on fire. He sounded the alarm, then laid the lantern he was carrying on the ground, and was about to enter the stable to loose the ponies when he was struck on the head with a billy by an unknown man. He lay unconscious, he supposes, for 10 or 15 minutes. When he recovered the fire was raging in all quarters of the main building, which was about 200 feet broad by 500 feet long.[34]

In the same story, the reporter asked Barnum about the fire. His lengthy response claimed that the fire had been a blessing in disguise, at least to the public. He stated, "Besides, it will give us a lot of free advertising. That, of course, will be some compensation for our loss." Barnum informed the reporter that a greater show would rise from the ashes. He stated, "I begin to think it was a good thing we were burned out after all."[35]

Barnum disclosed that the land in Bridgeport, on which the winter quarters had been constructed, had increased in value, and, consequently, he would not rebuild the winter quarters on it.

The reporter ended the story with the following:

> Sunday's fire was the seventh from which the old showman has been a direct sufferer. In October, 1852, his showy residence in Bridgeport, known as Iranistan was nearly destroyed by fire. Five years later the same house, reconstructed and refurnished, was completely destroyed, entailing a loss of about $125,000. In July, 1865, the American Museum, at Broadway and Ann-street, was burned, and in March, 1868, his new museum on Broadway, near Prince-street, was completely wiped out by fire. Three years later, December, 1871, the Hippotheatron was totally destroyed by fire, and in July, 1873, fire burned up a tent and all its furnishings while the show was in Chicago. Taken altogether, Mr. Barnum's losses will aggregate close to $1,000,000.[36]

What is troubling about these fires is that none seemed to bother Barnum. As he described in his autobiography, his reactions displayed unconcern, even when at least two of the fires may have been started by arsonists.

Although he lost money as a result of each fire, he rebounded financially quite successfully as a result of the publicity about each fire. Specific individuals called Barnum "the arsonist." Of course, this accusation was made in haste and not based on any evidence. However, fires followed Barnum throughout his professional life.

Barnum made enemies. It is not inconceivable to think that one or more of his enemies may have been responsible for one or more of the fires. For instance, he and James Gordon Bennett, the publisher of the *New York Herald*, had several confrontations, including a major dispute over real estate. Whether Bennett was responsible for one of the fires is debatable.

Barnum died in 1891.

From the advertising campaigns discussed, it is easy to summarize Barnum's philosophy of advertising: first, he realized that one needed to keep one's name or business before the public; second, he realized that unique or original devices could be used to produce conversation as well as attention; third, he realized that one needed to take advantage of every opportunity to bring about editorial comment or news; and fourth, he realized that one needed to provide more real value than one's competitors. Barnum's success, reputation, and number of imitators proved that he was correct not to use the more traditional methods of advertising of his day but the unusual methods of advertising that he perfected. Thus, the writer for *Printers' Ink* apparently overlooked the above, which undoubtedly had a dramatic influence on advertising.

According to Jennifer Wicke,

> He looms largest in American advertising partly because circumstances permitted his exploitation of the pure, self-reflexive poetics of advertising before industrial advertising had realized it in such monumental form. Under his hegemony, advertising came to be a form of social literature distributed to fashion as aesthetic space around products, which in Barnum's case were all theatrical and "aesthetic" spectacles, but for later advertisers were such nonspectacular goods as shoes, inks, machines, and plumbing tools.[37]

NOTES

1. "Barnum and Advertising," *Printers' Ink* (July 14, 1910), 193.

2. Frank Rowsome Jr., *They Laughed When I Sat Down: An Informal History of Advertising in Words and Pictures* (New York: McGraw-Hill, 1959), 29.

3. M. R. Werner, *Barnum* (New York: Harcourt, Brace, 1923), 15.

4. Frank Presbrey, *The History and Development of Advertising* (New York: Doubleday, 1929), 212.

5. *The Herald of Freedom*, December 12, 1832.

6. Benjamin Reiss, *The Showman and the Slave: Race, Death, and Memory in Barnum's America* (Cambridge, MA: Harvard University Press, 2001), 33.

7. Rowsome, *They Laughed When I Sat Down*, 30.

8. Werner, *Barnum*, 42.

9. E. S. Turner, *The Shocking History of Advertising* (New York: E. P. Dutton, 1953), 130.

10. P. T. Barnum, *Barnum's Own Story: The Autobiography of P. T. Barnum* (New York: Dover, 1961).

11. Harvey W. Root, *The Unknown Barnum* (New York: Harper and Brothers, 1927), 205–6.

12. Presbrey, *The History and Development of Advertising*, 216.

13. James W. Cook, *The Arts of Deception: Playing with Fraud in the Age of Barnum* (Cambridge, MA: Harvard University Press, 2001), 119.

14. Root, *The Unknown Barnum*, 208.

15. Root, *The Unknown Barnum*, 209.

16. Rowsome, *They Laughed When I Sat Down*, 30.

17. J. Bryan III, *The World's Greatest Showman: The Life of P. T. Barnum* (New York: Random House, 1956), 56.

18. Bryan, *The World's Greatest Showman*, 59.

19. Ruth Hume, "Selling the Swedish Nightingale: Jenny Lind and P. T. Barnum," *American Heritage* (October 1977): 99.

20. *New York Commercial Advertiser*, February 29, 1850.

21. Hume, "Selling the Swedish Nightingale," 103.

22. *New York Daily Tribune*, August 14, 1850.

23. Hume, "Selling the Swedish Nightingale," 104.

24. Hume, "Selling the Swedish Nightingale," 104.

25. P. T. Barnum, *Struggles and Triumphs or, Forty Years' Recollections of P. T. Barnum* (New York: Macmillan, 1930), 204–5.

26. Rowsome, *They Laughed When I Sat Down*, 30.

27. Barnum, *Barnum's Own Story*, 363.

28. "Barnum's American Museum Burns," *New York Times*, July 14, 1865.

29. "The Late Fire," *New York Times*, July 15, 1865.

30. Irving Wallace, *The Fabulous Showman: The Life and Times of P. T. Barnum* (New York: Knopf, 1959): 225–29.

31. Theodore James Jr., "World Went Mad When Mighty Jumbo Came to America," *Smithsonian* (May 1982): 138.

32. James, "World Went Mad," 146.

33. "A Great Loss to Barnum," *New York Times*, November 21, 1887.

34. "Barnum on Top as Usual," *New York Times*, November 22, 1887.

35. "Barnum on Top as Usual."

36. "Barnum on Top as Usual."

37. Jennifer Wicke, *Advertising Fictions: Literature, Advertisement, and Social Reading* (New York: Columbia University Press, 1988), 70.

Chapter Four

Lydia Pinkham and Her Vegetable Compound: The Advertising of a Patent Medicine

People who lived in the colonies depended on homemade remedies to cure illnesses. Generally, the formulas for these remedies passed from one generation to another. Or colonists visited physicians, who charged them for their Indian-type remedies; however, many colonists could not afford doctors. Or they could purchase patent medicines, which in most cases caused drunkenness.

Advertisements for patent medicines appeared in newspapers during the eighteenth and nineteenth centuries, partly because advertising paid the printers' expenses. Many newspapers, especially colonial newspapers, would have died after a few issues had it not been for these advertisements.

In the 1720s and 1730s, for instance, discussions about vaccination against smallpox appeared in newspapers. Containing a straightforward style of writing, most of these discussions appeared in advertisements created primarily to sell cures. By 1736, creativity had replaced the straightforward style of copy, as the following advertisement illustrates, for Dr. Bateman's Pectoral Drops, which appeared in the *Pennsylvania Gazette*, July 1, 1736:

> Dr. Bateman's PECTORAL DROPS, which are given with such great Success in all Fluxes, Spitting of Blood, Consumptions, Small Pox, Measles, Colds, Coughs, and Pains in the Limbs or Joints; they cure Agues, and the most violent Fever in the World, if taken in Time, and give present Ease in the most racking Torment of the Gout; the same in all sorts of Pains (be they ever so violent) they give Ease in a few Minutes after taken; they ease After-Pains, prevent Miscarriages, and are wonderful in the Stone and Gravel in the Kidneys, Bladder and Ureters; bringing away Slime, Gravel, and oftentimes

Stones of a great bigness, and are the best of Medicines for all Stoppages or
Pains in the Stomach, Shortness of Breath, and Straitness of the Breast, re-
enkindling the almost extinguish'd natural Heat in diseas'd Bodies, by which
Means they restore the languishing to perfect Health; Their manner of working
is by moderate Sweat and Urine. For Children's Distempers, no Medicine yet
discover'd can compare with it; For it cures the Gripes in their Stomach and
Bowels, by expelling Wind upwards and downwards. It causes weak and forward Children to take their natural Rest.

It is taken with great Success in the Rickets, and, in a Word, it hath
restored Hundreds of poor Infants to their strength and liveliness, that have
been reduced to meet Skeletons.

Sold by *Miles Strickland* in *Market-Street, Philadelphia*, price 3 s, a Bottle, with Directions.[1]

According to the advertising, this remedy cured more than thirty illnesses,
diseases, or abnormalities. Only three shillings a bottle, the product sold well
throughout the century. Other imported patent medicines were advertised
throughout the colonies, and most, like Dr. Bateman's Pectoral Drops, offered the consumer relief from practically any illness or disease.

As newspapers increased in size and number of pages, more advertisements for more medicines appeared. Some advertisers mentioned that their
concoctions were sanctioned by royalty. For instance, in the February 19,
1770, issue of the *Boston Chronicle*, the London Book-Store of Boston advertised the Essence of Pepper-Mint, by His Majesty's Royal Letters Patent.[2]
The product sold for one shilling four pence. In return, the consumer received "speedy relief" from colic, gout, and other illnesses.

During and after the Revolutionary War, advertisements for imported
medicines decreased. Americans realized that the need for medicines was
great. Consequently, they started advertising what they produced. Advertisements that listed medicines sold at apothecaries appeared weekly. Physicians
also served as dentists, veterinarians, druggists, and barbers and often advertised their services and cure-all potions.

In the nineteenth century, advertising for patent medicines occupied most
of the space in numerous newspapers. For instance, advertisements for Dr.
Ryan's Incomparable Worm-Destroying Sugar-Plums, Turlington's Balsam
of Life, Godfrey's Cordial, Steer's Genuine Opodeldor, Stoughton's Bitters
or Elixir, Antipertussis, Lockyer's Pills, James' Fever Powder, Dalbey's Car-
minative, and Anderson's Pills, just to name a few, appeared in newspapers
from New England to Florida. It seemed that certain names and labels could
ward off illnesses, even if the product could not.

Advertisements for mineral waters, such as Dr. Willard's Mineral Water,
Ballston or Congress Mineral Water, and Godwin's Celebrated German Water, were similar to advertisements for patent medicines—that is, the copy
was filled with outrageous claims. For instance, Dr. Willard claimed that the

water from his mineral spring in Connecticut could cure such maladies as "Erisipelas, Salt Rheum, Leprous Affections, and indeed almost every cutaneous complaint," including cancer, gout, paralytic disorders, and other diseases. [3]

In the 1830s and 1840s, specific patent medicines romanticized the American Indian through illustration, name, and advertising copy. For instance, Dr. Freeman's Indian Specific used the word to identify his product and to persuasively point out that the product's ingredients were from herbs that Indians used to cure consumption. Advertisements for Wright's Indian Vegetable Pills, which sold exceptionally well in the 1840s, contained the following: "THE ORIGINAL AND ONLY GENUINE INDIAN MEDICINE."[4]

Makers of patent medicines soon realized that it was more profitable to manufacture and advertise several remedies for several illnesses instead of producing one remedy and advertising it as a cure-all. Dr. Bardwell, for instance, had Aromatic Lozenges of Steel, Re-Animating Solar Tincture or Pabulum of Life, Genuine Ague and Fever Drops, and Annodyne Essence— all for different illnesses. Other companies, such as Michael Lee and Company of Baltimore, marketed numerous patent medicines.

Some companies manufactured gadgets that were to be worn. These gadgets supposedly used electricity. According to the advertisements, these devices could restore the nervous system as well as cure all kinds of diseases. Of course, the claims in these advertisements were false. These gadgets could not cure illnesses. Yet, like the copy in advertisements for patent medicines, the copy in these advertisements contained superlatives. Words or phrases such as "genuine," "original," or "nature's own" appeared often. Testimonies, too, appeared.

By the end of the nineteenth century, patent medicines and devices filled houses throughout the nation. Many patent medicines died in the early twentieth century because newspapers received advertisements from other manufacturers and businesses and because muckraking journalists discredited the patent medicine industry and consequently encouraged lawmakers to enact legislation that would eliminate or at least restrict their availability.

LYDIA E. PINKHAM AND HER VEGETABLE COMPOUND

Lydia E. Pinkham was born on February 9, 1819, in Lynn, Massachusetts, to William and Rebecca Estes, both Quakers. Pinkham, the tenth child of a dozen, is best known for concocting a vegetable compound that she targeted to women before the twentieth century.

Pinkham's father, a shoemaker turned gentleman farmer and owner of real estate, provided his family with physical comfort. Her mother introduced the family to the controversial ideas of Emanuel Swedenborg, a Swedish scientist and theologian who claimed to have experienced a spiritual world where people went after they died. Followers of Swedenborg were abolitionists, vegetarians, and abstained from drinking alcohol. Pinkham undoubtedly was influenced by Swedenborg's ideas. For instance, she joined the Lynn Female Anti-Slavery Society soon after it was founded.

Pinkham graduated from the Lynn Academy, then taught school for several years. In 1843, as a result of organizing the Freeman's Institute for the purpose of encouraging members to discuss various ideas, not just abolition, she met Isaac Pinkham, twenty-nine, a widower with a young daughter, who attended the meetings. They married later the same year. Remaining in Lynn, Pinkham gave birth to Charles Hacker Pinkham in 1844, Daniel Rogers Pinkham in 1849, and William Henry Pinkham in 1852. Another son had been born before Daniel Rogers, but he died when he was an infant.

Isaac Pinkham, a dreamer, worked at numerous jobs and often spent more than he earned. In 1857 he moved the family to Bedford, Massachusetts, and tried farming. Lydia gave birth to Aroline Chase Pinkham the same year. Three years later, the family returned to Lynn. Although the family earned a meager living during the years of the Civil War, Isaac's investments in land eventually brought the family some financial security. In 1873, however, a number of banks failed, and others, including those in Lynn, threatened to foreclose on mortgages. Isaac was sued and almost arrested for not being able to pay his debts; as a result, his health deteriorated. The family struggled but survived.

Lydia had been influenced by the American Eclectics—that is, doctors who practiced herbal medicine. Undoubtedly, she was influenced by Dr. John King's book *The American Dispensatory*, which concerned plants and their medicinal purposes. Reportedly, she added ingredients to a formula that she had found in the book, as well as to a formula provided by George Todd, who had borrowed money from the Pinkham family. As partial payment on the debt, he had offered the family the recipe for a home remedy.[5] Lydia had been brewing a medicine consisting of unicorn root, life root, black cohosh, pleurisy root, and fenugreek seed, which supposedly cured "women's weakness."[6] Lydia allowed members of her family and friends to test the formula. Apparently, the formula worked; "women's weakness" declined. However, Lydia did not think of advertising and selling the product. That thought occurred to Daniel, one of her sons, and Lydia E. Pinkham's Vegetable Compound began as a business in 1875. The first advertisements consisted of mere handbills printed by a local shop. In addition, a four-page pamphlet titled *Guide for Women* was distributed, which Lydia had written and which concerned feminine health (cleanliness, good nutrition, fresh air, and exercise), the problems with the medical profession, and the positive aspects of the vegetable compound. The product, which contained 18 percent alcohol, was brewed in the cellar and bottled.

The Lydia E. Pinkham Medicine Company, with William Pinkham as proprietor (primarily because he had no outstanding debts), officially organized in 1876, and Daniel and William traveled to various towns and cities to market the product. Eventually, druggists, who had been successful stocking other patent medicines, began ordering the vegetable compound. However, sales of the medicine were minuscule, particularly in cities such as Brooklyn, where Daniel tried several forms of handbills in addition to distributing the pamphlet. He also suggested that the advertising copy in the pamphlet include other parts of the anatomy, such as the kidneys, besides the uterus.

Daniel thought of adding a photograph of a woman to the handbills. The woman, he realized, needed to appear healthy and trustworthy. Daniel knew immediately that his mother's face displayed the motherly, if not grandmotherly, image he imagined. After discussing the idea with his mother, she agreed to pose for the photograph that eventually graced the product's labels and countless advertisements.

Later, Daniel placed one of the handbill's contents as an advertisement in the *Boston Herald*, for which his family criticized him because the advertisement was too expensive. However, the advertisement proved somewhat successful, and the family eventually hired T. C. Evans to create advertisements for newspapers.

According to Dan Yaeger, "Lydia Pinkham was transformed overnight from a mother and housewife into the very symbol of the product she made. Her visage gave life to the Vegetable Compound and provided the company with the image of stability, wisdom, wholesomeness, and healthy femininity."[7]

After her face graciously adorned advertisements for a year, sales of the product dramatically increased, and the family was offered six figures for the company and its appealing trademark; the family refused the offer, however.

According to Rita E. Loos, "Her advertisements were intimate in tone, appealing to the emotions."[8] Loos wrote, "Lydia had a variety of themes interwoven into her ads. One of these centered on political issues such as urging votes for the Greenback Party candidates. . . . Another dealt with the exploitation of women workers. . . . A third theme dealt with women's role in general."[9]

In 1881, after battling tuberculosis for two years, Daniel died; he was thirty-two. After Daniel's death, Lydia and Isaac assigned their interest in Daniel's estate to Charles, William, and Aroline. The three formed the partnership called Lydia E. Pinkham's Sons & Co. on October 19, 1881.[10] William, who was also ill with lung disease, died the same year; he was twenty-eight. The partnership was terminated; the company became known

as the Lydia E. Pinkham Medicine Company.[11] Lydia was stricken with
grief; in 1882 she suffered a stroke, then died several months later, in 1883.
She was sixty-four.

Nonetheless, the company continued to prosper under the family's guidance, and Lydia E. Pinkham's face continued to appear on labels and in
advertisements. In fact, editors of newspapers who did not have images of
certain prominent women, such as Queen Victoria, occasionally used the
image of Lydia E. Pinkham instead. Her image also inspired college students
to write songs about her and her product. The following is one example:

> Tell me, Lydia, of your secrets
> And the wonders you perform.
> How you take the sick and ailing
> And restore them to the norm.
> I will sing of Lydia Pinkham
> And her love for the human race;
> How she sells her vegetable compound,
> And the papers they publish her face. [12]

Other songs followed over the years, which helped keep Lydia E. Pinkham's
name and product before the public.

The following advertisement appeared in the *New York Times*:

LYDIA E. PINKHAM'S
Offers the
SUREST REMEDY
For the
PAINFUL ILLS AND DISORDERS SUFFERED BY WOMEN
EVERYWHERE.

It relieves pain, promotes a regular and healthy recurrence of periods and
is a great help to young girls and to women past maturity. It strengthens the
back and the pelvic organs, bringing relief and comfort to tired women who
stand all day in home, shop and factory.

Leucorrhea, Inflammation, Ulceration and Displacements of the Uterus
have been cured by it, as women everywhere gratefully testify. Regular physicians often prescribe it.

Sold by all Druggists. Price $1.00

Mrs. Pinkham's "Guide to Health" mailed to any lady sending stamp to the
Laboratory, Lynn, Mass. [13]

A line drawing of Lydia E. Pinkham was positioned to the left of the headline.

In addition to gracing newspaper advertisements, Lydia's face appeared
in pamphlets, drug store displays, and signs on barns, to mention a few.

Although her pen had advised countless female customers about their health over the years, even after her death advertisements encouraged women to write to "Mrs. Pinkham." As a result, thousands and thousands of women wrote letters to "Mrs. Pinkham," often seeking medical advice or hailing the wonders of the Vegetable Compound. Each letter received a personal reply. Other advertisements for the compound contained scientific information that was discussed in medical books, such as Dr. Frederick Hollick's *The Origin of Life* and Dr. John King's *The American Dispensatory*, and focused on numerous medical conditions, including leukorrhea and dyspepsia. Over the years, other maladies appeared on the list for which the compound was the perfect remedy. The advertising copy discussed symptoms that most individuals, especially women, experienced. Thus, to a certain extent, the advertisements manipulated readers into thinking they were ill. As a result of this manipulation, readers tried the compound. Other advertisements contained testimonials reportedly from customers whose illnesses had been cured by the compound. The Lydia E. Pinkham Medicine Company, of course, desired for women to use the compound, not see physicians, who were not necessarily well educated. Besides, almost all doctors happened to be men, and the company's literature, including advertisements, contained an antimale bias.

Harland Page Hubbard now created the advertising. He purchased space at very low rates and sold it to the Lydia E. Pinkham Medicine Company at very high rates. Eventually, the family learned of Hubbard's exorbitant charges and decreased the advertising budget. Sales dropped. In 1890 the family hired another agent, James T. Wetherald, and limited his commission. The advertising budget was increased; sales soared for at least several years, and the company earned a sizable profit.[14]

According to Donald Dale Jackson, "In 1898 the compound was the most heavily advertised product in the United States, its name as familiar as Coca-Cola and McDonald's are today."[15] In 1899, however, sales declined for the first time in nine years, probably as a result of the company's slashing its advertising budget earlier the same year. During the next ten years, sales continued to decline, no matter how much the company increased the advertising budget.

MEDIA'S CRITICISM OF PATENT MEDICINES

One explanation for the decline in sales is Cyrus Curtis, publisher of *The Ladies' Home Journal* and *Collier's Weekly*, who stopped accepting advertising for patent medicines in 1892. Another explanation is Edward Bok, editor of *The Ladies' Home Journal*, who wrote lengthy editorials against the patent medicine industry in the early twentieth century. For instance, "The

'Patent-Medicine' Curse" disclosed the amount of alcohol in different brands; "Why 'Patent Medicines' Are Dangerous" revealed that manufacturers of patent medicines were not obligated by law to list all ingredients on labels; and "A Diabolical 'Patent-Medicine' Story" disclosed the questionable marketing efforts for two patent medicines.

Bok hired Mark Sullivan to investigate Dr. Ray Vaughn Pierce and his product, Dr. Pierce's Favorite Prescription, primarily because Dr. Pierce had brought suit against *The Ladies' Home Journal* for libel. Bok had claimed that Dr. Pierce's product contained alcohol, opium, and digitalis. Dr. Pierce proved that his product did not contain opium or digitalis by having the product chemically analyzed.

Sullivan failed to find any evidence against Dr. Pierce or his product, and Bok lost the suit. However, Sullivan's investigation into patent medicines continued, and his investigative article about the patent medicine industry— specifically, the Proprietary Association, "The Patent Medicine Conspiracy against Freedom of the Press"—appeared in *Collier's Weekly* in 1905. Sullivan also informed the public that Lydia E. Pinkham had died in 1883 and had been buried in Pine Grove Cemetery in Lynn, Massachusetts.

Samuel Hopkins Adams, another investigator of the patent medicine industry, contributed several in-depth articles under the main title "The Great American Fraud" to *Collier's Weekly* in 1905. He revealed the amount of alcohol found in various patent medicines and claimed that women were in a constant stupor. He revealed the chemical formula for Liquozone in another article and discussed the exaggerated claims and false testimonials for the product in still another article. Additional articles about other questionable patent medicines followed.

Later, editors and writers of *Collier's Weekly* and *The Ladies' Home Journal* advocated federal regulation to control or prohibit patent medicines from being sold. Specific members in Congress had discussed such regulation for some time. Members of the American Medical Association, however, were divided. Certain members realized that a pure food and drug law could conceivably curtail sales of particular products by restricting advertising and possibly prohibit the manufacture of other products. Nonetheless, the Pure Food and Drug Act took effect the first day of 1907. As a result, all medicines that crossed state lines had to meet certain standards of purity and had to print accurate information on the packages and labels. Lydia E. Pinkham's Vegetable Compound was no exception. For the first time, the company had to reveal the amount of alcohol and delete the exaggerated claims from the package and label. However, the Lydia E. Pinkham Medicine Company, like other makers of patent medicines, realized that it was the responsibility of the consumer to notice the changes on the package and label. The company also realized that advertisements could imply what its advertisements had claimed, and the implications would be almost as effective as the claims had been. The company's advertising agent, James T. Wetherald, placed reading notices in various newspapers primarily to convince readers that the Pure Food and Drug Act eliminated dangerous drugs from the market. Wetherald emphasized that the Lydia E. Pinkham's Vegetable Compound was safe and healthy and de-emphasized the amount of alcohol, which was 18 percent. As a result of his efforts, sales increased over the years. In 1912, for instance, sales were above $1 million.

OTHER PROBLEMS

Critics of patent medicines continued to write articles and books, and Arthur J. Cramp, of the American Medical Association's Department of Propaganda, notified the Internal Revenue Service that because of Lydia E. Pinkham's Vegetable Compound's alcoholic content, the product should be taxed. The Internal Revenue Service informed the Lydia E. Pinkham Medicine Company that the product's formula had to be changed or the product would be taxed; the company complied and changed the formula. The Treasury Department accepted the change in 1914. However, the product's taste was not the same, and sales decreased during the next several years.

The company faced federal litigation in 1915, when a complaint concerning the product's effectiveness was filed. The company's lawyers claimed that the complaint applied to the chemical analysis of the old formula, not the new formula, and therefore was out of date. Eventually, the company faced a fine of $50, primarily for false claims that had appeared on labels. The company paid the fine and changed the labels.

In 1919, with the passage of the Volstead Act, the company feared that the government would classify the product an alcoholic beverage. Although the company thought of decreasing the amount of alcohol, the change was never made. In 1925, based on chemical analysis, the government pressured the company to stop marketing the product as a medicine exclusively for women. Later the same year, the company complied and changed the labels and advertisements.

In 1926 Lydia Pinkham Gove pitted herself and her mother, Aroline Gove, against the Pinkham side of the family for control of the company. Although Arthur Pinkham served as president of the company, the Goves controlled the finances. Lydia battled Pinkham, even though the company's board of directors had given him absolute control of the company's operations. However, when Wetherald died, Lydia created an advertising agency primarily for the purpose of saving the company money and concurrently played a role in the company's direction. Several family members, including Charles Pinkham, confronted Lydia, but she persevered by not supporting any advertising that had not met with her approval.

Eventually, the matter was brought before the courts when the Pinkhams initiated legal action in 1936. The court sided with the Pinkhams in the sense that the Goves were not to interfere in the business. Lydia, undeterred, refused to obey the court, and the Pinkhams filed another suit. Lydia had her day in court and lost. The judge sided with the Pinkhams.

In 1938 Congress passed the Federal Food, Drug, and Cosmetic Act. This legislation required the makers of patent medicines to list the ingredients on their medicines' labels. The same year, the Federal Trade Commission cited the company for its advertising. According to the Federal Trade Commission, the advertising exaggerated the product's benefits to women. The company used outdated medical research to support the claims of its advertising and lobbied the Federal Trade Commission, which allowed the product to be advertised as being helpful to women.

The company conducted an advertising campaign that addressed various female problems, and sales increased. In 1945, for instance, sales passed $2.5 million. The Food and Drug Administration, however, demanded medical evidence from the company that supported the claims made in the advertisements. The company conducted extensive research and claimed that the product indeed alleviated specific female symptoms. Although the Food and Drug Administration did not file a complaint against the company, it nonetheless scrutinized the company's advertising.

Sales of the product decreased dramatically in 1950. The American woman had changed, and the product was viewed as a pseudoremedy from the previous century. A modern, attractive female character replaced the face of Lydia E. Pinkham, who was dressed in clothes designed for the nineteenth century. However, sales continued to decrease. The company hired a research firm to conduct a market analysis in the late 1950s. The firm's report suggested that the company change the product and advertising. Apparently, the newly fashioned character did not appeal to the modern American woman. Although the company attempted another advertising campaign, sales sagged.

In 1968 the company was sold to Cooper Laboratories, a pharmaceutical company. Cooper Laboratories moved the facility to Puerto Rico to cut costs.[16] Today, the product is sold by Numark Laboratories, which purchased the product from Cooper Laboratories, as Lydia Pinkham Herbal Compound or Tablets. Lydia E. Pinkham's image graces the product's package. However, the product has become one that few female consumers purchase.

NOTES

1. *Pennsylvania Gazette*, July 1, 1736.

2. *Boston Chronicle*, February 19, 1770.

3. *New York Herald*, June 15, 1803.

4. Cedric Larson, "Patent-Medicine Advertising and the Early American Press," *Journalism Quarterly* 14, no. 4 (December 1937): 338.

5. Chaim M. Rosenberg, *Goods for Sale: Products and Advertising in the Massachusetts Industrial Age* (Amherst: University of Massachusetts Press, 2007), 111.

6. Jean Burton, *Lydia Pinkham Is Her Name* (New York: Farrar, Straus, 1949), 51.

7. Dan Yaeger, "The Lady Who Helped Ladies," *Yankee* 53, no. 9 (September 1989): 113.

8. Rita E. Loos, "Who Was Lydia E. Pinkham?" *New England Journal of History* 52, no. 3 (1995): 57.

9. Loos, "Who Was Lydia E. Pinkham?" 57.

10. Burton, *Lydia Pinkham Is Her Name*, 161.

11. Burton, *Lydia Pinkham Is Her Name*, 166.

12. Donald Dale Jackson, "If Women Needed a Quick Pick-Me-Up, Lydia Provided One," *Smithsonian* 15 (July 1984): 107.

13. *New York Times*, May 3, 1887, 2.

14. Stephen Fox, *The Mirror Makers: A History of American Advertising and Its Creators* (New York: Morrow, 1984), 18–19.

15. Jackson, "If Women Needed a Quick Pick-Me-Up," 107.

16. Sarah Stage, *Female Complaints: Lydia Pinkham and the Business of Women's Medicine* (New York: Norton, 1979), 11, 245–46.

Chapter Five

John Wanamaker and Retail Advertising

In the nineteenth century, primarily as a result of the Industrial Revolution, there "emerged a vast culture of consumption."[1] According to William R. Leach, "Advertising gave it shape; a new abundance of commodities established its foundation."[2] This culture emphasized service as well as competition and depended on the imagination of owners and operators of various businesses to promote the goods that they stocked.

The department store, unlike the small, cramped dry goods shop of an earlier period, exemplified this culture. Department stores opened in major cities throughout the United States after the Civil War. By the late nineteenth century, these stores occupied as much space as a city block and contained several stories, each of which was filled with numerous commodities for the prospective customer to examine. Numerous large department stores held street fairs and carnivals as well as tied promotional efforts to specific holidays or other days.

These department stores also emphasized decorations such as Egyptian temples, French salons, and Japanese gardens. Concurrently, these stores employed various colors and glass to highlight certain departments and commodities. The latter was also employed for displaying jewelry. Light, too, was employed for specific effects. The sales appeal of some products, for instance, was enhanced by light.

The department stores' show windows became a major instrument of promotion. People walking on sidewalks invariably were attracted to what was displayed in the stores' windows. In the early twentieth century, windows became ministages in the sense that they were used as props to highlight one or two products.

In the early twentieth century, the larger department stores often had zoos, restaurants, botanical gardens, beauty and barber shops, museums, fairs, post offices, and libraries, among other attractions and departments, to attract people's interest.

In addition, these large emporiums sold countless personal products as well as numerous commodities for the home. However, department stores "did not simply 'sell' commodities: they intervened with advertising skills to amplify the excitement of possibility inherent in the commodity form. They attempted to endow the goods with transformative messages and associations that the goods did not objectively possess."[3] By advertising, using displays, and stocking particular brands of goods, the large department stores made people, especially women, fashion-conscious. As women became important consumers of department store merchandise, owners and operators hired them as assistant managers and sales clerks. After all, they reasoned, women knew what women needed or desired.

JOHN WANAMAKER

John Wanamaker was born on July 11, 1838, to Elizabeth Kochersperger and Nelson Wanamaker near Philadelphia. His parents, Protestants, were devout Christians. His father was of German and Scottish descent, and his mother was of French Huguenot descent.

Wanamaker learned about money from his father and paternal grandfather, both of whom operated a brickyard. Wanamaker "turned" bricks before and after school, for which his father paid him seven copper cents. However, in 1849, because of competition, Wanamaker's grandfather retired from the brickyard and moved to a farm in Indiana. Wanamaker moved with his parents to the farm in 1850. Undoubtedly, farming was hard work. The family experienced a harsh, bitter, cold winter, and Wanamaker's grandfather died. Wanamaker's mother, whose family and friends lived in Philadelphia, grew homesick. Wanamaker's father realized that the family needed a change. Besides, farming had not been that productive.

Wanamaker, like his father, missed his grandfather very much. He stated, "My grandfather was a pioneer. I attended his funeral in Indiana. I will not in my lifetime forget the inscription on his gravestone, reading my own name on it. Standing at the grave, I prayed that I might become as good a man as he was."[4]

Nelson Wanamaker moved his family to Philadelphia, where he returned to making bricks. Wanamaker attended school until he was almost fourteen years of age. Then he became an errand boy for Troutman and Hayes, publishers of various reference books, for which he earned $1.25 a week.

In 1852 Wanamaker found employment at Barclay Lippincott, a clothing store; he earned $2.50 a week. Although his salary eventually doubled, his tasks were menial at best. Wanamaker grew frustrated; he desired to have the opportunity to employ his ideas about advertising and selling. Eventually, he was hired by Colonel Bennett, who owned Tower Hall, the largest clothing store in Philadelphia. Wanamaker earned $6 a week. More important, even though he was only 16 years of age, he was given the opportunity to apply what he knew and what he gradually learned.

At first, Wanamaker polished the large knobs on the front door. He was determined to prove to Colonel Bennett that he was willing to do any menial task in exchange for the opportunity to learn how to sell. Then he learned about stock and subsequently became a proud salesman. Always energetic, he was promoted; he was put in charge of the men's clothing department and persuaded Colonel Bennett to allow him to purchase specific items for the department, such as shirts and socks. Wanamaker learned to buy and save the store money. However, in 1857, as various businesses failed because of the economy, his health deteriorated. Tall and thin, he worked long hours at the store, then devoted hours to religious activities at the First Independent Church. He was advised by a doctor to leave Philadelphia and rest.

Years later, Colonel Bennett was asked about John Wanamaker. He replied,

> John was certainly the most ambitious boy I ever saw. I used to take him to lunch with me, and he would tell me how he was going to be a great merchant. He was always organizing something. He seemed to be a natural born organizer. This faculty is largely accountable for his great success in after-life. [5]

At nineteen years of age, Wanamaker traveled to the Northwest, where his health improved. After several months, he returned to Philadelphia, where he contemplated studying for the ministry. His pastor, Dr. John Chambers, had been an inspiration to him. Wanamaker realized that he did not have the formal education to become a minister, so he became involved in the Philadelphia Young Men's Christian Association (YMCA), which had been founded by George Stuart in 1854. Hired as a full-time secretary of the organization in 1858, Wanamaker earned $1,000 a year. His responsibilities included asking members to increase their contributions, which, he soon learned, was not an easy task. Certain members criticized him and the organization, and pastors of churches resented their members' giving contributions to the YMCA and not to their churches. Nonetheless, he persevered and recruited two thousand new members in his first year as secretary. His responsibilities also included the organization's engaging in evangelistic programs as well as helping the army during the Civil War. His responsibilities also included raising money to purchase the building in which the organization was located. Wanamaker remained active in the organization until 1887.

Wanamaker's first love, however, was Bethany Church and Sunday school, which he founded two years before he married Mary Brown in 1860. Wanamaker felt a certain pride for Bethany Church, and because of his religious convictions, he devoted considerable energy and money to its development and growth.

In 1861 Wanamaker approached Colonel Bennett about purchasing an interest in Tower Hall. Bennett, who respected Wanamaker and his abilities, refused Wanamaker's proposition. Wanamaker approached his brother-in-law Nathan Brown and proposed that they open a clothing store for men. Although family members and several friends attempted to discourage them, Wanamaker and Brown opened Oak Hall on April 8, 1861. Sales totaled $24.76 the first day. Wanamaker desired to stock merchandise that would have an immediate appeal. He traveled to New York to purchase goods on credit. When these goods were displayed in the store, the first advertisement appeared in the *Philadelphia Public Ledger* on April 27, 1861:

OAK HALL CLOTHING BAZAAR
Southeast corner Sixth & Market Streets
WANAMAKER & BROWN desire to say to their many friends and the public generally, that they open to-day with an entire new and complete stock of ready-made clothing; and having purchased their goods under the pressure of the times at very low rates, will sell them accordingly.[6]

Other brief advertisements for the store appeared in the same column as this advertisement and contained such headlines as "Oak Hall Clothing Bazaar," "Whole Suits for Three Dollars," "Right at the Corner," "John R. Houghton," and "Opens To-day." John R. Houghton, the store's cutter, encouraged his friends to visit the store.

The price for the suits attracted attention. However, profits from sales were not high, and advertising was expensive. During the first few months, the proprietors earned very little. Occasionally, even money for their lunches went to pay for advertising. According to Linda Kowall, "Store advertisements were generally simple notices of goods for sale, printed in microscopic type and buried inside the newspapers."[7]

After Bull Run, Wanamaker tried to serve his country by enlisting, but he was turned down because of his health. He secured contracts to clothe the officers of two regiments. This experience encouraged him to secure similar contracts for police officers, firemen, and military cadets months later.

Now a father of a son, Wanamaker enjoyed retailing, even though the business demanded most of his attention. His wife seldom saw him during the day but nonetheless listened to his ideas at night. Always supportive, Mary enjoyed being married to the young entrepreneur.

Owning a small store could be exhaustive and risky. Herbert Ershkowitz wrote,

> Whether the merchant was honest or unscrupulous, owning a small store was a hard way to make a living. With little capital, shopkeepers bought goods on credit from jobbers or other middle men who had purchased the goods from manufacturers or importers. Because shopkeepers often sold on credit while bearing high fixed costs, as many as 25 percent of all establishments failed each year.[8]

One of the store's first policies was to guarantee certain fabrics such as all-wool, which attracted new customers. Advertising quality goods helped establish Wanamaker and Brown as a reputable clothier. Wanamaker realized that price, too, should be advertised to appeal to certain prospective customers. However, problems in marketing became evident; sales suffered periodically. Wanamaker finally realized that the solution or at least part of the solution to lagging sales might be found by studying the consumer. To him, merchandising should be a public service, not an argument between the retailer and the customer over price. Thus, in addition to guaranteeing the quality of the goods in his store, Wanamaker ticketed every article. Although he was given credit for initiating the one-price system in retail merchandising, he claimed that A. T. Stewart, who owned a large department store in New York, was the first to employ the one-price rule for dry goods. In 1865 the firm announced that customers could return an article and get their money back, as long as the article had not been used. The policy of "money back" was revolutionary in the sense that he was the first retail merchant to have the policy; it was also revolutionary for Wanamaker and Brown's sales, which increased dramatically.

In addition to placing literate and folksy advertisements that captured the essence of small-town life in newspapers, Wanamaker employed outdoor advertising. He hired painters to paint "W. & B." in letters 12 feet high on boards all over Philadelphia. He had handbills distributed at county fairs. He used large balloons to attract attention to his store, as well as toy balloons, which were given to children. Other instruments that were used to announce Wanamaker and Brown included Oak Hall slates, pencils, tracing books, children's books, picture postcards, pen-and-ink sketches, calendars, clocks, and the cover as well as inside pages of the 1865 *City Directory*.

Nathan Brown, his partner, died in 1868, the year that Wanamaker and Brown became the largest retailer of men's clothing in the country. Wanamaker purchased his partner's interest in the business and established John

Wanamaker and Company in 1869 on Chestnut Street, which, to a certain extent, resembled the store owned by A. T. Stewart of New York. Wanamaker's new store was luxurious; it contained a skylight in the center, which was open, as well as carpeting, paintings, and mirrors. Wanamaker stocked lines of clothing that would not have sold in Oak Hall. He desired to attract a different clientele that preferred service and quality rather than price.

The store had six departments by 1874. These included gentlemen's ready-made clothing, youths' and boys' ready-made clothing, a department for children, ladies' coats and habits, measure goods, and a haberdashery.

The same year he placed the first half-page advertisement ever published in a newspaper, even though he depended, to a certain extent, on the store's windows to attract potential shoppers. However, the advertising for the Chestnut Street store was more restrained than the advertising for Oak Hall.

Although Mary had given birth to more children, the third son, Horace, had died in infancy, and the oldest daughter, Hattie, died when she was five years of age. The Wanamakers had four children who were bringing them considerable happiness, however. The Wanamakers also traveled, but most trips abroad were for purchasing goods for the stores.

Wanamaker opened additional stores in Pittsburgh, Pennsylvania, Washington, DC, and Richmond, Virginia, in the early 1870s but soon realized that these stores were not managed according to his wishes. As a result, he closed various branch stores in the mid-1870s and concentrated on those in Philadelphia.

In 1876 he opened the largest department store of its kind. Termed the Grand Depot, Wanamaker's "New Kind of Store" had been the Pennsylvania freight depot. Wanamaker had paid almost $500,000 for the land and the structure. This sum did not include the costs for renovation. The Grand Depot featured clothing, including men's. Wanamaker advertised the store's opening with fanfare, attempting to attract visitors who had come to Philadelphia for the Centennial Exhibition. Inside the store, "the spruced-up shed counters radiated outward in concentric circles, their arcs broken by aisles that crisscrossed the shed like grand avenues. Wanamaker embellished the façade with minarets and a Moroccan motif."[9]

Wanamaker focused on high volume and low cost, a focus that was extremely profitable, and to prevent sluggish sales periods, he advertised special sales, which, for the most part, moved goods. He wrote many of the advertisements for the store. Although display advertisements had become common, his advertisements, even when they were large, contained conversational language that discussed the bargains of the day.

According to William Leach, "Wanamaker claimed that his 'New Kind of Store,' as he put it, was built principally for profit but also in response to the needs of the people."[10]

In 1877 the Grand Depot offered additional lines of clothing, including women's. The emporium was termed a "dry goods store" by George W. Childs of the *Philadelphia Public Ledger*, as Wanamaker purchased additional lines of goods and added new departments. The Grand Depot's success was staggering. The number of employees increased from more than six hundred to more than twelve hundred within a year. Wanamaker introduced shoppers to electrical lighting in 1878. Electricity also helped him solve the problem of ventilation.

Wanamaker also published several journals that contained anecdotes, comments, and advice about shopping. These journals included *Everybody's Journal*, which had been published first for Oak Hall shoppers and employees, then for the general public at a cost of 10 cents. *The Farm Journal*, which appeared for the first time in 1879 for the Grand Depot, also attained respectability among the public. In 1879 *The Ladies' Journal*, which contained poems and articles, was targeted to women. In addition to these journals for the stores, Wanamaker published several religious periodicals for his church.

Wanamaker placed the first full-page newspaper advertisement of any retail merchant in 1879. Kowall wrote,

> This new "Wanamaker Style" of advertising—the bold use of consecutive full-page advertisements which were like news items themselves—marked the beginning of his unprecedented effort to make a science of advertising. To create advertisements . . . Wanamaker began to educate his advertising staff, sending them to visit factories, interview artists and become familiar with quality, sources of supply and manufacturing processes. In addition to its impact on modern advertising practices, the Wanamaker Style, soon emulated by other retailers, played a major role in the rapid rise of powerful and increasingly independent city daily newspapers by infusing them with the advertising dollars, which began to provide a substantial and reliable new revenue base.[11]

In 1880 Wanamaker hired John E. Powers, who had written advertisements for the Lord and Taylor department store in New York, to create advertisements that were honest, direct, and simple. Powers employed a typeface that was much more readable than other typefaces found in advertisements, and his advertisements undeniably were attractive. According to Daniel Pope,

> Powers' plain-spoken publicity featured descriptions of merchandise that were unprecedented for their detail and accuracy. His ads also reflected the cost advantages of Wanamaker . . . by clearly stating the products' prices and promoting the one-price-for-all, no-haggling policy Wanamaker had set.[12]

However, Powers was independent and, to a certain extent, not open to suggestions, even those proposed by Wanamaker. His closed-mindedness and candor forced Wanamaker to dismiss him in 1886.

By 1881 Wanamaker's Grand Depot had almost three acres of selling space on one floor, forty-six departments, and more than two thousand employees. Wanamaker had pneumatic tubes installed between the sales clerks and the cashier's office; as a result, cash transactions took less time. Other physical improvements, such as steam heating, carpeting, artwork, and music, occurred over the years, which made the Grand Depot one of the public's favorite places to shop. According to Neil Harris, "Wanamaker . . . filled his stores with pictures, careful to select and hang them to maximum effect. He objected to the crowding of pictures in museums, which he likened to a three-ring circus."[13]

Wanamaker was the first American retailer to place buyers of merchandise in various European cities. Wanamaker, who had hired his friend Robert Curtis Ogden to manage Oak Hall in 1879, invited Ogden to help him manage the Grand Depot. His oldest son was also involved in the management of the Grand Depot. Wanamaker's brothers managed the Chestnut Street store.

In 1886 he introduced the half-day Saturday to his employees. This reduced the workweek to five and a half days. (In 1914 Saturdays in July and August became full holidays.) He also provided medical benefits and a retirement system for his employees.

In 1887 Wanamaker entered the wholesale dry goods business when he purchased three wholesale businesses, one of which was the third largest in the country. By 1888 his new business had become prosperous.

Wanamaker, a Republican, dutifully supported Benjamin Harrison's campaign for president and, as a result, was respectfully asked by Harrison to serve as postmaster general of the United States. Although Harrison's advisers criticized Wanamaker in an effort to change Harrison's mind, Harrison refused to budge. After Wanamaker discussed the position with Harrison, he accepted and immediately recommended to Congress that a rural free delivery system be implemented throughout the United States so that every citizen, particularly those who lived in the country, would have access to the postal system. Congress allowed Wanamaker to test his idea in small towns, which he attempted to do without much financial support from the government. Later, Wanamaker requested a parcel post service, which legislators criticized and rejected. The service was implemented years later, however. Wanamaker was also criticized for recommending that postal rates for books and newspapers be increased. He also recommended that the government own and operate the telegraph and telephone systems. Owners of specific businesses and companies as well as certain congressmen felt relief when Wanamaker left Washington in 1893.

In 1896 Wanamaker established the John Wanamaker Commercial Institute, a school that served the young boys who worked at his retail stores. Eventually, the institute was expanded to include girls and older boys who had been deprived of a proper education. (The institute became the American University of Trade and Applied Commerce in 1908.)

When Wanamaker returned to Pennsylvania, he waged an unsuccessful battle against M. S. Quay. Quay, a successful politician, had considerable clout. In 1896, for instance, Wanamaker sought the Republican nomination for the U.S. Senate. Two years later, he sought the Republican nomination for governor of Pennsylvania. Controversy surrounded both races primarily because of the questionable nature of the campaigns. Voters learned little from the press about Wanamaker. Indeed, coverage, waged by Quay's political machine, could be classified as character assassination. However, Wanamaker gained some success when Quay's corrupt practices became known. Indicted, Quay was acquitted, but his popularity among voters rapidly declined. He lost the election.

Wanamaker entered the New York retail market in 1896, when he purchased A. T. Stewart and Company. He enlarged the advertising staff and demanded that every writer of advertising copy actually examine articles of clothing before writing a word. Wanamaker's advertisements, which were large and illustrated, appeared every day except Sunday in various daily newspapers. Wanamaker believed firmly in the power of advertising, especially during periods when sales decreased. He stated,

> When the times are hard and people are not buying, is the very time that advertising should be the heaviest. You want to get the people in to see what you have to sell, and you must advertise to do that. When the times are good they will come of their own accord. But I believe in advertising all the time. I never stop advertising.[14]

Under the watchful eye of Wanamaker, Robert C. Ogden and his staff maintained the New York store until it, like the other Wanamaker stores, became successful. Although many had predicted failure because of the store's location, which was at Ninth Street and Broadway, a part of town that was no longer attractive to merchants, Wanamaker was victorious.

Wanamaker purchased adjoining property and had a fourteen-story building erected. The building was connected to the older building, as well as to the recently completed subway system, and was designed to display furnishings for the home. For instance, the upper floors exhibited furniture, floor coverings, house furnishings, glassware, and draperies. The lower floors contained specialty shops for men. The building also contained the House Palatial, a private home consisting of twenty-two rooms; a large, magnificent restaurant; a three-story, thirteen hundred–seat auditorium; and a storage plant for furs.

The building, which opened in 1907, tripled the selling space of Wanamaker's in New York. Wanamaker used the older building for women's wear and dry goods. When Ogden retired, Wanamaker put his son Rodman in charge of the New York store.

Later in 1907 panic struck the financial center in New York, and Wanamaker's sales began to decrease. Concurrently, he feared that he could not complete the addition to his building in Philadelphia, which had been started, even though he was assured by his friends, including those who were loan officers in banks, that he would be given a loan if he so desired. Wanamaker weathered the financial storm. Unfortunately, certain small creditors requested payment. Wanamaker paid the few who demanded settlements and, primarily because of his deep religious beliefs, endured. Of course, he could have sold his business for millions and walked away, but he was determined to keep the business in his hands.

The same year, as if his financial problems were not enough to worry about, his home outside Philadelphia, Lindenhurst, was destroyed by fire. Wanamaker's loss was estimated to be more than $2 million. Wanamaker built a second Lindenhurst on the same property.

In 1908 sales did not necessarily improve, and the doomsayers predicted failure. Wanamaker, however, grew optimistic. He placed large orders, which helped wholesalers and manufacturers; he completed the building in Philadelphia. The same year his son Thomas B. Wanamaker, who had been ill, died; he was forty-seven. Wanamaker, already burdened with financial problems, became stricken with grief. He focused on his business.

In 1909 sales increased primarily because the panic that had gripped New York was over. This not only helped Wanamaker but silenced the doomsayers. Wanamaker, acknowledging that the business in New York was rebounding, returned to Philadelphia, where a new building was almost ready to open in time for the Golden Jubilee—the celebration of fifty years in business.

In October 1911, more than six thousand employees and family members helped Wanamaker celebrate fifty years of serving the public. Other luncheons and events sponsored by various organizations had been scheduled primarily for the purpose of honoring him.

Now in his early seventies, Wanamaker thought about subjects in addition to business. Some of his closest friends advised him to retire. Other close friends suggested that he let his son Rodman handle the business. Although he tried the latter, when he was in Philadelphia, he went to his office every day except Sunday. When he was in New York for any period of time, he maintained the same routine. Wanamaker realized that he could not give up something that for decades had been a major part of his life.

Wanamaker, who had remained active in politics, voiced his opinion when World War I erupted. He opposed Woodrow Wilson and supported Charles Hughes for president. In time he supported Wilson's position. He wrote brief, pro-American "editorials" that prefaced his businesses' daily advertisements. These editorials explained how Wanamaker's was helping in the war effort and what the average American citizen thought as he or she learned about specific developments or events. Wanamaker also aided the Red Cross and directed the Liberty Loan campaigns. He devoted considerable time, energy, and money to both causes.

In 1918, at eighty years of age, he served as one of the directors of the War Welfare Council. He continued his patriotic chore until the Treaty of Versailles was signed. After the war, American lives changed. Many were working for the first time. Wages of those who had been working for years suddenly climbed, and the cost of living increased. Prices of goods and services, too, increased, which worried Wanamaker. Could the average American afford to shop at Wanamaker's if prices continued to increase?

In response to this question, Wanamaker decided to offer every product in his stores at 20 percent off the ticketed price. The advertisement that announced this decision appeared on May 3, 1920. On May 8, a Saturday, a world's record was established for the amount of sales in a retail store: Wanamaker's sold more than a million dollars' worth of merchandise. Certain Philadelphia and New York merchants adopted a similar policy. In time the idea spread across the country. Wanamaker ended his sale July 2. The high cost of living actually slowed as a result of Wanamaker's brilliant scheme.

In 1921 he had been in business sixty years. To honor Wanamaker, celebrations occurred in Philadelphia and New York.

On December 12, 1922, he died from heart failure. Financiers and specific retailers attempted to persuade Wanamaker's heirs to sell the business, but the store remained independent for years. For instance, Rodman managed the business until his death in 1928. The company was then managed by trustees for the benefit of Rodman's children. Although the Stewart store closed in 1952 and the store next to it closed two years later, another store was built in New York and remained in the family's control.

In 1978, however, Wanamaker's, with sixteen stores and sales of more than $300 million a year, was purchased by the Carter Hawley Hale Stores, a California-based department store chain. This chain was acquired by Woodward and Lothrop before it filed for bankruptcy in the mid-1990s.

SUMMARY

In addition to his emphasis on advertising, which created "the image of an honest merchant whose word could be trusted,"[15] Wanamaker purportedly was the first retailer to offer vacations, with pay, to his employees; the first to introduce electricity and the telephone into a retail business; the first to open reading and resting rooms for his customers; the first to build a hotel for his female employees; the first to provide Christmas bonuses to his sales staffs; the first to build a camp for the boys who worked in his stores; the first to establish Saturdays in July and August as holidays for his employees, with pay; the first to offer medical services to his employees; the first to introduce the "satisfaction guaranteed or your money back" policy; and the first to install an elevator in a retail business.

According to Leach,

> He translated the new economy into a new culture for many Americans—we might call him one of this country's domesticators of commercial culture, a man who not only "revolutionized retailing," as he said himself, but who also legitimated fashion, fostered the cult of the new, democratized desire and consumption, and helped produce a commercial environment steeped in pecuniary values.[16]

NOTES

1. William R. Leach, "Transformations in a Culture of Consumption: Women and Department Stores, 1890–1925," *Journal of American History* 71, no. 2 (September 1984): 327.

2. Leach, "Transformations in a Culture of Consumption," 320.

3. Leach, "Transformations in a Culture of Consumption," 327.

4. Herbert Adams Gibbons, *John Wanamaker* (Port Washington, NY: Kennikat Press, 1971; originally, 1926), 1:21.

5. Thompson Brown, "Hon. John Wanamaker: From Messenger-Boy to Merchant Prince—A Romance of Business," *Our Day* 17, no. 113 (September 1897): 404.

6. *Philadelphia Public Ledger*, April 27, 1861, 1.

7. Linda Kowall, "Original and Genuine, Unadulterated and Guaranteed!" *Pennsylvania Heritage* 15, no. 1 (1989): 20.

8. Herbert Ershkowitz, *John Wanamaker: Philadelphia Merchant* (Conshohocken, PA: Combined, 1999), 35.

9. Maury Klein, "John Wanamaker," *American History Illustrated* 15, no. 8 (December 1980), 10–11.

10. William Leach, *Land of Desire: Merchants, Power, and the Rise of a New American Culture* (New York: Pantheon Books, 1993), 113.

11. Kowall, "Original and Genuine," 22.

12. Daniel Pope, *The Making of Modern Advertising* (New York: Basic Books, 1983), 134.

13. Neil Harris, *Cultural Excursions: Marketing Appetites and Cultural Tastes in Modern America* (Chicago: University of Chicago Press, 1990), 65.

14. Herbert Adams Gibbons, *John Wanamaker* (Port Washington, NY: Kennikat Press, 1971; originally, 1926), 2:25–26.

15. Ershkowitz, *John Wanamaker*, 119.
16. Leach, *Land of Desire*, 34.

Chapter Six

Albert Lasker and the Lord & Thomas Advertising Agency's Influence on Advertising

THE EARLY YEARS

According to Stephen Fox, "If the early twentieth century in advertising history can be described in a phrase, it would be: The Age of Lasker."[1] Lasker worked at, then owned, the Lord & Thomas advertising agency for more than forty years.

Albert D. Lasker was born on May 1, 1880, in Freiburg, Germany, to parents who were from Galveston, Texas. When Lasker was old enough to travel, his parents returned home.

Lasker's father, Morris, who had been born in Germany, moved to the United States when he was sixteen and eventually settled in Galveston, where he became a successful businessman and president of several banks. Although he loved his children, he was not demonstrative, and Lasker grew up feeling that he had to prove himself to his father. This sense of insecurity plagued Lasker for most of his life. Indeed, he suffered periodically from depression.

Lasker did not perform well in elementary school, primarily because he was interested in other things besides school work. He enjoyed earning money. Before his twelfth birthday, for instance, he founded a four-page weekly newspaper, which he wrote, edited, and published. Titled the *Galveston Free Press*, the paper earned a profit of $15 a week for more than a year. The paper contained aphorisms, a column on the theater, anecdotes, announcements, and a column by the editor. The paper also included advertisements. Lasker sold the space and then created the advertisements for the various merchants.

In high school, he edited the school magazine—one of the first in the United States—and managed the football team. In addition, he worked as a bookkeeper for his father and as a journalist for the *Galveston Daily News*, for which he covered sports, politics, business, crime, and the theater. Upon his graduation in 1896, he worked full-time for the newspaper. He left the *Daily News* when he turned in a review of a play that he had not seen but knew by heart. The play had not been performed because the Opera House had burned. Lasker immediately realized that he had made a serious mistake. Credibility was important to him. He moved to New Orleans and worked briefly for the *Times-Democrat*. Then he moved to Dallas, where he worked briefly for the *Dallas News*. When he returned to Galveston, his father suggested that he go into advertising. Lasker did not like his father's suggestion. He desired to edit and publish a small newspaper in Texas. His father finally agreed to buy a small newspaper for him on one condition—that he work in advertising for a brief period. Lasker agreed, but he never worked in journalism again.

LORD & THOMAS

Lasker's father knew Daniel Lord, a partner of the Lord & Thomas advertising agency in Chicago, and asked Lord to give his son a job. Lasker left Texas in 1898. In Chicago, he learned that Lord oversaw the agency's finances while Ambrose Thomas, his partner, oversaw the agency's daily operations. Lord introduced Lasker to Thomas, who informed him that he would earn $10 a week for three months. It would depend on how well he performed as to whether he would be offered a job after the probationary period.

Lord & Thomas offered two types of services. If clients wrote their own copy and desired space brokering, the agency would be paid a 10 percent commission. If clients desired advertising copy and space brokering, the agency would be paid a 15 percent commission. Although the agency seldom created advertisements for clients, it had an artist and a part-time copywriter.

Lasker worked as an office boy, learning everything he could about advertising and the agency. He found advertising to be challenging. At the end of the three-month probationary period, Thomas offered Lasker a job, and Lasker accepted. Journalism would have to wait.

Lasker rented a room in an agency's employee's home. Single and away from home, Lasker did not feel any parental pressure from his father. He occasionally drank and occasionally gambled when he was not working. In fact, he lost $500 to a gambler. Unfortunately, he did not have $500, so he went to see Thomas and explained what had happened. According to Lasker,

> I had never before sold anything to anybody, but I did a salesmanship job that day. I talked Mr. Thomas into advancing me $500—which was a fortune in those days. He went with me, and we settled with the gambler. Both he and I were sure that the gambler had cheated me, but the gambler had the due bill, and so we settled with him for $500. [2]

Now, Lasker could not leave the agency as planned. He owed Thomas too much money. The dream of owning a small newspaper faded.

Lasker had been working at the agency about a year when a salesman put in his resignation. Lasker learned that the salesman's territory included Indiana, Ohio, and Michigan. He spoke to Thomas about his interest in the position, and Thomas agreed to let him try it. Lasker worked hard. He persuaded new clients to advertise through Lord & Thomas and current clients to increase their advertising budgets. One client, the Wilson Ear Drum Company, had been with the agency for several years. Lasker learned that the advertisements for the company's Common Sense Ear Drums, which were sold by mail, had been quite small. The agency received a 10 percent commission. Lasker knew that he could improve the client's sales by improving the advertisements. He persuaded Thomas to allow him the opportunity to write copy. Then he went to see George Wilson, the owner of the company, and said,

> Suppose Lord and Thomas could multiply your sales. That would be very good for you, and it would multiply our volume of business with you, because you would spend more money. We will write a new kind of copy for you, but you must pay us fifteen per cent commission on all ads that contain the new copy. If at the end of ninety days the results haven't increased, we'll give you back the money, and your account will still be on a ten per cent basis. But as an earnest that you are interested, you will have to pay me a fee of $500. [3]

George Wilson agreed to Lasker's proposition, and Lasker hired Eugene Katz, a friend, to help him create several advertisements. Lasker had a photograph taken of the agency's artist cupping his ear. He showed "The Deafest Deaf Man You Ever Saw" advertisement to the client, George Wilson, who used it, and sales increased:

You Hear!
The only scientific sound conductors.
Invisible, comfortable, efficient. They

fit in the ear. Doctors recommend
them. Thousands testify to their
perfection and to benefit derived.
104 Trust Building, Louisville, Ky.[4]

The company had been spending $24,000 a year with Lord and Thomas. Within a year, the company spent three times this amount. The agency earned considerably more than it had from this account. Lasker had succeeded. He employed this bargaining technique on several clients. Sometimes it worked; sometimes it failed.

Lasker studied copywriting and wondered what caused some advertisements to work and others to fail. Eventually, the thought that advertising is news occurred to him. He would learn more about advertising several years later.

Around 1900, Lasker met Flora Warner, who was from Buffalo, New York. He was at least twenty-one, and she was at least twenty-two. Although he had paid his debt to Thomas and was earning considerably more than $10 a week, he realized that he could not support two people. However, he and Flora married two years later and lived in Chicago. After several months, primarily because he traveled and she did not know anyone, he suggested that she visit her family in Buffalo. During her visit, she grew seriously ill. Where she contracted typhoid fever is anyone's guess, but she remained in bed for more than a year. Lasker visited her periodically. Eventually, the medical bills forced him to meet with Thomas about a raise. Lasker informed him that he wanted $5,000 a year. Thomas asked if he wanted more, but Lasker refused. He informed Thomas that he desired to become a partner some day. Flora returned to Chicago in 1903. Their marriage eventually brought them three children, but Flora later contracted phlebitis and became a semi-invalid who needed medical attention for most of her life.

Lasker's salary had increased substantially when Lord retired. He purchased Lord's share of the agency and became a partner in 1904. Now, he had time to concentrate on copy.

John E. Kennedy sought a position as a copywriter with Lord & Thomas, so he sent a note to the agency that stated the following: "I can tell you what advertising is. I know you don't know. It will mean much to me to have you know what it is and it will mean much to you. If you wish to know what advertising is, send the word 'Yes' down by the bell boy."[5]

Kennedy waited patiently for a response downstairs in a saloon. Thomas dismissed the note, but Lasker responded, then met with Kennedy. Kennedy claimed that he had been a police officer in Canada. He had written copy for the Hudson's Bay Company's department store in Winnipeg; he had written advertising copy for a shoe company in Boston; and he had written advertising copy for Dr. Shoop's Restorative, a patent medicine. He informed Lasker that advertising was "salesmanship in print." He claimed, "Great advertising did the same work as a great salesman."[6] Whether Kennedy got this idea from Charles Austin Bates is anyone's guess. However, Bates had said several years earlier that "advertisements are printed salesmen."[7] Lasker desired to learn more from Kennedy, so he persuaded Thomas to hire him to write advertising copy.

From Kennedy, Lasker learned that consumers needed a reason to buy something. If a reason could be given and it was sound, consumers would react positively toward the product. To Kennedy, a good advertisement contained a logical explanation as to why the consumer should purchase the product. He knew almost instinctively how to attract the client's consumers. He used language that they understood. His advertisements were distinctive. He used heavy, italic type, underlined words, and capitalized letters in headlines. Through Kennedy, Lord & Thomas pioneered "reason-why" advertising, which other agencies adopted. Lasker learned that writing advertising copy did not come easy to Kennedy. Indeed, he would think a long time about the advertisement before he wrote one word. Then he would write the copy, then rewrite the copy, then rewrite the copy, and then rewrite the copy. Kennedy would do this again and again and again, until Lasker grew exhausted.

Kennedy also taught Lasker about using coupons or other devices to track responses. According to him, advertising copy needed to be tested to determine which piece of copy or which advertisement was the most effective.

Kennedy and Lasker created a speculative advertising campaign for the Nineteen Hundred Washer Company, which manufactured washing machines. The company's most popular advertisement depicted a woman chained to a washtub; the headline read, "Don't be chained to the washtub." Kennedy knew that the advertisement was negative and consequently would not work as well as an advertisement that was positive. He created an advertisement that depicted a woman sitting in a chair, reading a book, and turning effortlessly a handle of a washtub. The headline read, "Let This Machine Do Your Washing Free."[8] Lord & Thomas got the account.

Lasker and Kennedy worked on Van Camp's Evaporated Milk. They advised the company to change the product's name from "evaporated milk" to "sterilized milk." They persuaded the company to acknowledge the product's objectionable taste and claim it as a virtue. The company agreed, and the advertisements caused sales of the product to increase.

Lasker helped publicize Kennedy's discovery in the agency's house organ, *Judicious Advertising*, and in other publications. These articles appeared in the pamphlet *The Book of Advertising Tests*, which Lasker put together and advertised in magazines and newspapers. As a result, Lord & Thomas acquired more clients until it became one of the largest advertising agencies in the United States. According to a writer for the trade journal *Advertising and Selling*, Kennedy's discovery became "the foundation stone of successful advertising."[9] However, Kennedy owed much to Lasker; after all, if it had not been for him, he would not have been hired at Lord & Thomas.

After about a year, Kennedy negotiated a contract that allowed him to work part-time for the agency. About the same time, the agency established a department for outdoor advertising. This department required Lasker and his small staff of copywriters to produce additional work. Lasker reacted by hiring a few more writers. All new hires had to learn about Kennedy's ideas regarding effective advertising from Lasker. Unfortunately, one or two could not learn Kennedy's ideas and had to be fired, and one or two seasoned copywriters left because of better opportunities at other companies.

Lord & Thomas had nine copywriters, including Kennedy. However, Kennedy had developed a drinking problem. In fact, he would spend days, if not weeks, drinking alcohol; he would not do his work. Lasker tried to manage him as best he could. In 1906 Kennedy and Lord & Thomas parted company. According to Lasker, "Kennedy left us, for what reason I do not know, and I went on as best I could with the momentum of what I had learned from him and of what the others had learned. We were also learning lessons from the results we were getting."[10] Years later Lasker praised Kennedy's contributions to advertising:

> The history of advertising could never be written without first place in it being given to John E. Kennedy, for every copywriter and every advertiser throughout the length and breadth of this land is today being guided by the principles he laid down.[11]

Now, Lasker was in charge of editing all copy that was written for clients, even though he did not write any copy. He also introduced ideas for advertising campaigns.

When Thomas died in 1906, Lasker, together with Charles Erwin, purchased Thomas's share of the agency. Erwin remained for several years, then he sold his share of the agency to Lasker.

Lasker hired Claude C. Hopkins, one of the best copywriters of his day, in 1908, primarily to help increase sales for Van Camp's Pork and Beans. Hopkins had worked at several manufacturing companies in Michigan, Illinois, and Wisconsin. In addition, he had written advertising copy for one or two advertising agencies. Hopkins also owned part of the Liquid Ozone Company, the producer of Liquozone germicide, which he had advertised around the world. However, it was an advertisement that he had written for Schlitz beer that had caught Lasker's attention. Hopkins had toured the brewery before he had written a word of copy and had featured characteristics common to all breweries. He was the first copywriter to play up these characteristics, which differentiated Schlitz beer from its competitors.

Hopkins employed Kennedy's style but worked exceedingly fast, unlike Kennedy, who had worked very slowly and methodically. As he put it, he put in two years' worth of work each year he worked. Lasker paid Hopkins well—more than he had paid Kennedy. Lasker knew that Hopkins was worth every dollar.

For Van Camp's Pork and Beans, Hopkins visited the company in Indianapolis. He and Lasker employed tasting demonstrations, then created advertisements that provided reasons why women should purchase Van Camp's Pork and Beans. The advertisements asked consumers to compare Van Camp's Pork and Beans to other brands. The advertisements also differentiated Van Camp's Pork and Beans from its competitors. Consumers reacted positively to the advertisements and purchased Van Camp's. For other Van Camp products, Hopkins and Lasker used the power of suggestion as well as coupons for free samples.

Hopkins enjoyed visiting clients to observe the manufacturing processes involved. He visited Quaker Oats and observed how the company produced rice and wheat cereals, then, after getting approval from the client, he changed the name of one of the company's products from Wheat Berries to Puffed Wheat and employed the line "The cereal shot from guns." He described the production processes of these cereals in the advertisements. As a result, sales increased substantially.

He created memorable advertisements for various automobiles. He emphasized brand images in his advertisements. He realized the significance of conducting tests, using samples, and researching copy to determine which headline, which subhead, and which sentence of body copy attracted the most attention. Hopkins's advertisements were straightforward and simple, with few, if any, illustrations.

Hopkins enjoyed mail-order advertising, in which he eventually specialized. He employed testing through the use of coupons and samples to numerous campaigns. For another product, he learned what plaque meant. The advertisement played up beautiful teeth and how the consumer could have them. In addition, the advertisement offered a sample of the product. By using coupons and samples, he traced who responded, and this piece of information benefited the client.

Lasker learned a great deal from Hopkins and vice versa. Lord & Thomas acquired the California Fruit Growers Exchange account, and the agency coined the name "Sunkist" for the first advertising campaign, which encouraged people in Iowa to buy oranges. The California Fruit Growers Exchange adopted the name "Sunkist." Several years later Lasker learned that the citrus growers in the state produced so many oranges that they cut orange trees to limit the supply. Primarily to stop the destruction of orange trees and to sell the client's juicers, Lasker had advertising campaigns developed to encourage consumers to eat more oranges and to drink orange juice. Consumption of oranges increased so much that trees were spared.

Hopkins developed an "advisory board" at Lord & Thomas, which he advertised in the agency's house organ and other media. This advertising attracted new clients to the agency. In 1911, for instance, Lord & Thomas acquired the B. J. Johnson Soap Company account. The company manufactured soap products, including Palmolive, which, at the time, enjoyed only modest sales. When Lasker and Hopkins learned that the product's color—green—resulted from two ingredients, palm and olive oil, they realized an opportunity. First, they tested advertisements that offered consumers who purchased the company's laundry soap free bars of Palmolive. Second, they tested advertisements that touted Palmolive's beauty appeal. Third, they tested advertisements that contained coupons for bars of Palmolive. They tested other advertisements as well. Although these advertisements helped sell Palmolive, they focused on the advertisements that played up its beauty. Within several years, Palmolive became the leading brand on the market.

Although Lasker preferred that the agency handle clients that manufactured convenience goods, the agency was successful in handling clients that manufactured automobiles and tires. For each client, Lasker relied on the "reason-why" style of copy. For Goodyear, Hopkins created the phrase "No-Rim-Cut Tires," which informed consumers that Goodyear's straight-side tire, if punctured, would not cut the rim. Each advertising campaign was successful because Hopkins focused on the changes that occurred in the industry.

Lasker made several mistakes, however, in his professional career. For instance, he loaned money to one automobile manufacturer and invested in another. The latter cost him a fortune. Perhaps he had been naïve; after all, he was not that old at the time. Or perhaps he was merely caught up in the times. Industries were evolving or growing, and new products were being produced by the hundreds. Lasker learned quickly from his mistakes. Yet, he had a soft spot when it came to helping friends.

Lord & Thomas continued to prosper. Billings rose from $3 million in 1906 to $6 million in 1912, when Lasker became sole owner of the agency. The agency now had a branch office in New York, and Lasker made certain that this office paid for itself. As Don Belding pointed out, "He demanded maximum results from his men . . . and he did not let the agency stray into extracurricular activity and gather a lot of appendages, or barnacles as he called them."[12] In fact, Lasker fired a specific number of employees, or "deadwood," about every four years. This may be considered by many as a flaw in his character. Those who produced, like Hopkins, stayed with the agency until they left to pursue other opportunities or retired.

In 1916 the agency opened a branch office in Los Angeles in an effort to service the Sunkist account. The office soon attracted other clients, including the California Walnut Growers Association.

Before he became intrigued with politics in 1918, Lasker had contributed much to advertising. He had been partly responsible for the "salesmanship in print" and "reason-why" styles of copy. He had been partly responsible for "scientific" advertising. He had helped train personnel, some of whom had moved to other agencies or had founded agencies. He had promoted ethical principles and had been vehemently opposed to questionable or dishonest advertising.

For the next several years, Lasker worked first for the Republican Party, then the presidential campaign of Warren G. Harding, and finally for the U.S. Shipping Board, which, reluctantly, he agreed to direct. Lasker did not enjoy working for the federal government. He returned to the agency in 1923.

Hopkins had managed Lord & Thomas while Lasker served his country. The agency had opened a branch office in San Francisco before 1920 and another in London in 1922. However, the branch office in New York was not producing enough to cover its expenses. Personnel argued over which style of advertising to employ in advertising campaigns. Other agencies, such as the J. Walter Thompson Company, filled advertisements with colorful art, different typefaces, and borders. Headlines, to Lasker, seemed to play a secondary, instead of a primary, role in these advertisements, and body copy was not necessarily "reason-why." Lasker immediately learned that the agency was not the largest in the country. This fact bothered him immensely. The agency had lost some clients because of internal problems. Hopkins had created an art department. Lasker was opposed to having an art department because of costs. Hopkins, who had gotten along well with Lasker for years, suddenly realized that there were too many differences between them. He retired from the agency in 1924 and started a copywriting service. His auto-biography, *My Life in Advertising*, was published in 1927.

Lasker hired Ralph Sollitt, who had worked for the U.S. Shipping Board. Then he fired almost every employee in the branch office in New York. To make Lord & Thomas the largest agency in the United States, he had to take drastic steps. First, he talked at great length to his subordinates; he explained how Lord & Thomas was founded as well as what he had accomplished. In short, he presented his life to them and expressed the style of advertising that Lord & Thomas should create. Second, advertisements to attract new clients were created and subsequently published in trade journals. These advertisements were subtle compared to advertisements for other agencies, as the following illustrates:

Is Advertising Read?
Three examples that bring out the answer

THE word *halitosis* lay buried in the widely "read" dictionary of the English language scores of years until set in ordinary type in an advertisement it became a by-word of the millions.

As a result, a product 40 years on the market with moderate sales became a world leader. Bad breath became almost a fashion.

On the other hand, yeast was something merely to make bread with—until Fleischmann advertisements said otherwise.

Now we gain fair skins, robust health, cure ourselves of many of the common ills of mankind, and even look forward hopefully to Eternal Youth because of it.

For centuries women used makeshift hygienic pads. The subject itself was admittedly a forbidden one. A subject no one spoke about, much less wrote about, except in medical practice.

Then came Kotex. A sanitary pad. A product no woman had ever heard about. A product that admitted no definitely descriptive words in headlines to describe it.

Thus to learn what Kotex was intended for, the reader had to go *deep into the text* of the ads. Kotex headlines perforce had to be more or less indirect. No person could get the import of a Kotex ad *without reading virtually every word of the ad itself.*

That women did, everyone who follows advertising knows. Over 80% of the better class of women in America today employ Kotex. The makers of this product would be quick to answer whether or not advertising is read.

Thus Listerine, Fleischmann's Yeast and Kotex—at least three of the most notably successful products of the day—must be regarded as Simon Pure Advertising successes.

All had their basic selling stories, not in the headlines, but in the text of their ads. And readers had to read that text to be "sold." All stand as indisputable answers to the question, "Is Advertising Read?"

If people didn't read ads as carefully as news or feature matter, most of the successful concerns whose names are household words would be virtually unknown to the reading millions.

Men who have made money through advertising know how true that is. [13]

Lasker's style of advertising paid off. The agency captured new accounts in the 1920s. One was the International Cellucotton Products Company, a subsidiary of Kimberly-Clark, which made Kotex. Although the product had been on the market for some time, sales were slow. Instinctively, Lasker believed that Kotex could be sold successfully to women if the correct strategy was implemented. The agency created factual advertisements and persuaded several magazine publishers to accept them. Another advertising campaign was developed for newspapers. These advertisements informed women that Kotex would be available in plain packages in specific stores. Another advertising campaign was developed to inform organizations, including school boards, how girls could be taught feminine hygiene. The campaigns worked, and sales increased dramatically.

In 1924 Lord & Thomas captured another Kimberly-Clark product, which the agency named "Kleenex." However, Lasker was not as interested in this product as he had been in Kotex, primarily because he believed that Kleenex would never replace the handkerchief. Ernst Mahler, the inventor of the product, made Lasker realize the importance of the tissue when he asked, "A. D., do you enjoy putting germs in your pocket?"[14] Lasker persuaded Mahler to increase the size of the tissue, and the agency staff created a different size box. The advertisements sold Kleenex as the "handkerchief you can throw away."

Lord & Thomas earned millions of dollars from Kimberly-Clark. By the end of the 1920s, however, almost 60 percent of the agency's billings came from the American Tobacco Company account Lucky Strike. As Lasker recalled,

> The big cigarette companies had started some time between 1912 and 1923 to make the present type of cigarettes, domestic Virginia and Turkish tobaccos mixed. I think the first two to make it were Camels and Chesterfields. The American Tobacco Company was late in starting. Up to 1923, or even 1925, the American Tobacco Company must have had over fifty brands, and those fifty brands would be pushed and advertised—each with a little appropriation.[15]

Lasker acquired the Lucky Strike account from George Washington Hill, the son of Percival Hill, the president of the company, and persuaded Hill to invest more money in advertising the Lucky Strike brand. By doing so, the agency could conduct a national advertising campaign.

The first advertising campaign focused on "toasted," which had been stamped on the packages of the brand. This campaign differentiated the product from its competitors. One day, Lasker and Flora were eating in a restaurant. Because Flora had gained weight, she had been advised by her doctor to light a cigarette before each meal. When she lit a cigarette on this occasion, the proprietor informed Lasker that he could not allow a woman to smoke in public because it would offend others. This incident opened Lasker's eyes. Women were treated like second-class citizens. He realized that if he could change the public's attitude toward women's smoking in public, he could capture another target market. Lasker thought of women who lived in Europe; they smoked in public. Lasker thought of women who would capture the public's attention. He recalled,

> It was very natural that my mind went to the opera stars, because at that time there were only one or two American stars, and the rest were foreign.
>
> Then we developed what we called our "precious voice" campaign. As they were singers, they said, "My living is dependent on my being able to sing, and I protect my precious voice by smoking Lucky Strike."[16]

The advertisements contained colorful photographs of stars in their costumes. The stars accepted the assignments without pay. To them, the publicity was more important.

Almost overnight, women began to smoke in public. The taboo had been broken. Several months later, several companies that manufactured candies placed advertisements informing customers that smoking was not good for their health. Lasker reacted by seeing Hill, and, together, they came up with the line "Reach for a Lucky instead of a Sweet," which was employed in another advertising campaign.

Within a few years, Lucky Strike was one of the best-selling brands of cigarettes on the market, and Lord & Thomas earned millions of dollars from the account.

In 1926 the agency became Lord & Thomas & Logan when Lasker asked Thomas F. Logan, who owned the Logan agency, to consolidate with Lord & Thomas. Through Logan, Lord & Thomas acquired some excellent accounts, including Anaconda Copper and the Radio Corporation of America (RCA), which David Sarnoff, whom Lasker had met, directed. Sarnoff had been instrumental in creating the National Broadcasting Company (NBC) in 1926. As radio became popular, programs were developed and eventually sponsored by advertisers. Lasker had an hour-long program created for one of his accounts, Palmolive. When this proved successful, he had programs developed for other sponsors. By 1928, when Logan died, Lord & Thomas was responsible for about 50 percent of the advertising placed with NBC. Other programs were developed for other advertisers. These included *Amos 'n' Andy* for Pepsodent, *The Story of Mary Marlin* for Kleenex, and *Information Please* for Lucky Strike. With the help of radio, Lasker's Lord & Thomas advertising agency became one of the largest in the world in the 1930s.

While the country faced the Great Depression, Lasker's Lord & Thomas advertising agency continued but at a slower pace. In 1931 Lasker cut salaries by 25 percent. Two years later he fired more than fifty employees. Was the Great Depression taking its toll on Lasker? Was it age? Or was it worry?

In 1935 the agency captured the Frigidaire Corporation account. The company, a subsidiary of General Motors, manufactured refrigerators. The company's executives had a specific concept for the advertising in mind. However, the agency developed an advertising campaign based on the refrigerator's rotary compressor, which a copywriter named "meter miser." Sales were greater than senior executives' expectations.

In 1936 Flora died, and Albert Lasker, fifty-six years of age, was distraught. The love of his life had left him alone. What would he do? Advertising was no longer interesting to him. At the urging of friends, he traveled the world in 1937.

When he returned, he announced that he would move the agency's headquarters from Chicago to New York and that he would retire from the presidency of the agency in late 1938. Don Francisco, who had worked at Lord & Thomas for years, would be his successor. However, Francisco left Lord & Thomas to work for the federal government. Pearl Harbor had been bombed by the Japanese, and the country faced another world war. Lasker returned to the agency.

During his brief retirement, Lasker met an actress, Doris Kenyon, in California. After a few months they married. Unfortunately, within a few weeks, they realized that they had made a mistake. The marriage ended in divorce several months later.

In 1939 he met Mary Woodard Reinhardt, a business woman, in New York. They dated for more than a year, then married. Lasker realized that Mary had interests similar to his; she could talk to him about politics, business, and religion. He realized, too, that Mary's love saved him. His purpose in life changed as a result of her. She persuaded him to become involved in different causes, including cancer research and mental health research, which he did. In fact, he suggested that the Birth Control Federation change its name to Planned Parenthood. To him, considering the purpose of the organization, the original name was too narrow.

Two years later, he informed Mary that he had decided to retire from advertising. According to John Gunther, there were several reasons for his desiring to retire:

> First, he was . . . tired. Second, he was bored. Third, the new generation of executives with whom he had to deal seemed far beneath his standards. Fourth, he wanted to devote himself to public service. Fifth, he felt that shortages induced by the war effort were bound to curtail sales of consumer goods, on which his business largely depended. Sixth . . . Edward [his son] had made it clear that he did not wish to succeed his father in the business, and would not return to advertising after the war.[17]

Lasker met with his three senior executives, Emerson Foote, Fairfax Cone, and Don Belding. Lord & Thomas soon became Foote, Cone, and Belding. Lasker informed the agency's major clients of his decision and persuaded most to stay with the new company.

Lord & Thomas as an advertising agency ceased on December 30, 1942. Albert Lasker, who believed that a good advertisement must have a central idea, news, and enough creativity to make the central idea sing, died from cancer ten years later. He was seventy-two years of age.

Under Lasker's guidance, Lord & Thomas handled such clients as the Wilson Ear Drum Company, the Nineteen Hundred Washer Company, the Quaker Oats Company, the Pepsodent Company, California Fruit Growers Exchange (Sunkist), the B. J. Johnson Soap Company (Palmolive), the Van

Camp Packing Company, Goodyear Tire and Rubber Company, Kimberly-Clark, the Radio Corporation of America (RCA), and the American Tobacco Company.

NOTES

1. Stephen Fox, *The Mirror Makers: A History of American Advertising and Its Creators* (New York: Morrow, 1984), 40.
2. Albert D. Lasker, "Reminiscences," Columbia Oral History Collection (Columbia University, 1949–1950), 7.
3. Albert D. Lasker, "The Personal Reminiscences of Albert Lasker," *American Heritage* (December 1954): 78.
4. *Saturday Evening Post* 173, no. 28 (January 12, 1901): 18.
5. Albert D. Lasker, *The Lasker Story . . . As He Told It* (Chicago: Advertising, 1963), 19.
6. Jeffrey L. Cruikshank and Arthur W. Schultz, *The Man Who Sold America: The Amazing (but True) Story of Albert D. Lasker and the Creation of the Advertising Century* (Boston: Harvard Business Review Press, 2010), 56.
7. Fox, *The Mirror Makers*, 50.
8. John Gunther, *Taken at the Flood: The Story of Albert D. Lasker* (New York: Harper and Brothers, 1960), 60.
9. Fox, *The Mirror Makers*, 51.
10. Lasker, "Reminiscences," 79.
11. Lasker, *The Lasker Story*, 38.
12. Don Belding, "End of an Era in Advertising," *Advertising Agency and Advertising and Selling* (July 1952): 67.
13. Advertisement 37, April 21, 1927. From Foote, Cone, and Belding's file of Lord & Thomas original advertisements.
14. Gunther, *Taken at the Flood*, 155.
15. Lasker, "The Personal Reminiscences of Albert Lasker," 82.
16. Lasker, "The Personal Reminiscences of Albert Lasker," 84.
17. Gunther, *Taken at the Flood*, 269.

Chapter Seven

The Rise of Procter & Gamble and the Advertising of Ivory Soap

Cleanliness in the United States became somewhat of a concern in the late eighteenth century, and baths, which allowed total immersion, were installed in various cities. Prior to this time, men bathed in creeks, rivers, lakes, and oceans. For the most part, women, primarily because it was a social taboo, were denied this privilege. They bathed sporadically in private, usually with a piece of cloth and water. However, when bathhouses opened, most admitted women. These bathhouses emphasized cleanliness, not cold or mineral or spring water, which had been emphasized by so-called mineral spring spas that had been established by the 1770s.[1]

Interest in cleanliness dates to antiquity, but tradition was not necessarily the reason for cleanliness to become a major concern in the late eighteenth century. Although various religions had survived hundreds, if not thousands, of years and had perpetuated, to a certain extent, cleanliness of the body as well as the mind or spirit, most people had been hindered from practicing what their ministers occasionally had preached. Only the wealthy, for instance, could afford in-house bathrooms, and this was in the late eighteenth century, when tubs and elements of modern plumbing became available in specific cities of the country. However, the primary reason for cleanliness to grow in importance was the genteel code of behavior, which people adopted and/or taught to others. Manuals concerning gentility were published for the betterment of mankind. Some of these manuals actually appeared in the American colonies during the early eighteenth century; apparently, certain Americans desired to change their values and, subsequently, their culture. Certain American groups such as the American gentry patterned themselves after their European counterparts. The revolutionary innovations that ap-

99

peared in England, for instance, eventually were brought to America. Even certain sanitary habits made their way across the Atlantic. According to Bushman and Bushman,

> This wave of fashion reached the American shore in the 1790s intermingled with all the currents of influences that flowed so freely from England to America. Tubs in a variety of designs were on the market in London, and American tinsmiths made them available in Philadelphia at the same time. Regular, year-round bathing was certainly not routine even in the most elite households in either England or America by 1800.[2]

Cleanliness grew in popularity throughout the nineteenth century, and cold baths were claimed to benefit those with certain medical ailments, such as consequent indigestion, while warm or hot baths were claimed to benefit those with specific medical problems, such as anxiety. As the medical community learned more about the human anatomy, some physicians encouraged their patients and others to take warm or hot baths so that dirt and germs would be removed from the skin. However, most Americans did not take baths on a regular basis until around 1850 or later. Even though cleanliness "ranked as a mark of moral superiority and dirtiness as a sign of degradation,"[3] most Americans refused to take the time or did not believe that bathing was *that* important or even beneficial. Many Americans did not believe that bathing was necessary to function as a productive member of society. Nonetheless, if a person aspired to be accepted into the middle or upper class, he or she had to be clean; this was an absolute requirement.

As the nineteenth century passed, the demand for soap grew. As a result, specific companies introduced to the American public bars of soap for cleansing the body. One of these companies, Procter & Gamble, was founded in Cincinnati, Ohio.

THE MANUFACTURING OF SOAP IN AMERICA

The making of soap in America was done by the housewife for many years. She used the fats she collected and made soft soap that was used by every member of her family.

Eventually, craftsmen who knew how to make soap from fats and ashes arrived in the colonies. For many years, however, these craftsmen exported the soap ashes and made candles for the colonists.

According to Samuel Colgate, even though small soap-boiling establishments had been founded in large towns by 1795, most of these establishments earned very little from making and selling soap, because most soap was made at home.[4]

As the nineteenth century progressed, more Americans purchased soap from these small firms. In addition, these firms exported soap as well as candles. In 1835, for instance, exports of these products totaled $534,467.[5] Seven years later these firms were producing "50,000,000 pounds of soap, 18,000,000 pounds of tallow candles, and 3,000,000 pounds of wax and spermaceti candles."[6] Exports of these products totaled more than $1 million.[7]

The early soaps were made from various fats, such as stearine, palmitine, and oleine. Alkalis were mixed with the fats for the purpose of varying the hardness. Soda, for instance, made a harder soap than potash. Stearine mixed with soda made the hardest soap, while oleine and potash made the softest soap. Oils, too, were used in manufacturing soap. These included olive oil, palm oil, and linseed oil. Other ingredients were added, depending on the purpose of the soap.

THE FOUNDING OF PROCTER & GAMBLE

Procter & Gamble, one of the best-known companies in the world, was founded by William Procter and James Gamble in Cincinnati, Ohio, in 1837. Procter, a lean man with a black beard, knew how to make candles. Gamble, a short man with a clean-shaven face, knew how to make soap. Although Procter's name is presented first in the company's name, he was not the first of the two to arrive in the United States.

James Gamble was born in Ireland. His father, George Gamble, was a Methodist minister who desired to escape with his family the depression that gripped Ireland in 1819. George had heard about abundant prosperity in, of all places, Shawneetown, Illinois. Friends and others who had journeyed to America and to this small town had written to him about their good fortune. Determined to leave his unfortunate predicament behind, George loaded his family onto a ship and sailed across the Atlantic to America.

George and his family journeyed safely to Pittsburgh; however, their funds were in short supply. The only form of transportation that would take them west and that they could afford was a flatboat on the Ohio River, which they boarded after some hesitation. James, sixteen, got violently ill as the flatboat moved almost silently downstream. Finally, after several days, the boat stopped in Cincinnati, Ohio, and the family went ashore. James, still ill, needed to rest. Members of the family undoubtedly were amazed at the bustling city that bordered the river. Although shipbuilding dominated the edge of the river, the city had various brewing companies as well as other businesses. The slaughter of swine was a major industry. Cincinnati was a very busy city in the early nineteenth century, even though Horace Greeley and colleagues pointed out that

> Cincinnati . . . had in 1800 only four hundred inhabitants, the disputed title to the territory which then formed what was called the Northwest Territory having proved an obstacle in the way of its rapid settlement. With the settlement of this question, the West was opened freely to the tide of emigration which flowed from the Eastern States, caused by the attractions of the new life of a new country, and the opportunities it afforded for enterprise, together with that from Europe, composed of those who looked with hope to the new republic, and sought to live where the simple right of political representation which it required a revolution to obtain at home was freely offered to any one who desired it. [8]

The family remained in Cincinnati. At first, they used the excuse that James was ill. Then they used the excuse that Cincinnati offered employment. George, for instance, opened a greenhouse and occasionally preached. James worked briefly for his father, then became an apprentice to William Bell, a soap manufacturer. James Gamble worked for Bell for eight years. Then he and Hiram Knowlton, a friend, opened a soap and candle shop. The business, though small, was profitable, and James, who had met Elizabeth Ann Norris, the daughter of a successful candle maker, Alexander Norris, eventually married her. He was thirty.

Norris had another daughter, Olivia, who married William Procter the same year. Procter had owned a woolen goods store in England until burglars stole every item in the shop; Procter owed creditors approximately $8,000.

Procter promised to pay his creditors as soon as he could and sailed with his wife, Martha, to America. Like George Gamble, he, too, had heard about unlimited opportunity in the New World, except the place that he had heard about was called "the falls of Ohio," which was actually Louisville, Kentucky. Procter and his wife, like the Gambles, boarded a flatboat on the Ohio River; their destination was "the falls of Ohio." Unfortunately, before they could make it to Louisville, Martha contracted cholera. When the boat stopped in Cincinnati, Procter took his wife to one doctor, then another. The prognosis was the same: there was nothing that could be done for her. Martha died within several days. Stricken with grief and possibly feeling responsible for his wife's death, Procter buried Martha. However, he did not go to "the falls of Ohio." He remained in Cincinnati and accepted a position at a bank. Procter soon realized that his wages were insufficient; he could not live on what he earned and pay his creditors. He also realized that Cincinnati provided a very good opportunity to those who knew how to make candles.

Procter relied on the skills he had learned as a child. He made candles and sold them in a small store, which he rented. Procter, probably because he was alone, was consumed by his business. When he met Olivia Norris, he was earning a good living and paying his creditors. Procter realized that Olivia could fill the void that had been caused by Martha's death, so he asked her to marry him; Olivia graciously and formally accepted.

William Procter and James Gamble were brothers-in-law, and they were purchasing the same animal fats. In essence, they were competing for the same raw material to produce their respective products. This fact seemed illogical to their father-in-law. He persuaded them to become partners, even though he knew that Gamble had a partner.

In 1837 Gamble's partnership with Knowlton ended, and Gamble moved his share of the goods into Procter's store. Although Gamble and Procter had not signed a formal contract, they worked as partners nonetheless. The same year, they purchased the land for their candle and soap factory.

The firm, though small, prospered. Advertising was placed infrequently in local newspapers. The first advertisement, for instance, appeared in the *Cincinnati Daily Gazette* on June 29, 1838; it was two inches in length:

> Oils for lamps and machinery. A fine article of clarified Pig's Foot Oil, equal to sperm, at a low price and in quantities to suit buyers. Neat's Foot oil ditto. Also No. 1 & 2 soap. Palm and shaving ditto. For sale by Procter & Gamble Co., east side Main Street 2nd door off 6th Street. [9]

Gamble was responsible for production, and Procter was responsible for sales. Production was crude and primitive. Sales increased over the months, and the collection of fats and potash had to be extended to other areas outside Cincinnati.

Procter and Gamble, primarily because of competition, realized that if they purchased greater quantities of raw materials, they would not find themselves in the precarious position of not having any products to sell. They also realized that if they remained ethical in their advertising, they invariably would prosper. The principles of their Protestant religion were applied to their advertising and to their business overall.

The firm continued to prosper. By 1848, for instance, Procter & Gamble, though still small, was earning $26,000 annually.

STARS AND THE MAN IN THE MOON

The symbol that became the company's trademark actually germinated from the crude black crosses that illiterate wharf hands had painted on boxes of Procter & Gamble Star candles in 1851. The wharf hands painted the boxes for identification purposes. Eventually, wharf hands changed the crosses to stars, then painted circles around the stars. Later, part of a man's face was painted inside the circles.

Procter & Gamble approved of the "moon and stars" symbol and had it painted on each box; however, later, they decided to have the "man in the moon" removed, until a merchant in New Orleans rejected a specific shipment because he believed that the shipment of boxes contained imitations. William Procter learned of the merchant's legitimate concern and had the "man in the moon" added to the symbol. In addition, he requested that the cluster of stars number thirteen, for the original thirteen colonies, which had been represented by thirteen stars in the first flag of the United States.

In 1875 the company's executives realized the importance of the symbol and, several years later, as soon as it was possible, registered the trademark with the newly opened Patent Office. The design was sculpted at least twice, in 1882 and again in 1930. The design sculpted in 1930 was used on the company's products' packages until it was retired in the 1990s.

THE GROWTH OF PROCTER & GAMBLE

Horace Greeley and colleagues wrote,

> Fifty years after the opening of this century, less than the time allotted for two generations, the population of Cincinnati had increased from four hundred to nearly two hundred thousand persons, had built nearly a thousand steamboats, and shipped yearly nearly one hundred millions of dollars' worth of produce, importing nearly eighty millions of dollars' worth of materials from abroad. Beside this, the industrial enterprise of the city had built up a manufacturing interest which produced an aggregate of over fifty millions of dollars' worth of various articles, and the city has established railroad connection with more than ten thousand miles of railroad leading directly to or through it. [10]

Procter & Gamble's sales increased, and the two industrious partners realized that a larger facility was required. In addition to concentrating on their Star candles, which were made from pork fats, the partners developed two new soaps from the "red oil," or oleic acid, that was actually a by-product of the Star candle process. For instance, they used the red oil to produce a hard white soap that was referred to as Mottled German. Later, they used the red oil to produce a hard, rough soap called Oleine.

William Procter's oldest son, William Alexander Procter, left college in 1851 and went to work for James Gamble, his uncle, in the factory. William worked so diligently that the partners offered him 10 percent of the business six years later.

Although Procter and Gamble attempted several times to extract glycerin from the wastewater, they were not successful until 1858, when Richard Tilghman, a chemist, showed them how. Procter and Gamble licensed the process from Tilghman and eventually sold glycerin at a much lower price than their competitors.

George H. Procter, who had attended Kenyon College, joined the company as a sales representative and successfully increased the sales of Mottled German and Oleine soaps. To better illustrate Procter & Gamble's progress, Charles Cist, in his *Sketches and Statistics of Cincinnati in 1859*, wrote,

> Procter & Gamble . . . are probably engaged more extensively in manufacturing operations, than any other establishment in our city. They consume seven hundred barrels rosin, and three hundred tons soda ash; ten thousand carboys—or six hundred thousand pounds—sulphuric acid; one hundred and fifteen thousand pounds candle-wick, and thirty thousand barrels, of two hundred and fifty pounds each—or seven million five hundred thousand pounds—lard, annually, in their various products.
>
> Their sales have largely exceeded one million dollars yearly; and in consequence of the high price of the great staple, lard, will this year, doubtless, reach much higher figures than heretofore. They employ eighty hands, in the various departments of their business.[11]

In 1860, realizing that a war was imminent, Procter and Gamble sent William and James Norris Gamble, his cousin, to New Orleans to purchase a large supply of rosin, which was necessary for making soap. Procter and Gamble desired to have enough supplies on hand in case trade routes were cut off by troops.

When the Civil War erupted several months later, Procter & Gamble had more supplies than their competitors for making soap. The Union Army contracted with the company, and Procter & Gamble had to supply one thousand cases of soap a day. The company hired additional people and purchased more equipment and buildings to meet the terms of the contract.

Procter & Gamble faced numerous obstacles, however, including a fire that destroyed part of the factory and a shortage of rosin. Even though the factory closed every Sunday, the company met its commitment.

When the war ended, Procter and Gamble assumed that orders for their products would decrease substantially. That was not the case. Men, particularly those who had served in the Union Army, had used Procter & Gamble products for four years; therefore, many purchased the products after the war. In addition, certain merchants in the South had purchased the products before the war; even if they could not afford to pay cash, these merchants were extended credit by the company.

Procter & Gamble continued to grow and prosper; the company added new markets and developed new products. However, the founders of the company were in their mid-sixties. By 1867, when the company was thirty years old, both men relied on their sons to manage the business.

Procter & Gamble's production of candles peaked in 1867, then declined as more and more people used oil lamps to light their houses. Two years later, when a few speculators attempted to capture the gold market, President Ulysses S. Grant sold $4 million of the government's gold in an effort to drive down the price. As a result of the decrease, investors on Wall Street panicked, which caused the entire country to suffer. People saved what little money they had; many refused to purchase certain goods as well as pay their debts. Like other companies at the time, Procter & Gamble's sales decreased. Profits, too, plummeted, and the company suffered. It actually operated in the red for a year, even though it reduced the number of employees.

In 1868, Harley Thomas Procter, another son of William Procter, began to work as a sales representative at the company. Harley desired to see Procter & Gamble rebound. The company's sales did not increase until the early 1870s.

In the late 1870s, the company developed Ivory soap, which was heavily advertised by Harley Procter. As a result of his promotional efforts, the soap became the company's best-selling product. (The development and advertising of Ivory soap are discussed later in this chapter.)

Procter & Gamble's factory burned in January 1884, the year William Procter died. Partner James Gamble and members of the two families broke ground on a new, much larger factory, appropriately named Ivorydale, in 1885. The new factory's production capacity for soap was more than twice the production capacity of the former factory, which had been two hundred thousand bars a day. In addition to Ivory and several other brands, the company produced Lenox, a new laundry soap that had been developed by James Norris Gamble. Harley Procter was responsible for the product's advertising, which included in-store promotions. As a result of Harley's efforts, sales of Lenox increased; it became the company's second best-selling soap.

Also in 1885 the only son of William Alexander Procter, William Cooper Procter, who had attended the College of New Jersey (now Princeton University) and who had worked in the factory, informed his father that factory employees worked too many hours and suggested that the workers have Saturday afternoons off, with pay. Cooper, as he was called, argued that the workers would actually work harder as a result. Although Cooper's father and uncle disagreed, Harley Procter, who liked the idea, was able to persuade Cooper's father and James Norris that the company should at least test the proposal. The proposal was tested, but a minority of workers desired more. At this period, laborers across the country were uniting and making revolutionary demands of their employers. Procter & Gamble's employees went on strike numerous times during the next several years. In 1887 Cooper suggested that the company should allow its employees a share of the profits, a radical idea that was immediately rejected. However, specific writers who wrote for business magazines learned about the idea and requested interviews. Cooper firmly believed that his plan, if implemented, would result in greater productivity on the part of the employees.

The plan was accepted and explained to the employees later that year. A minority of workers thought that the plan was merely a ploy to get them to stop complaining and to work harder. Most employees, especially when the dividends were handed out several months later, appreciated the extra income. The plan did not necessarily persuade employees to work harder or more efficiently, as Cooper had predicted. Yet, the number of strikes decreased. Ida Tarbell discussed the plan in detail:

> As they frankly informed their employees, the purpose was to increase "diligence, carefulness and thoughtful cooperation" in order to enlarge earnings—earnings in which, of course, the employees would share. The sum divided was to bear the same relation to the total profits as the amount of wages, including the partners' salaries, bore to the total cost of carrying on the business. Only those who had been three months or more with the firm were to participate. The semiannual day of distribution was set aside as a holiday.
>
> In May, 1890, on the sixth dividend day, it was reported that profits of sixty thousand dollars had been distributed in the three preceding years, equal to about sixteen per cent of the wages paid. The "diligence, carefulness and thoughtful cooperation" which the firm sought had not, however, been fully secured. Certain changes were therefore made in the plan: the employees were divided into four classes, and dividends were to follow merit. But the revised regulations did not work out as well as the company desired. Just before and after dividend days enthusiasm was great; the diligence was all that could be asked. But gradually this wore off, to return only as the next celebration approached.[12]

The same year Harley James Morrison, a relative of the Procters and a graduate of Yale, was hired to help develop new products. Within three years, he persuaded Procter & Gamble executives to build a laboratory at Ivorydale. This laboratory was responsible for scientific inquiry that was conducted for the purpose of developing new products and improving old products.

The company, which was divided equally among the Procters and Gambles, continued to prosper under the second generation's guidance.

Later, in 1887, Cooper Procter was given a small interest in the company. Perhaps it was because of his receiving an interest in the company or that his previous idea was ultimately accepted and implemented that he suggested the partnership become a public corporation.

The first stockholders' meeting was held three years later, in 1890, and eleven members were elected to the board of directors. Five of these members included William Alexander Procter, James Norris Gamble, Harley T. Procter, David B. Gamble, and William Cooper Procter. Founder James Gamble was eighty-seven and too old to serve. Other members of the board were not related to the Procters or the Gambles and were not elected officials of the company. As a result, the management of the company remained in the families' control. Indeed, William Alexander Procter became president, James Norris Gamble became vice president, and William Cooper Procter became general manager.

Founder James Gamble died in 1891, and Harley T. Procter, forty-three, informed William Alexander Procter and other members of the families that he was retiring. They attempted to persuade him to remain, but he was determined to move to New England with his wife, which he did. However, he returned to the company periodically, particularly whenever he was needed or whenever the board met. The advertising campaigns for which he had been responsible continued. Full-page advertisements with illustrations of Ivory appeared in the major publications of the day, and the company continued to prosper.

Although William Alexander Procter was president, his son William Cooper Procter was general manager and consequently searched for professionals who knew how to manage specific departments and employees. In 1892 he initiated a stock-purchasing plan for employees that was guaranteed by the company and later coupled with the profit-sharing plan.

Procter & Gamble continued to expand as a result of developing new products and sales. In 1903, for instance, the company built another plant in Kansas City. In 1906 the company built Port Ivory in New York. Ivory and Lenox soaps were the company's best-selling brands, but other companies were advertising successfully other brands of soap, such as Pears'. Procter & Gamble responded to these companies by developing products such as P&G White Naphtha and by increasing its advertising budget.

William Alexander Procter, who had been grieving for several years for his deceased wife, killed himself in 1907. His son, William Cooper Procter, became president at a time when numerous companies closed or decreased the number of employees as a result of several large banks' closing in New York. Procter & Gamble weathered the storm that gripped the nation. Cooper, who actually learned about hydrogenation from E. C. Kayser, a German chemical engineer who had turned liquid cottonseed oil into a solid, purchased the rights to use Kayser's hydrogenation process and subsequently had a facility built at Ivorydale in 1908. The product that was developed in the new facility was Crisco, a new vegetable shortening, which ultimately could be found in most American kitchens.

During World War I, Procter & Gamble, in an effort to compete successfully against Lever Brothers, expanded into Canada when it had a factory built in 1914 in Hamilton, Ontario. The facility produced Ivory soap and Crisco.

In 1917 the plant in Kansas City closed when picketers dared any employee to cross the picket line. Cooper Procter boarded a train for Kansas City, met with a committee of employees, and listened attentively to their demands. As a result of the meeting, Cooper agreed to an eight-hour workday, which would be enacted as soon as the war ended. The committee agreed to his terms, and the plant immediately reopened.

Cooper Procter enacted the Employees' Conference Plan, which encouraged a representative body of employees to meet frequently with upper management to discuss issues and resolve problems, in 1918. The Employees' Conference Plan worked until 1937, when the U.S. Supreme Court ruled that the National Labor Relations Act of 1935 was constitutional. Conference committees had to be abolished. Procter & Gamble complied.

In 1920 the company started selling its products directly to retailers nationwide. (It had sold its products to retailers in New York City on an experimental basis for several years.) According to Alecia Swasy,

> Wholesalers watched the volatile prices of fats and oils, which were used to make Ivory soap and Crisco shortening. Like any smart buyer, they would stock up on P&G brands when raw material prices were low and stop buying when prices soared. The inventory could then be resold to small shopkeepers at a profit, regardless of P&G's pricing. That buying schedule made for erratic production at P&G plants.[13]

The plan was fought by various companies, especially wholesalers. Nonetheless, Procter & Gamble increased its sales staff and opened various warehouses across the country. Unfortunately, a recession hit the country in the early 1920s, and Procter & Gamble lost at least $30 million.

In 1923, however, the company rebounded. Its direct selling plan, for instance, had been improved and had been accepted by more companies. Its manufacturing output had increased. Employees realized they had a certain security.

In addition, the company introduced new products, such as Ivory Flakes, for washing dishes and laundering certain fabrics; Chipso, for various kinds of cleaning, including laundering; and Camay soap, for the bathroom. This brand of soap competed with Ivory and was heavily advertised. Samples were delivered door-to-door, and housewives were asked to write to the company to inform executives about the product.

The same year, the company established an Economic Research Department primarily for the purpose of studying the commodities markets. The department, under Dr. D. Paul Smelser, conducted surveys of various kinds and learned what consumers believed about new and old products manufactured by Procter & Gamble. Other forms of market research were used to learn about advertising, particularly its effectiveness. Regional market tests were conducted before any new product was sold nationally. Several products failed these tests and were discontinued.

Although William Cooper Procter was president of the company, he realized that he was growing older. Richard R. Deupree was made general manager in 1927, then a vice president a year later. He had been hired in 1905 as an office boy and had served as a salesman, manager of the Bulk Soap Sales Division, manager of western sales for all consumer products, general sales manager, and a director. Procter allowed Deupree to assume responsibility of managing the company. In 1930 William Cooper Procter was named chairman, and Deupree was elected president. Procter was sixty-eight, and Deupree was forty-five. In 1933 Deupree, at Cooper's urging, enacted a five-day, forty-hour workweek at every Procter & Gamble factory. A year later William Cooper Procter, seventy-one, died.

The Great Depression gripped the country. Although Procter & Gamble's sales plummeted, Deupree refused to slash the company's advertising budget. Indeed, Deupree and the company's advertising manager, Ralph Rogan, through the Blackman Company, an advertising agency in New York, had advertised Crisco on several radio programs as early as 1923. Eventually, as radio grew in popularity, Procter & Gamble advertised other products, such as Ivory, on several early serials, or "soap operas," which were actually developed for the company's products. The company was also responsible for developing the "slice of life" advertising format that was adopted later by other companies.

By the time the company was one hundred years old in 1937, Procter & Gamble's products were known to millions, and sales of specific products had more than doubled when the Great Depression ended. Between 1933 and 1935, for instance, net earnings increased 66 percent.

In 1937, when the company celebrated its centennial birthday, the Ohio River flooded parts of Cincinnati, including parts of Ivorydale. Even though Mother Nature was unkind to some of Procter & Gamble's facilities, the company was experiencing phenomenal growth, with eleven factories in the United States and five in four other countries. Procter & Gamble's growth was primarily the result of research in its manufacturing, advertising, and sales departments and in the quality of its personnel.[14]

THE ADVERTISING OF IVORY SOAP FROM THE 1880S TO THE 1930S

During the 1870s James Norris Gamble and Procter & Gamble's first full-time chemist were attempting to make a hard white soap that would be as good as the castile soaps of Europe. The company purchased a formula from another soap manufacturer and then experimented with it. Major changes were made to the formula. Finally, in 1878, James Gamble announced that his laboratory had achieved what had seemed to some in the company impossible. He and his associates had created a formula that met everyone's expectations. Although the new soap was to be marketed as P&G White Soap, Harley Procter instinctively realized that the name was not unique or memorable. He informed other members of the family that the product needed a name that people would remember. They gave the task of naming the product to him. Harley eagerly read Dr. Roget's thesaurus and the dictionary. Nothing. He read countless lists of names for other products, including soaps. Nothing. Finally, at church one Sunday morning the minister read Psalms 45:8: "All thy garments smell of myrrh and aloes and cassia, out of the ivory palaces whereby they have made thee glad." The word "ivory" remained in Harley's mind, probably because it was white, and Harley realized that white symbolized cleanliness, if not purity. He also realized that "ivory" was expensive. Harley decided that "Ivory" would be the best name for Procter & Gamble's white soap. According to the editors of *Advertising Age*, "Harley Procter . . . asked a New York chemist to analyze the three leading brands of castile soap, then asked that same chemist to evaluate Ivory. By the chemist's own definition of purity, Ivory was purer than the castiles, with only 0.56% impurities."[15] Later, he asked chemistry professors at several major universities to analyze Ivory.

Before the soap was successfully marketed, according to legend, one of the men who handled one of the crutchers forgot to stop the machine when he went to lunch. Crutchers contained arms that mixed the ingredients for the soap. Upon his return, the mixture was frothy and overflowing the vat. However, another employee decided that the ingredients had not been changed and subsequently used the mixture for soap, which was eventually shipped. One or two months later merchants were requesting the "soap that floats." Unfortunately, no one at the company knew which brand of soap these merchants were requesting until a thorough investigation revealed the "accidental" mixture, which was repeated. The company then produced the "soap that floats."[16] However, according to Davis Dyer, Frederick Dalzell, and Rowena Olegario, "By 1878, the company had been experimenting for at least a dozen years with floating soaps."[17] If Dyer and colleagues are correct, then the story above may be apocryphal.

Although Harley Procter, who was sales manager for the company, was informed that Ivory would float, he was not necessarily impressed. He, along with his sales staff, carried samples of the product to wholesalers in the Northeast and Midwest. Then he placed an advertisement in a trade journal that targeted grocers. When he became a partner of the company in 1881, he requested funds for advertising directly to consumers, which was a relatively new concept to American manufacturers. Procter & Gamble had been spending about $1,500 a year on advertising to merchants. The company's executives agreed to listen to his rationale but were not convinced that his explanation was sound. Harley reiterated his idea, and in 1882 the partners increased the advertising budget to $11,000. Immediately, Harley, who had been responsible for the notch in the middle of the large-size bar so that the consumers could break it into two smaller bars and who had been responsible for the checkerboard wrapper with the word "Ivory" and the company's trademark, created the first consumer advertisement for Ivory soap. Harley focused on the soap's color as well as its gentleness. Of course, he included the fact that it was 99.44 percent pure. The advertisement appeared in the December 21, 1882, issue of the religious publication *The Independent*:

> THE "IVORY" is a Laundry Soap, with all the fine qualities of a choice Toilet Soap, and is 99 44–100 per cent. **pure.**
>
> Ladies will find this Soap especially adapted for washing laces, infants' clothing, silk hose, cleaning gloves and all articles of fine texture and delicate color, and for the varied uses about the house that daily arise, requiring the use of soap that is above the ordinary in quality.
>
> For the Bath, Toilet, or Nursery it is preferred to most of the Soaps sold for toilet use, being purer and much more pleasant and effective and possessing all the desirable properties of the finest unadulterated White Castile Soap. The Ivory Soap will "**float**."
>
> The cakes are so shaped that they may be used entire for general purposes or divided with a stout thread (as illustrated) into two perfectly formed cakes, of convenient size for toilet use.
>
> The price, compared to the quality and the size of the cakes, makes it the cheapest Soap for everybody for every want. TRY IT.
> **SOLD EVERYWHERE**[18]

The illustration, which was above the copy, contained a pair of hands tying a string around a large bar of soap. The string was in the notched area.

One of Harley Procter's first advertising campaigns consisted of full-page advertisements in *The Century* and other magazines. Each of these advertisements featured one or two testimonials from one or two chemistry professors who had analyzed one or two bars of Ivory. In another campaign, each advertisement contained an illustration and some verse. According to Alfred Lief, "by associating little girls, mamma's helpers, with the soap, and creating a merry mood through fantasies of the animal kingdom, the ads . . . cultivated an impression of universal acceptance of Ivory for its purity and safety."[19] Harley also advertised the product on outdoor displays.

Another advertising campaign consisted of advertisements placed in the more popular women's service magazines, such as *Good Housekeeping* and *The Ladies' Home Journal*. In each advertisement, Harley urged readers to purchase a bar of Ivory for each room in the house. He did not use the fact that Ivory soap would float and the "99 44–100 percent pure" claim in every advertisement, however.

The fact that Ivory would float was not emphasized in advertisements until about ten years later. Nonetheless, Harley's early advertisements were so successful that certain Procter & Gamble competitors mentioned Ivory by name in comparative advertisements for their respective products.

In the March 1886 issue of *The Ladies' Home Journal*, a quarter-page advertisement announced the Ivory soap etching, which was available for 54 cents to cover packaging and postage, from Procter & Gamble.

Beginning in 1887, advertisements featuring babies in illustrations became well known and attracted attention. The Ivory babies, as they were called, implied that the soap was so mild that mothers could use it to wash their infants.

One of the first premiums offered to consumers was the Ivory soap "Watch Charm," which was a small facsimile of a bar of Ivory soap with a gold-plated ring, for the centerpiece from twelve soap wrappers. This advertisement appeared in the January 1889 issue of *The Ladies' Home Journal*.

In addition to these advertisements, Harley persuaded the company to sponsor a contest for amateur poets. The writer of the best poem would receive $300. The contest generated thousands of submissions, and sales of Ivory increased substantially. Harley's ideas for selling Ivory seemed endless, at least to others in the company.

According to Davis Dyer and colleagues,

> By this point, Procter & Gamble had clearly found the pitch for Ivory. The ads were taking on a distinct look. They gave most of the page over to a single image, well-crafted and high-minded, even artistic, cultivating an impression of gentility and aesthetic taste. . . . Ivory was tapping into complex iconography, identifying itself with concepts—purity, femininity, domesticity—that were acquiring a peculiar resonance in an age of rapid industrialization and urbanization, among a population of consumers adjusting themselves, sometimes uneasily, to participation in mass markets.[20]

In the January 6, 1894, issue of *Harper's Weekly*, the company placed a one-third-column advertisement that contained the words "Ivory soap" with an illustration of the notched bar. Two lines of copy—"It Floats" and "For

Table Linen"—immediately followed. Other advertisements during this period were similar in the sense that each mentioned an article found in the
kitchen or dining room that could be cleaned with Ivory soap.

In the January 5, 1895, issue of *Harper's Weekly*, the following advertisement appeared:

Ivory
99 44/100 Pure
Why not wash with pure white Ivory Soap and have pure white linen?
"Whatever is worth doing at all, is worth doing well."[21]

This advertisement emphasized the color and the article on which the product
could be applied.

In 1896 the advertisements for Ivory discussed uses other than cleaning,
as the following illustrates:

TO BICYCLISTS:

Many of those who have made the discovery have requested us to notify
wheelmen generally that there is no better chain lubricant than Ivory Soap; it is
the most cleanly application and is perfect for this use.

An additional block of copy in smaller-size type discussed the product's
ingredients:

The vegetable oils of which Ivory Soap is made, and its purity, fit it for many
special uses for which other soaps are unsafe and unsatisfactory. Ivory Soap is
sold by more dealers and used in more households than any other.[22]

The last sentence informed the consumer that unless she had Ivory in her
home, she was not purchasing the preferred brand.

In the December 1897 issue of *The Ladies' Home Journal*, a quarter-page
advertisement contained a large illustration of Mrs. S. T. Roper, an authority
on the selection and preparation of food, who endorsed Ivory:

With the increase of wealth and luxury there comes an increased demand for a
better and safer cleansing agent for household use. A large number of house-
keepers have discarded the ordinary colored soaps and are now using only a
pure soap of the best quality. Mrs. S. T. Roper, widely known as an authority
on the selection and preparation of food and other articles of household consumption, says [the quotation was in smaller-size type]: "In looking over the
field I am sure that the housewife can afford without a second thought to throw
away her alkali powders, drop her ammonia bottle, and use Ivory Soap for all
purposes, with far better results than could be obtained from combinations of
which she knows but little."[23]

Advertisements featuring other authorities discussing Ivory appeared in magazines at this time and were similarly designed.

Harley Procter pioneered the use of preprinted color inserts in the early magazines when in 1900 he hired the Procter and Collier Company, which was actually a printing firm in Cincinnati. The firm, which had been founded by Percy Procter, William Alexander Procter's younger brother, and Allen Collier, was hired to produce four-color advertisements. These advertisements contained colorful illustrations that had been drawn by the most popular artists of the day, such as Alice Barber Stephens and Maxfield Parrish. Reproductions of these commissioned works of art were available for Ivory wrappers. The Procter and Collier Company held the Procter & Gamble account for more than twenty years, until the Blackman Company earned the account in 1922.

Before 1910, advertisements for Ivory were encouraging consumers to use the product five or six times a day to improve their complexion.

In the July 1910 issue of *The Ladies' Home Journal*, the following advertisement occupied a full page:

> No matter whether you bathe in the morning or at night, in warm water or cold, *you should use Ivory Soap.*
> It floats. It is pure. It lathers freely. It rinses easily. It *cleans!*
> Can you think of any other qualities that a bath soap should have?
> **Ivory Soap. . . . . It Floats.** [24]

The copy emphasized the name of the product and the fact that the product cleans. The phrase "Ivory Soap . . . It Floats" was printed in large, bold letters. A large illustration of a woman preparing to take a bath was above the block of copy. She was holding a bar of Ivory in her left hand and looking at the reader.

In 1911 Harley Procter announced to consumers that Procter & Gamble would offer $1,000 for the most unusual uses of Ivory in homes. As a result, Procter & Gamble received thousands of suggestions, and Harley used some of these in advertisements. Later, the company published and advertised the booklet *Unusual Uses of Ivory Soap*, which contained some of the suggestions that had been mailed to the company. Other booklets followed, including *Questions Often Asked*.

The company's position toward advertising was stated in a full-page advertisement that was published in the May 15, 1911, issue of *Saturday Evening Post*:

> Advertising has been a factor—an important factor—in the success of Ivory Soap.
> But—would you buy Ivory Soap if you could get better soap for the price you pay for Ivory? No!

Would you buy Ivory Soap if you could get another soap, as good as Ivory, for less than you pay for Ivory? Of course not.

Advertising is merely an evidence of a manufacturer's faith in the merit of an article.

Continuous advertising is proof of the public's confidence in it.

Ivory Soap has been advertised, *continuously*, for more than thirty years. [The last paragraph of copy was in smaller-size print.]

For bath, toilet and fine laundry purposes; for the nursery; for shampooing; for everything and anything that necessitates the use of a better-than-ordinary soap, Ivory Soap is unequalled.[25]

In 1915 the company's advertisements for Ivory claimed that the product was gentle enough for babies, as the following advertisement illustrates:

Babies and Ivory Soap seem to belong to each other. It is natural to think of Ivory Soap in connection with a baby's tender skin and it is almost impossible not to think of baby's bath when recalling the many particular things which Ivory does so well. [The remaining blocks of copy were in smaller-size type.] The sensitive little body demands a soap that is mild and pure, above all else. To most people Ivory has come to mean the mildest and purest soap that can be made. Users of Ivory Soap now think of it as the soap for all better-than-ordinary purposes. They know that it is capable of the most exacting things— that even the tender skin of a new baby is unhurt by its use.

The Ivory Soap "Baby Book" is a valuable treatise on the raising of healthy, happy children. You may have a copy free of charge by addressing The Procter & Gamble Company, Dept. 3–B, Cincinnati, Ohio.
Ivory Soap. . . . It Floats. . . . 99 44/100% Pure[26]

The block of copy appeared on an illustration of an unopened scroll. A large illustration of a woman and her babies was in a frame that rested above the scroll. The advertisement's design undoubtedly was influenced by artists who had drawn or painted religious artifacts or figures centuries before.

In the 1920s, the advertising focused on hair, specific articles of clothing, and skin and how Ivory could be beneficial to all three. In 1925, for instance, in the "Beauty Is Fragile" advertisement, the copy discussed what specialists advised for the skin as well as the scientific basis for using soap.[27]

The focus of the advertisements remained the same during the 1930s. In the January 1930 issue of *The Ladies' Home Journal*, the following advertisement was published:

She pays $780 for nice hands—mine cost me next to nothing!
I don't have $780 a year to spend on a maid—like my nice next-door neighbor, Alice G—, who has two cars and never even washes out a handkerchief! My hands are *my* maids, and with a baby and husband to care for, you can imagine how busy they are.

Perhaps you're like me . . . you enjoy tending babies and home. But at a bridge or tea, you don't want your hands to look useful and stodgy. You want them to be ornamental! Don't I know? For the first year after I was married my hands looked like two neglected orphans. And how I sighed over them!

Strangely enough when my baby came I realized what was the trouble. Every day I put her little clothes through Ivory suds. And my hands always felt soothed afterward. (They usually were like graters after my Monday washing with ordinary "kitchen soup.")

So I decided to try Ivory for all my work. And at the end of a week, I felt as if I had a new pair of hands. Don't say hands can't speak! For they were thanking me for changing my dishwashing and cleaning and clothes—washing into gentle Ivory baths!

If you try my plan, as I hope you will, you'll find Ivory is thrifty because it keeps things like new. It doesn't fade colors . . . or rob paint of its gloss . . . or discolor linoleum as strong soaps do.

But I have my best reward when my neighbor drops in for a chat and a cup of fragrant tea. For I can't help noticing then (I'm only human!) that my hands look as carefree as hers!

Catherine Carr Lewis[28]

The block of copy was conversational and informal, but the focus was similar to that of previous advertisements.

In the mid-1930s the company used advertisements that contained large illustrations at the top and small boxed illustrations at the bottom. For the most part, the large illustrations were faces or hands.

The early advertisements for Ivory were successful in generating sales. The various ideas that germinated in Harley Procter's mind were revolutionary in the sense that many had not been attempted by anyone. As Charles Goodrum and Helen Dalrymple pointed out, Harley (1) knew that with the company's white soap, he had a specific, identifiable brand; (2) realized that he needed to advertise to consumers—the individuals who purchased products—to explain why the product was better than its competition and to express how the product was beneficial; (3) knew that the product was 99.44 percent pure and therefore could use this fact in the advertisements; (4) realized that the product's strength was its unquestionable value or quality and consequently implied this characteristic or attribute in the advertisements; and (5) knew that advertising to consumers was important, if not crucial, to increasing awareness and sales.[29]

When Harley left the company, the advertisements for Ivory basically remained the same, consistent with those that Harley had created. The advertisements focused on the same characteristics and attributes of the product that Harley thought were important. In short, the advertisements "described why the product was better than any other and how it could be used to benefit the purchaser."[30]

NOTES

1. Richard L. Bushman and Claudia L. Bushman, "The Early History of Cleanliness in America," *Journal of American History* 74, no. 4 (March 1988): 1215.

2. Bushman and Bushman, "The Early History of Cleanliness," 1220–21.

3. Bushman and Bushman, "The Early History of Cleanliness," 1228.

4. Samuel Colgate, "American Soap Factories," *One Hundred Years of American Commerce: 1795–1895*, ed. Chauncey M. Depew (New York: Greenwood Press, 1968; originally, D. O. Haynes, 1895), 2:422.

5. Colgate, "American Soap Factories."

6. Colgate, "American Soap Factories," 423.

7. Colgate, "American Soap Factories," 423.

8. Horace Greeley et al., *The Great Industries of the United States: Being an Historical Summary of the Origin, Growth and Perfection of the Chief Industrial Arts of This Country* (Hartford, CT: J. B. Burr and Hyde, 1872), 925.

9. *Cincinnati Daily Gazette*, June 29, 1838.

10. Greeley et al., *The Great Industries of the United States*, 925.

11. Charles Cist, *Sketches and Statistics of Cincinnati in 1859* (Cincinnati, OH: n.p., 1859), 266.

12. Ida M. Tarbell, *The Nationalizing of Business 1878–1898* (New York: Macmillan, 1936), 174–75.

13. Alecia Swasy, *Soap Opera: The Inside Story of Procter & Gamble* (New York: Times Books, 1993), 239.

14. Oscar Schisgall, *Eyes on Tomorrow: The Evolution of Procter & Gamble* (Chicago: Ferguson, 1981), 133–34.

15. Editors of *Advertising Age*, *Procter & Gamble: The House That Ivory Built* (Lincolnwood, IL: NTC Business Books, 1988), 10.

16. Nancy F. Millman, "The Saga of P & G's Ivory Soap: Keeping a Brand Afloat 100 Years," *Advertising Age*, April 30, 1980 (originally, July 2, 1979), 50; Alfred Lief, *"It Floats": The Story of Procter & Gamble* (New York: Rinehart, 1958), 7–8.

17. Davis Dyer, Frederick Dalzell, and Rowena Olegario, *Rising Tide: Lessons from 165 Years of Brand Building at Procter & Gamble* (Boston: Harvard Business School Press, 2004), 24.

18. *The Independent*, December 21, 1882.

19. Lief, *"It Floats,"* 12.

20. Dyer, Dalzell, and Olegario, *Rising Tide*, 38.

21. *Harper's Weekly* (January 5, 1895).

22. *The Ladies' Home Journal* (May 1896).

23. *The Ladies' Home Journal* (December 1897).

24. *The Ladies' Home Journal* (July 1910).

25. *Saturday Evening Post* (May 15, 1911).

26. *The Ladies' Home Journal* (May 1915).

27. *The Ladies' Home Journal* (May 1925).

28. *The Ladies' Home Journal* (January 1930).

29. Charles Goodrum and Helen Dalrymple, *Advertising in America: The First 200 Years* (New York: Harry N. Abrams, 1990), 51, 54.

30. Juliann Sivulka, *Stronger Than Dirt: A Cultural History of Advertising Personal Hygiene in America, 1875 to 1940* (Amherst, NY: Humanity Books, 2001), 91.

Chapter Eight

Elliott White Springs and the Mid-Twentieth-Century Advertising Campaign for the Springs Cotton Mills

The advertising campaign for the Springs Cotton Mills was one of the most successful advertising campaigns during the late 1940s and early 1950s. It also was one of the most controversial advertising campaigns of this period. The campaign was created for the Springs Cotton Mills and its Springmaid brand of fabrics and sheets. Sparked by the company's owner, Elliott White Springs, the advertisements in the campaign gained notoriety because of the language and illustrations, both of which contained or implied sexual connotations. The campaign increased brand awareness and, subsequently, sales.

SEX IN ADVERTISING

Sexual suggestion has been used by advertisers for years. According to Robert Atwan, Donald McQuade, and John W. Wright, "Sex as a selling tool lies at the core of America's economy of abundance, and advertising has been instrumental in putting it there."[1] However, does sex, whether implied or otherwise, actually help sell a product?

According to John M. Trytten, "Sex doesn't sell the product (except for certain specific products)."[2] Furthermore, he claimed that sex did not sell products as well as good stories about those products.[3]

In *Fashion and Eroticism: Ideals of Feminine Beauty from the Victorian Era to the Jazz Age*, Valerie Steele discussed Freud's concept of the libido and looking, as well as Flugel's concept of women's fashion and eroticism. She wrote,

> Women's fashion is said to attract by means of the selective exposure, concealment, and emphasis on the various erotic "zones" of the female body. These can be the secondary sexual characteristics (such as the breasts, hips, and derriere), or parts of the body that acquire sexual connotations (such as the legs, feet, back, waist, shoulders, and so on). According to this theory, male sexual interest in these portions of the anatomy fluctuates, "and it is the business of fashion to pursue [the shifting erogenous zone], without actually catching it up." The fashionable exposure or emphasis must be extreme enough to be exciting, but not so overt as to be widely considered obscene. [4]

Steele claimed that if the body were exposed to view, it would leave nothing to the imagination and consequently would be perceived as ordinary and eventually hardly noticed. Thus, she claimed that fashion maintained "erotic interest in the body by ensuring that interesting variations cause the viewer to *see* the body with renewed interest and awareness." [5]

She also discussed the attractiveness of underclothes:

> Sensations of softness and warmth and of silky materials gently rubbing against the skin, an intimate connection with the body, a combination of secrecy and visual effect, and a justifiable sense of luxury—a "little fortune"—were all components of lingerie that contributed to reinforcing a sense of femininity. [6]

Elliott White Springs intuitively knew that nudes were not as attractive to the reader as women who were dressed, and he rationalized that language, if suggestive, would be noticed by women as well as men. Concurrently, he apparently thought that teasing the reader with a provocative illustration and suggestive language rather than with a photograph would have a positive effect.

WHO WAS ELLIOTT WHITE SPRINGS?

Elliott White Springs was born to Grace and Leroy Springs in Lancaster, South Carolina, in 1896. His father owned a cotton mill, which was successful. Then he opened other mills. When his father-in-law, Samuel Elliott White, retired, he operated his mill as well. According to Burke Davis, Leroy was "imperious, opinionated, hard-drinking, and quarrelsome." [7] In fact, whenever he and Elliott were together they bickered.

In 1905 Elliott suffered from typhoid fever. Two years later, his mother died, which affected him throughout his life. In 1908 Elliott was sent to an academy in Asheville, North Carolina, where he became an athlete and wrote for the school magazine. His father insisted that he earn excellent grades. Perhaps because of his father's pressure or because he missed his mother, he developed stomach problems. Then he was sent to Culver Military Academy in Indiana, where he continued to write and experience stomach problems.

Leroy married Lena Wade in 1913. Although Elliott now had a stepmother, he still missed his mother. He attended Princeton University, where he grew interested in frequenting bars and clubs in Princeton, New Jersey, and New York City. Before he graduated in 1917, the United States was preparing for war. Against his father's wishes, Elliott volunteered for the Aviation Section of the U.S. Army Signal Corps so that he could train as a pursuit pilot. Elliott and other pilots sailed to England, where they received more training and partied whenever they could. In 1918 the squadron was sent to France. Elliott, like other pilots, experienced dogfight after dogfight as well as several crashes. Before World War I ended, he had downed eleven German planes. When he returned stateside, he settled in New York City and partied, which caused his father to admonish him. Then he found employment as a test pilot for a manufacturer of small planes. However, when his plane crashed in a U.S. cross-country race, he gave up flying and went to work for his father. Arguments with his father sent him packing more than once.

Elliott did not enjoy working at the mills. In 1921 he and a friend from the war sailed to Europe. He met Frances Hubbard Ley of Massachusetts, who was sailing to Europe, and he spent as much time as he could with her. Elliott grew to love her. When he returned home, he wrote to her. Eventually, they became engaged. They married in 1922.

Elliott and Frances moved into his maternal grandfather's house in Fort Mill, which Elliott had renovated. His maternal grandfather had died several years earlier. In 1924 Frances gave birth to a son, and Elliott insisted that they name the child Leroy, after the child's grandfather.

In 1925 Elliott came across Mac Grider's brief diary, which Grider had given to him. Grider, another pilot whom Elliott had known during the war, had been killed in a dogfight. Elliott started writing short stories based on his experiences in the war. These stories were published in several magazines. Then he wrote a novel in the form of a diary about the war. Titled *War Birds: Diary of an Unknown Aviator*, Elliott used "John MacGavock Grider" as the author; he used his own name as the editor. The novel was serialized in *Liberty* in 1926. Immediately, it received considerable attention, and George Doran offered Elliott a contract to publish the series as a novel, which Elliott accepted. Although the film rights were sold, the novel was never made into a movie. Grider's family claimed that Elliott had used Grider's diary without permission; reluctantly, he agreed to pay for the rights to the diary, even though the novel had been based on his experiences and not Grider's experiences. Leroy disliked the novel, especially the passages that were about him, and criticized Elliott.

Elliott continued to write short stories for magazines and novels for publishers. In 1927 his father offered him a vice president's position at one of the mills; Elliott accepted. A year later his father and stepmother moved to New York City, where Leroy played the stock market. Although Elliott was furious with his father for gambling in the stock market, Leroy and Lena remained in New York until Lena had surgery in 1930 and subsequently suffered emotionally. Leroy died in 1931.

Elliott became president and chief executive officer of the company upon his father's death. At the time, the company, which had produced unbranded cotton cloth since its founding in 1888, was worth more than $7 million, with annual sales slightly more than $8 million.[8] Like many businesses, the Springs Cotton Mills suffered during the 1930s as a result of the Great Depression.

Nonetheless, Elliott was determined to have fun while managing his business. According to him, presidents of cotton mills could be divided into three classes:

> First, there is the Honorable Gentleman. He attends all conventions, sits on the platform at all banquets, and will always agree to shut down for the good of the industry. . . .
>
> Next, there is the Bastard, Second Class. He runs his plant at capacity until his warehouse is full of cloth and his office full of bankers. Then he tries to get rid of them by selling all his goods in one day. . . .
>
> Lastly, there is the Bastard, First Class. He runs his mills twenty-four hours a day, six days in the week, fifty-two weeks in the year. When he goes to New York he lunches alone at the Automat.[9]

Elliott considered himself to be in the third category. As president, he consolidated the five scattered cotton mills in Fort Mill, Lancaster, Kershaw, and Chester, South Carolina, into the Springs Cotton Mills. Then he applied his creative skills to the Lancaster and Chester Railway, a slightly less than thirty-mile line that his father had purchased primarily to ship goods to and from the mills. Elliott purchased the private car "Loretto," which had belonged to Charles Schwab before his death, and made the car Lancaster and Chester's regional office. Next, he created a map that contained a network of railroad lines that crisscrossed fifteen states and labeled it the "Lancaster & Chester Railway System." He added, in much smaller type, "and connecting lines."[10] Elliott had a vice president for every mile of track. The vice presidents were personal friends who were prosperous in other endeavors. This humorous marketing concept helped the small railway earn a profit every year thereafter.

Unlike some other presidents of cotton mills, Elliott never closed one mill during the Great Depression. When World War II erupted, the Springs Cotton Mills filled orders for the War Production Board and earned the coveted Army and Navy "E" Award for excellent performance on war contracts.[11] According to Elliott, the Japanese could detect ordinary camouflage cloth because of its lack of endemic odors. Thus, his company perfected a process in which camouflage cloth was impregnated with the scent of the jungle. The company produced other types of cloth with special characteristics for the War Production Board.

Before the war ended, Elliott had prepared his company to become a major marketer of consumer goods by differentiating his finished cotton products through branding and advertising under the Springmaid label. In addition to building a cotton finishing plant, a foundry, and another facility to test various fabrics, processes, and equipment, he opened Springs Mills, Inc., in New York in 1945, primarily to sell Springmaid products. Prior to this year the company's products had been sold through other companies in New York.[12]

Elliott started advertising Springmaid products the same year. He became disillusioned with the advertising campaign within a year. For instance, in 1946 he wrote to the Gatch Advertising Agency, which had created the campaign: "Your advertising campaign needs pepping up. We have had too many pictures of horses with some very tiresome text underneath to prove, in six paragraphs, that the horses are thoroughbreds, and so are our sheets."[13]

In the same letter, Elliott criticized the agency's campaign and other advertising campaigns, claiming, "Many advertisements are an insult to second grade IQ and are just as dull as yours."[14] Then he explained several advertisements that should be considered by the agency. The first depicted a girl on a street corner with the wind blowing her skirt. The copy explained that the company had developed a special cotton fabric that was windproof. The second depicted a girl striking a match on the seat of her pants. The copy explained that the company had developed a special cotton fabric for the abrasive trade. The third depicted a girl being pinched at a party. The copy explained that the company had developed a crease-proof cotton fabric.

Elliott requested that the agency have an artist create a series of subtle, sexy advertisements that incorporated illustrations, not photographs. Although the agency attempted to please Elliott, he rejected the artist's sketches, as the following excerpt from a letter illustrates:

> What I wanted was a subtle picture of a girl with her skirt agitated by the wind.

> You send me down a picture of a girl standing over an air jet with her skirts blown over her head like Coney Island! It's about as subtle as the Can Can. [15]

The agency's artist returned to the drawing board; however, upon receiving the sketches, Elliott reiterated what he had emphasized in his previous letter. The Gatch Advertising Agency failed in its efforts, and Elliott searched for other advertising agencies, without success. Eventually, he procured illustrations from several artists and wrote the accompanying copy. The new advertising campaign—which was handled by Hill Wolfe, the head of the company's advertising department in New York, and the advertising agency Erwin, Wasey and Company—began in May 1948 in several magazines, including *Charm, Cue, Esquire, Fortune, Holiday*, the *New York Times Magazine*, and the *Saturday Evening Post*. The first part of the campaign promoted the company's specialty fabrics.

THE CAMPAIGN AND ITS REPERCUSSIONS

A writer for *Tide*, a trade publication, discussed the campaign's purpose within two months: "The general idea of this activity is to get positive national identification for the traditional Springmaid label. There are, however, a number of secondary ideas. The principal one, as the company puts it, is to 'liven up' textile advertising." [16]

The writer of the article mentioned that there were at least three versions of a particular advertisement because of the copy: "The copy is so unusual that the agency has made it permanent operating procedure to check every word with the magazine involved before the insertion contract is drawn up. Where it feels that a publisher's squeamishness is justified, or when it particularly wants to get the copy in, the agency makes required alterations." [17]

Writers for other mass-circulated magazines, including *Time*, discussed the campaign and its creator. This publicity helped stimulate interest among specific members of the press and, more important, among readers.

One of the first advertisements in the campaign depicted a young, attractive woman ice-skating with one leg up in the air; her panties were exposed to the reader and to two elderly gentlemen seated on a bench. The headline "Perfume and Parabolics" introduced four paragraphs of copy. The first paragraph explained that the Springs Cotton Mills developed a fabric for camouflage that was used during World War II. Unfortunately, the Japanese detected it. The second paragraph explained that the fabric was then dyed and impregnated with various odors, which resolved the problem of detection. The third and fourth paragraphs read,

> This process has been patented, and the fabric is now available to the false bottom and bust bucket business as SPRINGMAID *PERKER*, made of combed yarns, 37" wide, 152 x 68 approximate count, weight about 3.30, the white with gardenia, the pink with camellia, the blush with jasmine, and the nude dusty.
>
> If you want to achieve that careless look and avoid skater's steam, kill two birds with one stone by getting a camouflaged callipygian camisole with the SPRINGMAID label on the bottom of your trademark.[18]

The words "false bottom" and "bust bucket" certainly would be offensive to many women and to specific editors of trade papers that critique advertisements.

Just as in every advertisement in the campaign, the advertisement contained the name and address of the manufacturer as well as the Springmaid logo.

Another early advertisement in the campaign depicted a young, attractive woman standing barefoot in a puddle of water. Wearing a halter top and a short skirt that has been blown by the wind, she has tossed leaves of various colors about her. The headline "Be Protected" introduced two paragraphs of copy:

> During the war, The Springs Cotton Mills was called upon to develop a crease-proof cotton fabric. It was used with great success as a backing for maps, photographs, and other valuable assets. This fabric has now been further perfected and made available to the torso-twister trade.
>
> After a convention, a clam-bake, or a day in the Pentagon Building, you need not eat off the mantel if you have your foundation covered with SPRING-MAID *POKER* woven of combed yarns 37" wide, 152 x 68 count, in tearose, white, nude, and black, light and medium gauge. If you bruise easily, you can face the future confidently with the SPRINGMAID trademark.[19]

The advertisement appeared in magazines that were read by men and women. Although the copy may not have been offensive, the illustration, because it revealed the young, attractive woman's panties, may have offended some readers, especially women.

Another early advertisement in the campaign depicted a young, attractive woman dressed in a tied blouse and a revealing skirt, skipping rope. The headline "Fortify Your Foundations" introduced one paragraph of copy that had been excerpted from an article. The article supposedly had appeared in *The Bawl Street Journal*. The paragraph read, "One of the most interesting sets of questionnaires came from Congress. So far, he said, he has been unable to fit this group into any previously known category. He sounded a note of warning to young females, however, saying his researches indicated that any such person subject to bruises should wear at least two thicknesses of girdles before venturing on Capitol Hill. A chest protector would also be valuable in a pinch, he added."[20] *The Bawl Street Journal*, of course, did not exist. Again, Elliott was having fun with the copy, as the excerpt illustrates.

Another early advertisement in the campaign also featured the excerpt from the article that had appeared in *The Bawl Street Journal*. The illustration featured a young, attractive woman standing in water. She had a surprised expression on her face, which was caused by one large duck and two small ducks swimming nearby. The young woman had pulled up her dress. Of course, her panties were revealed to the reader. The headline "Beware the Goose!" playfully introduced three paragraphs of copy, which, for the most part, described the company's cotton fabric. The words "hip harness" and "bosom bolster" were used to identify certain prospective businesses.[21]

Another advertisement in the campaign had an illustration that depicted three cheerleaders jumping in front of a crowd of spectators. The headline "Safe in the End Zone" introduced two paragraphs of copy, which concerned "Mediker," a special fabric that was developed during World War II for the medical department. The copy claimed that the fabric was useful for self-applied bandages.[22]

In another advertisement, the illustration depicted a young, attractive woman carrying two bags of groceries; however, she was having difficulty walking because her panties had fallen to her ankles. The headline "Watch the Butter Fly" introduced three paragraphs of copy, which discussed the "Sticker," a special cotton fabric that contained rubber. Actually developed for hospital use, the product was being offered to makers of underwear. The copy also mentioned the cloth's measurements and colors. The advertisement's last two paragraphs read,

> Don't depend on buttons and bows, but switch to *STICKER* and let the SPRINGMAID label protect you from the consequences of embarrassing accidents such as pictured above.
> We stick behind our fabric and feel its tenacity so strongly that we call it an insurance policy to provide full coverage. Our only competition comes from a tattoo artist.[23]

Considering the publicity in various magazines and trade publications, the advertising campaign was a success, at least to Elliott. Elliott started advertising the company's sheets. One of the first advertisements for sheets contained two paragraphs of copy that rhymed. The illustration depicted an early American military officer with a sword on his hip and a young, attractive housekeeper or maid in a bedroom. An older man could be seen through the opened bedroom door; he was standing on stair steps peering in. The headline "Bundling without Bungling" introduced the copy:

When knightly bundling was in flower and great-grandpa was in his bower, he often played heck with a sheet for he slept with spurs upon his feet. And when a nightmare made him twitch, the damsel really had to stitch. But both the sheets and great-grandma survived the calls of great-grandpa. Since boots and spurs are not in vogue and guest rooms are today the mode, your sheets must still stand rips and tears of laundries, kids, and derrieres. But mending sheets is now passé; our whistle bait has a better way, and sheets don't face such knightly slaughter. A colonial dame's great-granddaughter selects our own FORT SUMTER sheets to spur beaux on to spurless feats.

Unlike old times when couples bundled and in the process often bungled, we make our SPRINGMAIDS much the best and proved it in a strenuous test. We took our own FORT SUMTER brand, woven and finished by skillful hand. Each sheet was washed 400 times—a test like this would slick new dimes. Two hundred times they were abraded, yet none were either worn or faded. That's equal to a generation of wear and tear and vellication. In speaking of FORT SUMTER covers, we really wish all fabric lovers, when homeward bound from some dull party, would test SPRINGMAIDS—they're all so hardy that you can get a running start and dive in—they won't come apart. The moral is, to each of you: No matter what you say or do, remember that in cold or heat, you can't go wrong on a SPRINGMAID sheet. [24]

The copy has more than one inference, which was, of course, Elliott's intention. In short, the advertisement was selling more than sheets; it was promoting sexual intercourse.

Another advertisement depicted an early American military officer escaping from an upstairs window. A young, attractive woman whom the officer had been visiting appeared distressed, as her apparent grandfather was about to cut the sheet by which the officer was escaping. The headline "Bungled Bundling" introduced two paragraphs of copy. The first paragraph read,

In olden times throughout this land our maidens made their sheets by hand. They used a spinning wheel until it was replaced by cotton mill. Then, lovers found more than one use for strong sheets that could stand abuse. They used them to avoid grandsire and thereby to escape his ire. Our knight slid often down a sheet with eyes on girl and spurs on feet. But sometimes luck just wasn't there when grandpa's hatchet cut through air. Today we weave FORT SUMTER sheets in such a way that always meets with every family's bedroom need from restful sleep to militant deed. [25]

The remaining paragraph, also in rhyme, explained the strenuous test that was applied to the company's sheets.

Another advertisement had an illustration of a young, attractive woman who had leaped from a window of a burning building. Four firemen, holding a sheet, were about to catch her. Smiles graced the faces of the firemen as they stared at the woman in distress; her dress had been blown to her waist. Her panties and stockings were visible to the firemen and to the reader. The headline "We Love to Catch Them on a Springmaid Sheet" introduced four paragraphs of copy that discussed the quality and durability of the company's sheets.[26]

Another advertisement for Springmaid sheets contained an illustration of a young, attractive Indian squaw and a young Indian chief in a hammock made from a sheet. The chief appeared exhausted, and the attractive squaw appeared happy. The illustration suggested that the chief and the squaw had just had sexual intercourse. The headline "A buck well spent on a Springmaid Sheet" introduced three paragraphs of copy that discussed the quality and durability of the company's sheets.[27]

Elliott used sexual innuendo primarily to capture the reader's attention, then used double entendre or puns to tease and inform the reader about Springmaid products. The feminine figures that dominated the advertisements were often leggy and shown in unusual situations. The figures captured the reader's attention and invariably forced the reader to not only glance at the headline but read the copy. Concurrently, the company's logo was prominently displayed.

The copy in these and other advertisements in the campaign was soon scrutinized by several writers in trade magazines. For instance, in the August 27, 1948, issue of *Tide*, the copy was considered "ribald" and ineffective, as the following excerpt illustrates:

> Its copy in consumer magazines has astonished a rather large number of people in and out of advertising by its disarming use, in describing articles of female underclothing, of expressions like "false bottom and bust bucket," "ham hamper and lung lifter," "hip harness and bosom bolster."[28]

According to the writer, "Agency men who have seen the copy are most upset (90%) by it; advertisers are two-to-one against it."[29]

As if criticism by writers in specific trade publications had not been enough, several magazine publishers refused to run the advertisements altogether because of phrases such as "ham hamper," "lung lifter," and "rumba aroma." Newspaper publishers, however, seemed less concerned about the copy. According to Elliott, the publishers of the *New York Times*, the *New York Herald Tribune*, and several other newspapers accepted the advertisements without any changes in the art or the copy.[30]

In the September 10, 1948, issue of *Tide*, Charlotte Montgomery discussed the controversy surrounding the campaign. She explained the advertisements—that is, the illustrations ("semi-nudes") and the copy ("baffling")—then asked whether the advertisements were directed to consumers. Finally, she added, "I wonder if someone is using a very expensive method to amuse his friends, collect pictures for his whoopee room and cause talk that may flatter egos but can do more harm than good in the long run."[31]

Charlotte Montgomery was not alone in her criticism. Elliott and the company received numerous letters from readers who had read the advertisements, and many complained, as the following excerpt illustrates: "Your illustrations and copy are both vulgar—and I feel, as do many with whom I have spoken—that you are certainly doing yourself more harm than good."[32]

In the December 3, 1948, issue of *Printers' Ink*, the writer of the column "Aesop Glim's Clinic" discussed truth as well as good taste in advertising. According to the writer, advertising needed both, primarily to improve its image in the public's mind. The writer mentioned the Springs Cotton Mills' campaign, stating that it was "a flagrant . . . example of bad taste."[33] The writer claimed that if the advertisements were addressed to women, then the advertisements failed because of the illustrations and copy. The writer claimed that if the advertisements were addressed to the garment industry, then the advertisements failed because they appeared in the wrong publications.[34]

In the December 10, 1948, issue of *Printers' Ink*, the president and publisher of the magazine condemned the controversial campaign in his column "The Publisher Speaks":

> The only thing that worries me is that the advertiser himself and some others will be deceived by the fact that his campaign is talked about. They will dig up the old chestnut about "Better to be talked about badly than not talked about at all." We may see a slight epidemic of double-entendre advertising. And that, I think, would be bad for the cause of advertising as a whole.[35]

Roland Smith, a professor of advertising at the time, criticized the campaign in the article "After Hours: Publicity Isn't Advertising," which appeared in the December 17, 1948, issue of *Printers' Ink*. Smith claimed the campaign merely provoked publicity. He added, "It seems to me that Springs Mills is making enemies for its products as rapidly as it's making a few friends."[36]

As the controversial campaign was discussed by members of the press, it became increasingly popular. Before 1949, for instance, Elliott was receiving approximately fifty letters a day. According to him, 98 percent were favorable toward the campaign.[37] In addition, the advertisements had appeared in the following magazines: *American Magazine, Charm, Collier's, Coronet, Cosmopolitan, Cue, Esquire, Fortune, Harper's Magazine, Holiday, Hotel Management, Life, Look, Mademoiselle, Newsweek, New Yorker, The Pathfinder, Promenade, Pic, South Carolina Magazine, Saturday Evening Post, Southern Agriculturist, Town and Country, Time,* and *Vogue,* which indicated that publishers, even some who had rejected the advertisements initially, had grown more tolerant toward the illustrations and copy or that the agency had been successful in responding to specific requests, as mentioned.

THE RESULTS OF THE CAMPAIGN

The advertisements for this particular campaign appeared in magazines through 1951. In that period—1948–1951—Starch readership surveys revealed greater copy recall and greater brand recognition for the Springs Cotton Mills' advertisements than for any other campaign.[38] Thus, Elliott had accomplished one objective: national brand name awareness. Sales of products with the Springmaid label increased as a result. In 1948, for instance, sales were about $105 million. By the end of 1951, sales had increased to approximately $120 million. Elliott employed photographs of celebrities, including Gypsy Rose Lee, in a similar advertising campaign. Testimonials, the advertisements continued to promote Springmaid sheets. A similar advertising campaign featured "leaders" of high society. In 1959, when Elliott died from pneumonia and cancer and executives of the company decided to discontinue his humorous style of advertising, sales had increased to $170 million. The company had become one of the largest makers of sheets.[39]

The use of attractive figures depicted in unusual situations had been productive. Not only had Springmaid become a household name, but the company's products sold extremely well. The advertising had been effective no matter what the pundits claimed.

NOTES

    1. Robert Atwan, Donald McQuade, and John W. Wright, *Edsels, Luckies, and Frigidaires: Advertising the American Way* (New York: Dell, 1979), 326.

    2. John M. Trytten, "Sex in Advertising: The Easy Way Out!" *Sales Management* (May 28, 1973): 36.

    3. Trytten, "Sex in Advertising," 36.

    4. Valerie Steele, *Fashion and Eroticism: Ideals of Feminine Beauty from the Victorian Era to the Jazz Age* (New York: Oxford University Press, 1985), 34.

    5. Steele, *Fashion and Eroticism*, 42.

    6. Steele, *Fashion and Eroticism*, 208.

    7. Burke Davis, *War Bird: The Life and Times of Elliott White Springs* (Chapel Hill: The University of North Carolina Press, 1987), 7.

    8. *The Story of the Springs Cotton Mills: 1888–1963* (Fort Mill, SC: Springs Mills, 1963), n.p.

    9. "Playboy of the Textile World," *Fortune* (January 1950), 66.

    10. "Textile Tempest," *Time* (July 26, 1948), 72.

    11. *The Story of the Springs Cotton Mills*, n.p.

    12. *The Story of the Springs Cotton Mills*, n.p.

    13. Elliott White Springs, *Clothes Make the Man* (New York: Little and Ives, 1949), 84.

    14. Springs, *Clothes Make the Man*, 85.

    15. Springs, *Clothes Make the Man*, 90.

    16. "Springmaid," *Tide* (July 16, 1948); reprinted in Springs, *Clothes Make the Man*, 120.

    17. "Springmaid," in Springs, *Clothes Make the Man*, 120.

    18. *Coronet* (August 1948).

    19. *Coronet* (November 1948).

20. *Coronet* (December 1948).

21. *Coronet* (February 1949).

22. *Coronet* (August 1949).

23. *Coronet* (December 1949).

24. *Coronet* (June 1949).

25. *Coronet* (April 1950).

26. *Coronet* (February 1950).

27. *Coronet* (June 1950).

28. "Tide Leadership Survey," *Tide* (August 27, 1948), 53.

29. "Tide Leadership Survey," 53.

30. Springs, *Clothes Make the Man*, 228.

31. Charlotte Montgomery, "The Woman's Viewpoint," *Tide* (September 10, 1948), 24.

32. Springs, *Clothes Make the Man*, 137.

33. "Aesop Glim's Clinic," *Printers' Ink* (December 3, 1948), 75.

34. "Aesop Glim's Clinic," 75.

35. C. B. Larrabee, "The Publisher Speaks: Bad Taste Leaves a Bad Taste," *Printers' Ink* (December 10, 1948), 5.

36. Roland B. Smith, "After Hours: Publicity Isn't Advertising," *Printers' Ink* (December 17, 1948), 124.

37. Springs, *Clothes Make the Man*, 152.

38. Charles Goodrum and Helen Dalrymple, *Advertising in America: The First 200 Years* (New York: Harry N. Abrams, 1990), 77.

39. *The Story of the Springs Cotton Mills*, n.p.

Chapter Nine

Stanley B. Resor and the J. Walter Thompson Company: 1908–1961

Stanley Burnet Resor guided the J. Walter Thompson Company for more than five decades. Under his leadership, the company became the largest advertising agency in the world. As president, he advocated his beliefs about advertising. For instance, he strongly believed that advertising should be based on scientific research. He also believed that advertising should be ethical. He hired college-educated men and women, including a few with doctorates, and he opened additional branch offices in the United States and abroad.

JAMES WALTER THOMPSON

The company was named for its second owner, James Walter Thompson, who was born in Pittsfield, Massachusetts, in 1847. His father, a contractor, was hired to build a bridge across the Sandusky River, a project that would last a long time; consequently, he moved his family to Fremont, Ohio. Thompson attended school, then, after his father died, he enlisted in the U.S. Marine Corps. He served two years aboard the *U.S.S. Saratoga*. In 1868, after military service, he traveled to New York, where he found a job as a bookkeeper at Carlton and Smith, an agency that purchased space in popular religious publications, then sold it at a higher price to advertisers. This company had been founded by William J. Carlton and Edmund A. Smith after the Civil War. However, Smith left the company after two or three years.[1]

Taking care of the company's books did not interest Thompson. He desired to be a salesman. He spoke to Carlton, who agreed, and subsequently became an effective salesman for the company. Although Carlton was happy buying space in religious publications, Thompson realized that the agency could increase its revenue if salesmen were allowed to approach other magazines, especially those directed at women. Thompson believed that magazines were in homes longer than newspapers. He also believed that women purchased most of the goods, especially goods for the home. He also believed that women controlled the money in most households. Consequently, he believed that advertisers should be interested in purchasing space in these publications. He approached Carlton; reluctantly, Carlton allowed Thompson to approach other publishers. Many publishers of general and women's magazines refused to sell as much space as he desired. Thompson was determined, however. He persuaded a few, including the publishers of *Godey's Lady's Book* and *Peterson's Magazine*, to sell several pages worth of space to him.

Thompson's assumptions about women were correct. Eventually, more publishers realized that revenue from selling space for advertising could help pay for their publications. As a result, Thompson became successful.

By 1878, buying and selling space for advertising no longer appealed to Carlton, an avid reader of books; indeed, he had become interested in publishing. Consequently, he sold the agency to Thompson for $1,300 ($500 for the agency and $800 for the equipment and furniture).[2]

Thompson continued on the path that had brought him success. He developed the "J. Walter Thompson's Illustrated Catalogue of Magazines Compiled for the Use of Advertisers," which he expanded over the years. The "catalogue" became well known among advertisers, and Thompson's company grew as a result. In fact, within a few years, his company was representing numerous publications in North America and several in South America.

In 1888 the company published *Advertising in America*. The publication explained the advertising market in the United States and was directed to manufacturers abroad, particularly those in Europe. In essence, Thompson desired to expand his business by informing advertisers overseas about the publications his firm represented.

Although he added newspapers before 1890 primarily to interest advertisers who refused to advertise in magazines, he was partial to magazines. According to Pamela Walker Laird, "As late as 1889 . . . Thompson handled 80 percent of national magazine advertising as special agent for almost all American magazines."[3] Because of his relationship with publishers, he encouraged them to use higher-quality paper; he also encouraged them to hire artists who had exceptional ability.

Thompson opened a branch office in Chicago in 1891. He opened another in London before 1900. His agency was the first in the United States to have an office abroad. In addition to hiring more people to sell space in publications, Thompson hired people to look after the needs of the agency's clients and to create the clients' advertising. The agency actually helped several clients design packages for products; it also helped several clients develop trademarks. As more clients entered his offices, the agency increased in size.[4]

STANLEY B. RESOR

Stanley Burnet Resor was born to Mary Wilson Brown Resor and Isaac Burnet Resor in Cincinnati, Ohio, in 1879. His father's family had started a small company that manufactured wood- and coal-burning stoves in the early nineteenth century. Resor attended the city's public schools, then, after graduation, matriculated to Yale University in New Haven, Connecticut. He helped pay for his college education by tutoring students. During the summers, he went door-to-door selling religious literature, including a history book about the Bible.

At the end of his senior year, Resor received the James Gordon Bennett Prize in Economics. When he earned his bachelor's degree in 1901, he intended to continue his education because of his desire to teach economics. However, his family's company was manufacturing stoves that were competing against modern-designed stoves that used gas; as a result, the family's income decreased.

Resor was forced to find a job. First, he worked in a bank, which was not exciting. Second, he worked as a salesman for the Lodge and Shipley Tool Company, which manufactured tools. Resor felt inadequate. As far as he was concerned, selling machine tools required technical training or at least some understanding of machines, which he lacked. Third, he worked in a printing shop, which was not exciting. Finally, in 1904 his older brother, Walter, who was working for Procter and Collier, an advertising agency that handled the advertising for Procter and Gamble, helped him land a job with the agency. Although he did not have any experience as a copywriter, Resor learned to write advertisements for soap products at Procter and Collier. Ambitious and highly motivated, he acquired a reputation for being a hard worker. Furthermore, he proved that he could plan imaginative advertising campaigns.

Resor also met Helen Lansdowne, who worked at the agency.[5]

HELEN LANSDOWNE

Helen Lansdowne was born in Grayson, Kentucky, in 1886. Her parents eventually had nine children. Her mother was the daughter of a well-educated Presbyterian minister. However, contrary to her father's beliefs about marriage, she left her husband and moved the children to Covington, Kentucky, where two brothers lived. One of the brothers hired her as a clerk; the other helped the family by providing money whenever it was needed.

Helen graduated from high school in 1903; she was valedictorian of her class. Although an excellent student, she did not have the money to attend college. Instead, she found employment at the World Manufacturing Company, which produced products for the home that were sold by mail. Within a year, she accepted a position as an auditor of bills at Procter and Collier. She found auditing bills to be monotonous and uninspiring. When a position became available at the *Commercial Tribune*, a newspaper in Cincinnati, she applied and was hired. She wrote copy for retail advertisements.

Helen enjoyed writing advertising copy, but she desired to broaden her experience. In 1906 she left the newspaper and accepted a position at the Street Railways Advertising Company. She enjoyed her job and within several months was offered a position in the company's offices in New York. Stanley Resor, whom she had met while working at Procter and Collier, asked her to return to the agency. She accepted. She worked with Resor on several advertising campaigns. For instance, she wrote advertisements for BRENLIN window shades. The brand name was developed by Resor. She wrote advertisements for Higgin metal screens for windows. Resor targeted these advertisements to members of the middle class. The advertisements encouraged readers to imitate the habits of wealthier people. She wrote advertisements for Red Cross shoes.[6]

STANLEY RESOR

Charles E. Raymond was a vice president and was in charge of the Chicago office of the J. Walter Thompson Company. He had noticed some work by Resor and had been impressed. He contacted Resor and asked if he and his brother would be interested in managing the company's office in Chicago. Resor and his brother refused; they did not necessarily want to leave Cincinnati. Raymond informed him that J. Walter Thompson would open an office in Cincinnati, if he and his brother would manage it.

Stanley and Walter agreed and opened the office in 1908. Resor persuaded Helen Lansdowne to join them as the copywriter. Resor realized that an office could offer clients more services than just space in publications. He believed that an office could provide copy and art. He also believed that a business that specialized in advertising should analyze a client's business problems, including the distribution and pricing of its products. Resor believed that advertising could become part of each client's overall sales strategy. He claimed, "Advertising must be shaped to fit directly into people's daily lives and must present a product in terms of added health or improved personal appearance, or economy, or some other basic want."[7]

Resor was influenced by Thomas Henry Buckle, who had written the *History of Civilization in England*. In short, Buckle believed that human nature was predictable when historical laws were applied. According to Buckle, if one had enough factual information about people, then one would know how they would behave. He was also influenced by William Graham Sumner, who claimed that humans evolved slowly and were driven by primitive urges, such as fear, hunger, sex, and vanity.[8]

Although the brothers performed well as managers, it was Helen's creativity that impressed the senior executives, including J. Walter Thompson, at the main offices in New York. For instance, in 1910, her advertising for Woodbury's Facial Soap, which informed women about skin problems, appealed to consumers so much that it helped substantially increase sales of the product within a few years.[9] In fact, she was promoted and invited to work in New York in 1911.

One of her first assignments in New York was Procter and Gamble's Crisco, a new shortening. Executives at Procter and Gamble apparently believed that Procter and Collier was too small to develop the introductory advertising campaign for the product. Helen traveled to Cincinnati several times to meet with Procter and Gamble's board of directors. Although she was surrounded by men in business suits, she discussed the advertising with confidence. In the advertisements for Crisco, Helen presented scientific claims in an editorial fashion. As a result, the scientific claims appeared as natural elements in an advice or beauty column.[10]

Stanley and Walter found themselves without a copywriter. Helen informed Stanley about James Webb Young, who, several years before, had been a classmate of hers. Young had dropped out of school and had worked at numerous jobs, from office boy to book salesman. Stanley interviewed him and was impressed enough to hire him as a copywriter. Under the Resors, the office in Cincinnati was productive. Young, highly talented, became a very good copywriter.[11]

In 1912, after four years of soliciting new accounts to writing copy, Stanley was invited to the main offices in New York. Walter was promoted and made manager of the office in Boston. James Webb Young was promoted to manager of the office in Cincinnati. He hired Henry Stanton as an account representative in charge of new accounts. Stanton had worked as a sales manager for Procter and Gamble. Resor continued to impress the senior executives at the company; he was promoted to vice president and became the company's general manager. Resor applied what he believed to advertising. According to James Playsted Wood, "He conducted empirical research to find out what needed to be done to and for a product to promote sales."[12] He tested several advertising claims to determine which claims had the most impact. He also developed a few brand names for clients, including "Yuban," for coffee for the Arbuckle Brothers Company, and "Kelvinator," for refrigerators for the Electro-Automatic Refrigerating Company. Helen wrote the copy for the advertisements.

Resor commissioned a market study that contained statistical information on retail establishments and towns throughout the country. This study was published as *Population and Its Distribution* in 1912. It was updated periodically and used for clients' advertising campaigns.

Helen wrote advertising copy for other products, including Lux Flakes and Cutex nail polish. The advertisements for the former product were educational in the sense that consumers learned about the product's benefits. The advertisements for the latter product were educational as well; women not only learned about the product's benefits but were instructed on how to care for their nails. The advertisements included coupons for samples, which women appreciated.

J. Walter Thompson was astonished by his company's growth. In 1916 he doubted if it could grow any larger. Indeed, the company had 177 employees in five offices (New York, Boston, Chicago, Cincinnati, and Detroit; the office in London was closed because of World War I). These employees were servicing three hundred clients. The company's annual billings were almost $3 million.[13] Now, almost seventy years old, the "commodore," as he was called because of his interest in yachts, was no longer interested in advertising. In this respect, he was similar to William J. Smith, his former boss. He offered the company to Resor, Charles E. Raymond, and Harry E. Ward for $500,000. Ward and Resor had met at Yale and become friends. Although Resor and Raymond put up some of the money, Ward, who worked at Irving Trust, was able to borrow the most.[14]

Within months, Raymond retired and sold his interest in the company to Young and Stanton.[15] Resor became president. Immediately, Resor dismantled the company by changing its focus. As a result, more than two hundred accounts were let go. Many employees lost their jobs. One or two branch offices were closed.

STANLEY AND HELEN RESOR

In 1917 Resor asked Helen Lansdowne to marry him, and she accepted. Many women who married before 1920 did not work outside the home. Helen, however, did. Although she eventually gave birth to three children, she remained with the company as a vice president. She was primarily in charge of the creative function, including the production of the advertisements, which she enjoyed. As the wife of the president and principal owner of the company, she was directly involved in whatever decisions were made regarding the agency.

Stanley was responsible for the administration of the company. He believed in building consensus when it came to managing the agency. He did not like or encourage the development of organization charts. He preferred creating a working environment in which every employee felt at ease enough to go to any other employee—no matter what his or her title—for advice or help. Resor believed that senior executives were on hand to "backstop" junior executives in the service to their clients. Consequently, he insisted that every office door remain open during working hours. In addition, he did not believe in the company having formal committee meetings. In fact, such occurred only when solutions to specific problems could not be found otherwise.[16]

James Webb Young and Henry Stanton were promoted and invited to the main offices. Gilbert Kinney, who had worked previously at the company, was invited to return. The Resors, with input from these three and others, frequently discussed the direction of the company.

The company concentrated on national clients that manufactured products for women. There were exceptions, of course, especially if the clients sold products abroad. The company also concentrated on magazines that appealed to women. Helen realized that women purchased most of the products sold in department stores, drug stores, and grocery stores; consequently, she knew that the agency's advertising had to be based on a thorough understanding of women's motivations. In essence, the agency had to learn about this group's opinions toward specific products. Furthermore, the agency had to learn about this group's buying habits or purchasing patterns.

The company had established a Statistical and Investigation Department (research department) in 1915 as a result of Stanley's belief that advertising had to become more scientific to solve the marketing problems of its clients. Helen realized that her husband had been motivated by his formal education and his strong beliefs about advertising's image and about advertising as a profession.

Later, in 1917, Resor cofounded the American Association of Advertising Agencies, which encouraged advertising agencies in the United States to not only become members of the organization but adhere to its policies regarding advertising. Resor acknowledged that advertising's image was low as a result of the promotion of questionable products such as patent medicine.[17] He also acknowledged that advertising as a business, unlike law and medicine, was not considered a valuable profession. According to Peggy Kreshel, "Resor . . . realized that the ability of advertising to ultimately attain professional stature was very much dependent upon the opinion that big business had of the soundness of advertising methods, and of the advertising industry's ability to provide solutions to practical problems encountered in business practice."[18]

Consequently, to improve advertising's image and worth, he strongly advocated that companies develop advertising based on sound research and that they follow ethical principles.

In 1918 Young and Stanton moved to the office in Chicago, where they managed the company's entire western operation. Kinney became treasurer of the company and worked closely with Resor in the main offices.[19]

Resor established the "University of Advertising" within the company. All new hires were subjected to every aspect of the agency by actually working several months in each department. The typical new hire spent more than two years in the program. Resor insisted that every employee, not just new hires, become familiar with the ideas presented in the *History of Civilization in England*, by Henry Thomas Buckle.[20]

The Thompson T-Square was developed and was based on the following five questions:

> What are we selling?
> To whom are we selling?
> Where are we selling?
> When are we selling?
> How are we selling?[21]

The questions had to be answered before any advertising was created. Generally, one or more employees in the research department conducted interviews to help determine the answers. Other instruments were developed as well.

Helen was instrumental in the founding of the agency's Women's Editorial Department. She was involved in the hiring and mentoring of the women who worked in the department. She established high standards. She insisted that everyone in the department understand that effective advertising was based on knowing how products were manufactured. She understood the importance of research. She and her female companions created advertisements that imitated or mirrored the pages found in her preferred magazines, including *The Ladies' Home Journal* and *Saturday Evening Post*. Her team, many members of which had college degrees, developed advertisements that "combined the visual and sensual with the informative. Beautiful, often romantic, pictures accompanied a compact but informative text, touting the product and frequently offering a bargain or free sample."[22] As Juliann Sivulka wrote, "Instead of a rational argument, they often relied on an intimate, personal style to strongly dramatize the disadvantages of not using the advertised product and the social incentives for using it."[23] The agency used the "reason-why" approach for years for numerous advertising campaigns. In addition to creating advertising campaigns for various products, Helen and her team created campaigns for charitable organizations, such as the American Red Cross and the Young Men's Christian Association (YMCA).

The company prospered as the number of major accounts increased. As a result, Resor opened additional branch offices and hired additional employees. When World War I ended, he reopened an office in London. Libby, McNeill and Libby was the office's first big account. Yet, unlike many advertising agencies, Resor refused to have employees prepare advertising campaigns on speculation for potential clients. He knew that these campaigns would not necessarily represent the client or the client's product or service, primarily because the agency would not have all the facts about the company, the product or service, and the consumer. He also knew that these campaigns demanded employees' time, which would be wasted if the potential clients did not hire the company after the campaigns were presented. Resor felt that such time could be better spent on the agency's current accounts. In addition, he refused clients that were responsible for products that contained high alcohol, including liquor distilleries.[24]

JOHN B. WATSON

In 1920 Resor interviewed John B. Watson, the behaviorist psychologist who had been dismissed from his position at Johns Hopkins University because of an affair. Although impressed with Watson's academic credentials, he tested Watson's ability to work in advertising by having him study the rubber boot market along the Mississippi River. Watson traveled to the South and interviewed people. When he returned to New York, his affair and divorce had been discussed in the newspapers.

Although Resor had learned about Watson's past, he was impressed by his results. He checked Watson's references, then offered him a full-time position; Watson accepted. Resor realized that Watson, because of his formal education and experience, could help improve the image that many business-men had of advertising. He also realized that Watson could help the agency conduct scientific research for its clients.

Resor had Watson sell Yuban coffee to grocery stores in Pennsylvania and Ohio for several months. Watson, the former academician, found himself trudging from merchant to merchant like other salesmen. Upon his return, he had to spend time in each department of the agency, just like other new hires. To learn about consumers, he spent weeks behind a counter at Macy's.

When he returned to the agency, he helped employees with their advertising campaigns. Finally, in late 1921, he was given several accounts of his own. His primary task was to conduct research to determine what the advertising message should be and to whom the message should be directed.

The same year, he and several other psychologists founded the Psychological Corporation, which publicized the skills of applied psychologists so that leaders of businesses and industries might learn about them. Watson and other psychologists believed that businesses and industries could hire these applied psychologists for specific tasks. Soon the corporation had different divisions, including the Division of Market and Advertising Research, which measured consumer trends. [25]

Watson interviewed people about life insurance and learned that the majority of people did not care for individuals who sold life insurance. As a result, Watson believed that a national advertising campaign could change the image that people had of life insurance.

He tested smokers to determine if they could identify their preferred brands of cigarettes, which most could not. He realized that some products, like cigarettes, were preferred by consumers for other reasons, including the atmosphere in which the product had been depicted or the idea the consumer had of the product. [26]

He assisted the creative staff as they developed advertisements for Johnson & Johnson Baby Powder. The advertisements informed mothers that the brand was hygienic, that it could be used before the child was one year old, and that it could be used often. The testimonial advertisements targeted the middle- and upper-class consumers and appeared in women's magazines.

Watson informed the makers of a specific brand of toothpaste that the product had a terrible taste. The client improved the product, and Watson assisted the creative team as it developed the advertising campaign that introduced the new improved brand. [27]

Watson became a spokesperson for Resor and J. Walter Thompson. He was an effective speaker, often making a positive impression. He traveled all over the United States and Canada on behalf of the company.

Watson was promoted to vice president in 1924. Although he had other obligations because of his title, he provided insight whenever Helen or other copywriters needed it. For instance, he provided some insight when Helen and her team developed the advertising for Maxwell House coffee. Each advertisement focused on a scene from history, such as a societal ball in a Southern mansion. The design of these advertisements was elegant and appealing. Each created a fantasy. He provided assistance when campaigns were developed for other accounts. Watson believed that three motivations were responsible for most actions: fear, love, and rage.[28] As mentioned, Resor had been influenced by Sumner, who had a similar belief.

STANLEY AND HELEN RESOR

In 1922 Resor hired Paul Cherington, who had taught at the Harvard Business School. Cherington knew about marketing and became the director of the company's research department. He conducted numerous consumer surveys that provided the agency with valuable information. Cherington, according to Juliann Sivulka, "taught the agency to construct advertising text and slogans in a way that helped sales and expanded the market."[29]

In 1923 Helen persuaded Edward Steichen, a well-known artistic photographer, to shoot photographs for advertisements. Most advertisements at this time contained illustrations. If an advertisement contained a photograph, the photograph generally lacked emotional appeal. Helen made certain that Steichen could improve the artwork by providing products that offered possibilities. The first product was Jergen's Lotion. Steichen shot photographs of Helen's hands as she peeled potatoes. The advertisement was directed at women who did their own housework. Steichen worked on other advertisements, including those for Eastman Kodak and Woodbury's Facial Soap. Helen and her team persuaded other famous photographers, including Margaret Bourke-White, to work for J. Walter Thompson.[30]

From 1923 to 1924, Resor served as president of the American Association of Advertising Agencies. He wrote "What the American Association of Advertising Agencies Does to Make Advertising Scientifically More Effective," which was published in 1924. Although he was solicited by numerous professional associations and trade organizations to speak about advertising, generally he refused these invitations because he did not feel at ease behind lecterns or podiums. Besides, he realized that the company employed other individuals, such as Watson, who were more effective speakers. However, he spoke more than once when he served as president of the American Association of Advertising Agencies.[31]

Helen's creative team resurrected a very old technique that had been used in advertising—the often-used but reliable endorsement or testimonial. For instance, the advertisements for Pond's Cold Cream and Pond's Vanishing Cream were based on scientific evidence. Indeed, the agency's research department investigated female consumers by means of hundreds and hundreds of questionnaires and numerous interviews throughout the country. As a result of the findings, Helen and her team decided to discuss the reason for using Pond's in the copy. They also decided to employ members of high society instead of celebrities or so-called experts. The advertisements created a new image for Pond's facial creams and increased sales substantially. Testimonial advertising campaigns were used to sell Fleischmann's Yeast, Lux Flakes, and other products as well. Helen and her team were encouraged to rely on scientific research; much of the advertising they developed was based on a female perspective and psychological appeals. Helen and her team were responsible for most of the agency's drug, food, soap, and toiletry accounts.

In an effort to educate the company's employees, Helen commissioned historian Lewis Mumford to develop a list of three thousand books. The collection started in 1927. However, not every title was purchased. After a few years, Helen noticed that a number of titles had disappeared from the agency, and she consequently stopped the collection.[32]

In 1927 the company moved to the Graybar Building, which was next to Grand Central Station. Helen had commissioned designers and interior decorators to design and decorate the open areas, the walls, and the offices. The offices reflected the individuals who occupied them. At the time, the agency's annual billings were $23 million. The agency, which had four branch offices as well as the main offices, employed more than 430.[33]

As a result of capturing the General Motors Export Company account, the agency expanded internationally. Indeed, between 1927 and 1933 more than twenty offices were opened in Africa, Australia, Europe, India, South America, and Southeast Asia.[34] The Women's Editorial Department contributed to the company's internationalization efforts. In fact, Helen and her creative team applied concepts that had driven successful advertisements directed at women in the United States to advertisements that were developed for overseas markets. For instance, the advertising for Pond's in foreign markets employed the same concept—testimonial and social prestige—that had worked in the United States.

Although each overseas office was managed by someone from the United States, Resor insisted that each office manager hire staff members native to the country where the office was located. Resor was the first advertising agency president in the United States to think about advertising on an international basis. As the Great Depression gripped the country, however, the company's annual billings declined several million dollars; consequently, the agency closed several offices abroad.

In the late 1920s the creative staff developed the "tabloid style" of advertising primarily as a result of *True Story*, a magazine that had become extremely popular among female readers. *True Story* was filled with dramatic stories about characters that seemed real. Indeed, the stories were "confessions" by characters. As a result, the creative staff developed advertising that was "confessional" in the sense that the advertisements seemed to copy the stories found within the magazine.[35] For other advertising, the creative staff employed testimonials that implied fantasies. For instance, for Woodbury's, the advertising implied that the product could do more than just provide women with beautiful skin.

In 1929 the Resors purchased four hundred acres along the Snake River in Wyoming, where they built a ranch, which they visited almost every summer thereafter. They also expanded the ranch by purchasing additional acres over the years. In addition to a residence, the ranch had dairy barns, chicken and turkey coops, cattle, and horses. It also had the best equipment available.[36]

Helen influenced several women who worked in the agency's Women's Editorial Department. These included Aminta Casseres, Margaret "Peggy" King, and Ruth Waldo, among others. Not only did she set an example by exhibiting confidence, but she also encouraged these women to exert their independence. She realized that these women were working in a male-dominated profession, even at J. Walter Thompson, yet were intelligent and well educated and had abilities that their male counterparts did not necessarily have. It was important to her to see them succeed.[37] Several women from the department worked in offices overseas. A few became vice presidents.

J. Walter Thompson, like other agencies, developed advertising campaigns that included radio, not just print media. In fact, in 1930 the company had almost eighteen clients sponsoring more than twenty hours of radio programs a week. Such programs included the "Fleischmann Yeast Hour," "Kraft Music Hall," and "Lux Radio Theater." The agency produced nine popular programs on NBC radio in 1933. Products were advertised in brief "spots" that were often "live mini-dramas" complete with original jingles. These "live mini-dramas" allowed listeners to eavesdrop on a conversation between two individuals who discussed the benefits indirectly related to a product, such as Fleischmann's Yeast.[38]

In 1935 the company had the following major accounts: Chase and Sanborn coffee, Corning Glass, Cream of Wheat, Eastman Kodak, Guinness, Johns-Manville, Lux Flakes, Lux Toilet Soap, Northam Warren, Penick and Ford, Pond's, Scott Paper, Sharp and Dohme, Shell Oil, Standard Brands, Swift, and Libby, McNeill, and Libby, among others.[39]

The same year, John B. Watson's wife died. Eventually, he resigned from J. Walter Thompson and accepted a vice president's position at William Esty and Company, a new advertising agency. He worked in advertising another ten years, then retired.

In 1939 Resor established the J. Walter Thompson Consumer Panel, which had been tested for several years. The Consumer Panel provided valuable information about consumers and their purchasing habits. Indeed, hundreds and hundreds of American families were selected on the basis of their representation of the country's population and on such criteria as city or town size, geographic location, purchasing power, and other information. They were canvassed periodically about their purchases within a specific number of days. The agency not only used the data but sold the information to clients. [40]

By the time the United States entered World War II, Walter Resor, who had managed the branch office in Boston for years, died. Stanley, with Helen's help, continued to guide the company. The agency's billings reached $40 million. The company did its part during the war. For the federal government, Helen and her team developed an advertising campaign that encouraged women to work in factories for their loved ones who were serving in the military. [41] The agency's regular clients included Eastman Kodak, Lever Brothers, Planter's peanuts, Pond's Extract Company, Purolator, Scott Paper, Shell Oil, Swift and Company, Universal Pictures, and Libby, McNeill and Libby, among others. Billings were more than $73 million when the war ended in 1945. The agency captured additional accounts, including the Ford Motor Company. Two years later, J. Walter Thompson passed $100 million in annual billings; it was the first advertising agency to do so. [42]

In 1949 Resor received the Gold Medal Award, which was sponsored by the trade publication *Advertising and Selling*. The award had been established by Edward Bok in 1924. According to the sponsor's representative, Resor was considered "Advertising Man of the Year" because he had done more than anyone to improve the image of advertising. [43]

In 1954 the agency passed $200 million in annual billings. Although the company had produced one of the first variety programs and one of the first dramatic programs for television, it had slipped primarily because television, which had grown in popularity after World War II and had become an important medium to advertisers, demanded more creative ideas from advertising agencies. No longer could agencies employ the ideas that had been successful on radio. J. Walter Thompson, unlike several companies, seemed to be tied to the past. Disagreements between senior executives occurred. A year later, Resor became chairman of the board. Norman H. Strouse, who had been with the company for years, became president and eventually changed the agency's direction. Indeed, J. Walter Thompson responded to the creative revolution that was occurring in television advertising.

Helen made occasional appearances at the company after 1958. Resor retired from the agency in 1961. The company had more than six thousand employees in more than fifty offices in the United States and abroad. It had annual billings in excess of $350,000,000. Stanley and Helen sold their stock in the company to the employees' trust. [44]

According to a writer for *Advertising Age*, "It was during his long tenure that the agency emerged as a creative marketing force, that it pulled far away from competition on the domestic scene, and that it became the leading worldwide advertising agency."[45]

He died in late 1962. Helen died in 1964. Both were inducted into the American Advertising Federation's Advertising Hall of Fame in 1967.

The J. Walter Thompson Company became a publicly held corporation in 1969. Eleven years later, the J. Walter Thompson Group, a holding company, was organized. J. Walter Thompson, the advertising agency, was the largest subsidiary. In 1987 the J. Walter Thompson Group was purchased by WPP Group, a holding company in Britain.

NOTES

1. "In First 100 Years, Thompson Spurs Rise of Magazines, Agency Concept, Ad Role in Sales Strategy," *Advertising Age* 35, no. 49 (December 7, 1964): 31.

2. Donald L. Thompson, "J(ames) Walter Thompson (October 28, 1847–October 16, 1928)," *The Ad Men and Women: A Biographical Dictionary of Advertising*, ed. Edd Applegate (Westport, CT: Greenwood Press, 1994), 320; also Mark Tungate, *Ad Land: A Global History of Advertising* (Philadelphia: Kogan Page, 2007), 25.

3. Pamela Walker Laird, *Advertising Progress: American Business and the Rise of Consumer Marketing* (Baltimore: The Johns Hopkins University Press, 1998), 169.

4. "In First 100 Years," 32; also Tungate, *Ad Land*, 25.

5. Laurence Wile Jacobs, "Stanley B. Resor: 1879–1962," *Pioneers in Marketing: A Collection of Twenty-Five Biographies of Men Who Contributed to the Growth of Marketing through Thought and Action*, ed. John S. Wright and Parks B. Dimsdale Jr. (Atlanta: Publishing Services Division, School of Business Administration, Georgia State University, 1974), 109–10; also, James Playsted Wood, "A Pioneer in Marketing: Stanley Resor," *Journal of Marketing* 25, no. 6 (October 1961): 71.

6. Ann Maxwell Keding, "Helen Lansdowne Resor (February 20, 1886–January 2, 1964)," *The Ad Men and Women: A Biographical Dictionary of Advertising*, ed. Edd Applegate (Westport, CT: Greenwood Press, 1994), 262–63; also Denise H. Sutton, *Globalizing Ideal Beauty: How Female Copywriters of the J. Walter Thompson Advertising Agency Redefined Beauty for the Twentieth Century* (New York: Palgrave Macmillan, 2009), 16–17.

7. "Resor Retires after 53 Years at J. W. Thompson," *Advertising Age* 32, no. 9 (February 27, 1961): 8.

8. Robert Sobel and David B. Sicilia, *The Entrepreneurs: An American Adventure* (Boston: Houghton Mifflin, 1986), 219.

9. Stephen Fox, *The Mirror Makers: A History of American Advertising and Its Creators* (New York: Morrow, 1984), 81; also Sutton, *Globalizing Ideal Beauty*, 17.

10. Sutton, *Globalizing Ideal Beauty*, 111.

11. Elsie S. Hebert, "James Webb Young (January 20, 1886–March 3, 1973)," *The Ad Men and Women: A Biographical Dictionary of Advertising*, ed. Edd Applegate (Westport, CT: Greenwood Press, 1994), 355; also Keding, "Helen Lansdowne Resor," 263.

12. Wood, "A Pioneer in Marketing," 72.

13. "In First 100 Years," 32; also Jacobs, "Stanley B. Resor," 110.

14. Jacobs, "Stanley B. Resor," 110; also John N. Ingham, *Biographical Dictionary of American Business Leaders: Volume N–U* (Westport, CT: Greenwood Press, 1983), 1155.

15. Jacobs, "Stanley B. Resor," 110; also Wood, "A Pioneer in Marketing," 72.

16. "J. Walter Thompson Company: Known Also in the Trade as 'Thompson,' as 'J. Walter,' and as 'JWT,' but by Whichever Name the Largest Advertising Agency in the World," *Fortune* 36 (November 1947): 214.

17. Francesco L. Nepa, "Resor, Stanley Burnet," *American National Biography*, ed. John A. Garraty and Mark C. Carnes (New York: Oxford University Press, 1999), 18:354; also Fox, *The Mirror Makers*, 89–90.

18. Peggy J. Kreshel, "The 'Culture' of J. Walter Thompson, 1915–1925," *Public Relations Review* 16, no. 3 (1990): 82.

19. "In First 100 Years," 36.

20. Fox, *The Mirror Makers*, 83–84.

21. Jacobs, "Stanley B. Resor," 111–12; also Kreshel, "The 'Culture' of J. Walter Thompson," 85–86.

22. Sobel and Sicilia, *The Entrepreneurs*, 220.

23. Juliann Sivulka, *Soap, Sex, and Cigarettes: A Cultural History of American Advertising*, 2nd ed. (Boston: Wadsworth, Cengage Learning, 2012), 152.

24. "J. Walter Thompson Company," 228; also "Resor Retires after 53 Years," 8.

25. Kerry W. Buckley, "The Selling of a Psychologist: John Broadus Watson and the Application of Behavioral Techniques to Advertising," *Journal of the History of the Behavioral Sciences* 18 (July 1982): 209.

26. David Cohen, *J. B. Watson: The Founder of Behaviorism—A Biography* (London: Routledge & Kegan Paul, 1979), 178–79.

27. Cohen, *J. B. Watson*, 182–83.

28. Cohen, *J. B. Watson*, 188.

29. Sivulka, *Soap, Sex, and Cigarettes*, 150.

30. Jackson Lears, *Fables of Abundance: A Cultural History of Advertising in America* (New York: Basic Books, 1994), 325, 327; also Keding, "Helen Lansdowne Resor," 266.

31. Daniel A. Pope, "Stanley Burnet Resor: 1879–1962," *Dictionary of American Biography, Supplement 7: 1961–1965*, ed. John A. Garraty (New York: Charles Scribner's Sons, 1981), 642; also Kreshel, "The 'Culture' of J. Walter Thompson," 87; also Fox, *The Mirror Makers*, 91.

32. Keding, "Helen Lansdowne Resor," 267.

33. "In First 100 Years," 36; also Ingham, *Biographical Dictionary of American Business Leaders*, 1155–56.

34. Sobel and Sicilia, *The Entrepreneurs*, 221; also Ingham, *Biographical Dictionary of American Business Leaders*, 1156.

35. Roland Marchand, *Advertising the American Dream: Making Way for Modernity, 1920–1940* (Berkeley: University of California Press, 1985), 56.

36. Lauren Whaley, "The Plan 75 Years in the Making," *Planet JH Weekly* (May 7, 2004), http://www.planetjh.com/news/A_100042.aspx.

37. Sutton, *Globalizing Ideal Beauty*, 16.

38. Marchand, *Advertising the American Dream*, 106.

39. William E. Berchtold, "Men Who Sell You," *New Outlook* 165, no. 1 (January 1935): 29.

40. "J. Walter Thompson Company," 224.

41. Karen Egolf, "Resor, Helen Lansdowne: 1886–1964, U. S. Advertising Pioneer," *The Advertising Age Encyclopedia of Advertising*, ed. John McDonough and the Museum of Broadcast Communication and Karen Egolf (New York: Fitzroy Dearborn, 2003), 3:1352.

42. Ingham, *Biographical Dictionary of American Business Leaders*, 1157; also Nepa, "Resor, Stanley Burnet," 354.

43. Nepa, "Resor, Stanley Burnet," 355.

44. "In First 100 Years," 36.

45. "In First 100 Years," 36.

Chapter Ten

The Development of Advertising Education in the United States: A Brief History

The academic discipline "advertising" has a relatively long history. Indeed, the discipline began in the late nineteenth century, when prominent members of the academy as well as members of specific professions saw the need for developing curricula that would prepare people for the new world that embraced industry and new businesses. As Quentin J. Schultze wrote,

> Educators and businessmen together established the nation's first advertising courses and programs. . . . Although businessmen were the prime movers in the development of such instruction, they were motivated primarily by a symbolic ideal of professionalism, and ironically, that preoccupation with professionalization hindered their ability to grasp the complexities of creating professional education for business in the early twentieth century. [1]

Before advertising was ever taught in a classroom, people learned about it on the job. For instance, in the nineteenth century, department stores hired experienced copywriters to train selected employees about developing advertisements for newspapers. However, learning to write and illustrate successful advertisements for businesses and products took time. Even John E. Powers, one of the best copywriters of the late nineteenth century, experimented to determine which advertisements worked. In short, professional copywriters, not just those they trained, learned about advertising each day they developed one or more advertisements. As Schultze wrote,

> Advertising instruction in the last decade of the 19th century was a combina-
> tion of self-teaching and inchoate methods of formal instruction, including
> agency apprenticeships, on-premise retail advertising training and trade jour-
> nal and textbook instruction.[2]

The population of the United States increased after the Civil War. In the late nineteenth century, there were more newspapers. In addition, there were several magazines that appealed to the masses. Advertising by retailers and manufacturers increased. Retailers and other businesses, including advertising agencies, hired more people who knew how to advertise. Subsequently, demand for individuals who understood advertising increased. According to Frank Gordon Coolsen, "Since the public and endowed institutions were not willing or able to provide instruction, the field was left open for exploitation. The correspondence schools rose to meet the occasion and developed creditable courses in advertising."[3]

HISTORY OF ADVERTISING EDUCATION

Correspondence Schools and the Advertising Education Debate

The Page-Davis School of Advertising was one of the first correspondence schools to offer advertising. Edward T. Page worked for a retailer as a copywriter, and Samuel A. Davis worked for a wholesaler as the manager of the advertising department; both of these businesses were in Chicago. Page and Davis offered their advertising course beginning in 1896.

Thomas J. Foster founded the International Correspondence Schools in 1891. About ten years later, the school offered the most comprehensive correspondence course in advertising. Although George F. Lord, the company's advertising manager, initiated the first courses in advertising, S. Roland Hall wrote most of the courses, which consisted of several books in the International Library of Technology series. Hall's work was comprehensive. Indeed, his concepts were used by others who wrote books about advertising, especially books about writing copy and designing advertisements.

George W. Wagenseller, a copywriter in Philadelphia, offered the Wagenseller Correspondence Course of Advertising. Wagenseller wrote *The Theory and Practice of Advertising*, which was published in 1902. The book contained numerous lessons and problems. In addition, the book contained a coupon worth a dollar toward the cost of the course, for which Wagenseller encouraged the reader to send.[4]

Of course, numerous other correspondence schools offered courses in advertising. However, some professionals who worked in advertising criticized these schools. They believed that advertising, especially copywriting, could not be learned from such courses. Their views were expressed in *Printers' Ink*, which was read by countless professionals.

However, young professionals who worked in advertising believed that advertising needed to be elevated to professional status. According to Schultze, "They realized that formalized and standardized education was a prerequisite for professional status."[5] Consequently, they approached various institutions about offering courses in advertising.

Although arguments between the old and young professionals appeared in the pages of several publications, in 1905 Earnest Elmo Calkins, who had worked at the Bates advertising agency before he and Ralph Holden opened an advertising agency, argued for professional advertising education in the pages of *Profitable Advertising*. In fact, in the second part of the two-part series, he provided a curriculum that was suitable for a college or university. Of course, older professionals criticized his idea, and administrators, particularly at private business schools, rejected it primarily because it required three years.

A year later, representatives of local advertising clubs from throughout the country formed the Associated Advertising Clubs of America. The organization developed a list of several purposes, including the elevation of the profession by encouraging formalized advertising education. Members of the organization disagreed, however, as to how advertising education should be handled. They agreed that professionals, not academicians, should be responsible for instruction in advertising. The organization's "Committee on Lectures" developed a "Standard Course" for local clubs to offer. As a result, several members approached their local YMCA (Young Men's Christian Association) organizations and offered courses in advertising.

Within a few years, members of the Associated Advertising Clubs of America realized that courses in advertising were offered by correspondence schools, YMCAs, and several colleges and universities. Yet, these courses differed greatly in content. Eventually, they agreed that colleges and universities should provide advertising education. Their idea was opposed by older professionals and numerous academicians. The latter group believed that advertising was not worthy of being in institutions of higher learning. Yet, a few departments or schools of commerce as well as journalism had been founded at several colleges and universities. Some of these departments or schools offered part of a course or a course devoted to advertising. In addition, a course about advertising could be found in more than one department of psychology as well as other departments and schools on several college and university campuses. Advocates for advertising education believed that advertising should be housed in journalism because of its relationship to newspapers and magazines or in commerce because of its relationship to business.

Colleges and Universities Offer Journalism and Advertising

Formal journalism education started in the late nineteenth century, after the American Civil War. Although one or more individuals had the desire to establish a program that would educate future journalists prior to the war, they were not successful. According to De Forest O'Dell, "Professional education for journalism came into being in the United States in 1869 as the result of a thirty-nine-year conflict between the American social order and the Penny Press."[6]

The Penny Press had been introduced in England as a result of the Industrial Revolution's impact on society and had been brought to the United States, where cities grew in population as more factories opened. Newspapers enjoyed new readers. Specific publishers and editors learned that sensational news, such as crime and sex, appealed to readers' interest. Other publishers and editors waged a moral war against the Penny Press in an effort to retrieve subscribers.[7] Prominent members of society realized that certain aspects of society were evolving; they believed that journalism should change as well. Since professional education existed for engineering, law, and medicine, education was "chosen as society's means of control over a rebellious organism."[8]

General Robert E. Lee, who had become president of Washington College (now Washington and Lee University) in Virginia, initiated journalism education. Lee had led the Army of Northern Virginia during the Civil War. When the war ended in 1865, he accepted the position at Washington College. Lee realized that the Civil War had taken its toll on the South and that the South needed rehabilitation to survive. Lee also realized that journalism education might help young men of the South find jobs. As president, Lee had helped build the college by introducing new departments and professional schools, including law and equity as well as civil and mining engineering. He requested that the board of trustees allow instruction in journalism to be offered by the institution. The board approved. In 1869 Lee introduced the School of Journalism. Although fifty scholarships were to be offered to young men who desired to learn how to be editors as well as printers, only a few scholarships were awarded. The program was covered by the press, but many journalists were negative in their stories. Lee died in 1870, and the program in journalism, which had not grown in popularity, died eight years later. It was revived in 1925, however.[9]

After Lee's death, editors at newspapers and magazines published articles—some pro, most con—about journalism education. For instance, Frederic Hudson, the former managing editor of *The New York Tribune*, wrote,

> Such an establishment as *The New York Herald*, or *Tribune*, or *Times* is the true college for newspaper students. Professor James Gordon Bennett, or Professor Horace Greeley would turn out more real genuine journalists in one year than the Harvards, the Yales, and the Dartmouths could produce in a generation.[10]

Educators were not deterred, however, particularly those at the land grant colleges and universities, which had been established under the provisions of the Morrill Act of 1862. The bill, which was introduced by Representative Justin Smith Morrill of Vermont and signed into law by President Abraham Lincoln, authorized granting to each state thousands of acres of public land. The law stipulated that the revenue from the sale of these lands had to be used to endow and support at least one college that offered, among other subjects, agriculture and mechanic arts.

John A. Anderson, president of Kansas State College of Agriculture and Applied Science (now Kansas State University), helped establish a course in printing in 1874. Journalism became formally established in 1910.

The first president of Cornell University, Andrew Dickson White, provided an outline of a program in journalism. According to White, the program would offer a certificate. Unfortunately, the program was abandoned at Cornell, although lectures in journalism were given in 1876 and one or two courses in journalism were offered by the English Department in 1888.

David Russell McAnally, the head of the School of English at the University of Missouri, introduced journalism to students in 1878, with "History of Journalism—Lectures, with practical explanations of daily newspaper life."[11] A few years later "Materials of Journalism," which focused on "practical procedures," followed.[12] Occasionally, other courses in journalism were offered by other professors at the university.

Instruction in journalism was sporadic, to say the least, as indicated in Table 10.1.

According to Paul L. Dressel, "By 1890, the modern conception of a newspaper with a capable staff and huge circulation had emerged, and the need for trained personnel led to interest in journalism education."[13]

At this time, prominent members of the press, including Charles Dana of *The New York Sun*, Joseph Pulitzer of *The New York World*, and Charles Emory Smith of *The Philadelphia Press*, were claiming that the basis of journalism could be taught by competent professors who had practical experience in journalism.

154   *Chapter 10*

Table 10.1.   Institution and Year Journalism Was First Offered (a. Abandoned in 1878; b. Printing)

Institution	Year
Washington College (Washington & Lee University)	1869[a]
Kansas State College of Agriculture and Applied Science (Kansas State University)	1874[b]
University of Missouri	1878
University of Denver	1882
Cornell University	1888
University of Kansas	1891
State University of Iowa (University of Iowa)	1892
Indiana University	1893
Kentucky University (University of Kentucky)	1893
University of Nebraska	1894
University of Michigan	1895
Bessie Tift College	1898
Temple University	1899
University of Chicago	1899
University of Oregon	1901
University of North Dakota	1903
Iowa State College of Agricultural and Mechanic Arts (Iowa State University of Science and Technology)	1903
University of Washington	1907
South Dakota State College (South Dakota State University)	1908
University of Colorado	1909
Oklahoma Agricultural and Mechanical College (Oklahoma State University)	1910
Columbia University	1912
Louisiana State University	1912
University of Georgia	1913
Pennsylvania State College (Pennsylvania State University)	1914
University of Minnesota	1915
University of Florida	1916

Eugene Camp of *The Philadelphia Times* encouraged the University of Pennsylvania to develop a curriculum in journalism. In 1893, Professor Joseph French Johnson of the university's Wharton School of Finance and

Commerce (originally, Wharton School of Finance and Economy) became the director of the newly developed program of professional training for newspaper work, which was the first comprehensive curriculum in journalism offered in the country. Johnson had worked at the *Chicago Tribune*.

Johnson's program consisted of the following:

- Journalism—Art and History of Newspaper Making.
- Journalism—Law of Libel, Business Management, Typographical Union, Cost and Revenue, Advertising, Method of Criticism, etc.
- Journalism—Newspaper Practice, Exercises in Reporting, Editing of Copy, Conversations, etc.
- Journalism—Current Topics, Lectures on Live Issues in the United States and Foreign Countries.
- Journalism—Public Lectures by Men Engaged in the Active Work of the Profession.[14]

The curriculum contained five courses in journalism, and one of these courses—"Journalism—Law of Libel, Business Management, Typographical Union, Cost and Revenue, Advertising, Method of Criticism, etc."—contained information about advertising.

Dr. E. M. Hopkins, who was chair of the Department of Rhetoric and English at the University of Kansas, offered a course in journalism in 1891. No other courses in journalism were offered at the university, however, until 1903.[15] During this period, other colleges and universities offered one or more courses in journalism (see Table 10.1).

In 1896 E. W. Stephens, the publisher of the *Columbia Herald*, addressed members of the Missouri Press Association and encouraged them that Missouri and the nation needed programs in journalism. The members responded by adopting a resolution that in 1898 persuaded the president and the board at the University of Missouri to establish a "Chair of Journalism." Although the university catalog listed a Department of Journalism, it existed only on paper for several years. As mentioned, courses in journalism had been offered in the School of English for years, however.

In 1898 the board of directors created a School of Journalism at Bessie Tift College (now extinct) in Forsyth, Georgia. The courses varied but most focused on a specific form of writing. The program was revamped in 1923. Also in 1898 the University of Missouri offered a course in journalism— "Newspaper Making"—that provided information about advertising.[16]

In 1902 the College of Commerce and Administration of the University of Chicago offered a major in journalism, which lasted until 1911. The primary course in journalism was offered in the Department of Sociology, however.[17]

In 1902 the Department of Rhetoric and Oratory (Department of English) of the University of Illinois offered "Rhetoric 10," the first course in journalism. Part of the course focused on advertising.[18] In 1903 the same department at the University of Illinois introduced a second course in journalism, "Rhetoric 12."

Joseph Pulitzer, who had become a successful publisher and editor and who had desired to endow a school of journalism since 1892, announced in the *New York World*, August 16, 1903, that he had endowed a school of journalism at Columbia University. Pulitzer expressed his position on education for journalism in an article that appeared in the *North American Review*. Pulitzer described a program that focused on (1) style, (2) law tailored for the journalist, (3) ethics, (4) literature, (5) truth and accuracy, (6) history tailored for the journalist, (7) sociology, (8) economics, (9) "the enemies of the republic," (10) arbitration in its broad sense, (11) statistics, (12) modern languages, especially French and German, (13) science, (14) the study of newspapers, (15) the power of ideas, (16) principles of journalism, and (17) the news.[19]

Pulitzer's idea for an endowed school of journalism had been discussed at length in a brochure that had been given to the presidents of Harvard University and Columbia University. The president of Columbia responded positively to Pulitzer's plan. Harvard's president, Dr. Charles W. Eliot, had been off campus. Eventually, he responded, but his curriculum stressed the business side of journalism. Pulitzer was not necessarily interested in Dr. Eliot's proposed curriculum, although it was listed in the *World*. Dr. Eliot's proposal consisted of the following:

1. Newspaper Administration (the organization of a newspaper office and functions of various departments and services).
2. Newspaper Manufacturer (study of printing presses and other mechanical devices used in publishing).
3. The Law of Journalism.
4. Ethics of Journalism.
5. History of Journalism.
6. The Literary Forms of Newspapers (approved usages in punctuation, spelling, abbreviations, typography, etc.).[20]

Dr. Eliot's proposal focused on editorial work, operation of the business office, operation of the advertising office, and operation of the mechanical department. He suggested that other departments at the university, including English, history, government, geography, and economics, could offer courses relevant to journalism. In essence, these "background" courses would be coordinated with the journalism program.

Dr. Eliot also was listed in the *World* as a temporary member of the Advisory Board for the new school of journalism at Columbia. He could not serve as a permanent member because of his position at Harvard, however.

Basically, Pulitzer's plan emphasized a liberal arts education, while Dr. Eliot's plan emphasized practical courses or so-called skills courses. Although some early programs in journalism offered courses that were based on Pulitzer's ideas, most early programs in journalism offered courses that were based on Dr. Eliot's ideas. Eventually, the curriculum in journalism was broadened; more liberal arts types of courses were offered, while skills types of courses were limited.[21] Programs in advertising, particularly those found in departments or schools of journalism or mass communications, have embraced these concepts in the kinds of courses offered.

Pulitzer and the *World*, by including Dr. Eliot and his curriculum in the stories about the endowed new school, brought academic credibility to the new school, which received praise as well as criticism from journalists throughout the country. In 1904 the National Editorial Association announced that it supported Pulitzer and his endowment. Pulitzer died in 1911, and the building housing the new school was finished in 1913. The first few courses had been offered in 1912. Although Columbia's School of Journalism offered courses to undergraduates for years, in 1931 it became a graduate program.

In 1905 a chair in journalism was established at Iowa State College of Agricultural and Mechanic Arts. The same year Dr. Frank Scott developed the first four-year curriculum in journalism at the University of Illinois. His curriculum was influenced by Pulitzer and Dr. Eliot at Harvard.

The same year Dr. Willard G. Bleyer introduced journalism on the campus of the University of Wisconsin. "English 19. Newspaper Writing" was offered initially in the English Department. Bleyer was influenced by Pulitzer, Dr. Eliot, and his own formal education. Basically, Bleyer agreed with Pulitzer in that he thought a program in journalism could help students understand the role of the press in society or how the press had affected society. He also believed that students should learn the skills of journalism as well as how journalism had been practiced. More courses in journalism were added to the curriculum, which became part of a two-year program.

In 1906 a Department of Journalism was established at the University of Missouri. However, Dr. Eliot's proposed curriculum was the basis for the first school of journalism, which was founded two years later at the university. Walter Williams was named dean of the school of journalism, which offered an undergraduate program that focused on practical skills. Williams mentioned advertising in "The Journalists' Creed": "I believe that advertising, news, editorial columns should alike serve the best interests of the readers; that a single standard of helpful truth and cleanness should prevail for all; that the supreme test of good journalism is the measure of its public service."[22]

Advertising became part of the school's curriculum, with "Advertising and Publishing," which was offered in 1908, as the school's first course in advertising.[23] The school of journalism offered the first degree in advertising in 1910. The courses included "Principles of Advertising," "The Writing of Advertising," "Current Problems in Advertising," "The Soliciting of Advertising," and "Rural Newspaper Management."[24] The school of journalism's curriculum was copied by other universities.

Leon Flint, a faculty member at the University of Kansas, developed the first course in advertising in 1908.

In 1910 the University of Washington, which had offered a few courses in journalism since 1907, offered its first course in advertising.[25] The curriculum in advertising expanded within a few years.

An editorial in the *Journalism Bulletin* claimed that one school and three departments of journalism existed by 1910. These included the school at the University of Missouri and departments at the universities of Wisconsin, New York, and Washington. The editorial also claimed that one or more courses in journalism were offered at the following colleges and universities: Bessie Tift College, Cornell University, DePauw University, Indiana University, Kansas State College of Agriculture and Applied Science, Ohio University, University of Colorado, University of Illinois, University of Michigan, University of Nebraska, University of North Dakota, University of Oklahoma, and University of Pennsylvania.[26] As this chapter indicates, the writer of this editorial was incorrect. There were institutions of higher education offering one or more courses in journalism in 1910 that had been overlooked. In addition, a Department of Journalism had been authorized in 1909 at the University of Kansas and was established soon thereafter. In fact, the program offered another course in advertising in 1910.

Journalism education continued to grow in popularity. In 1911 a Department of Journalism was established in the College of Arts and Sciences at Indiana University. Although students could enroll in courses, they could not major in journalism until years later. In 1912 as many as five courses in journalism were offered at the University of Oregon. However, the university's School of Journalism was not established until four years later.

Also in 1912 Willard G. Bleyer became chair of the newly established Department of Journalism at the University of Wisconsin. The same year, Walter Williams, dean of the School of Journalism at the University of Missouri, reported that thirty-two institutions offered courses in journalism. Three of these institutions had professional schools of journalism, while seven others had departments of journalism.[27] Williams' report may have been too conservative, considering how popular journalism had become.

Although a course in journalism had been offered by the Department of English for several years, a School of Journalism was not established at the University of Oklahoma until 1913. Theodore Brewer, the head of the Department of English, served as the first director.

Although the president of the University of Kentucky had recommended that a Department of Journalism be established in 1908, the department was not founded until 1914. Enoch Grehan served as the first head or director. The same year, a School of Journalism was established at the University of Texas and offered several courses in journalism and at least one in advertising. The same year, a School of Journalism was established at the University of Montana.

In 1914 a course in advertising was offered in the Department of Rhetoric at the University of Oregon.

In 1915 a Department of Journalism was established at Louisiana State University, and a School of Journalism was founded at the University of Georgia. S. V. Sanford served as the first director at the latter program.

According to James Melvin Lee, by 1918, ninety-one institutions offered courses in journalism. By 1920, 131 institutions offered courses in journalism.[28] It is conceivable that these figures are too conservative, considering how popular the subject had become throughout the country.

In 1915 John B. Powell, who taught courses in advertising at the University of Missouri, learned that twenty-six colleges and universities offered one or more courses in advertising. Powell's figure was too conservative, however, according to an article that was published in *Printers' Ink.* The writer mentioned at least two additional institutions that offered courses in advertising.[29]

A year later Bruce Bliven, a faculty member at the University of Southern California, reported that thirty-seven colleges and universities offered one or more courses in advertising.[30]

In May 1921, Daniel Starch reported about nineteen institutions that had responded to a survey. According to Starch, "Each of the institutions gives a first or general course. Six of these institutions designate this course advertising; five designate it as principles, elements, or essentials of advertising; seven as psychology of advertising; and one, publicity and advertising."[31] Starch found that numerous institutions offered specialized courses:

> Five insitutions offer a course in advertisement writing or copywriting; five offer a course in advertising design, advertising display, or typography of advertising; three, in advertising campaigns; three in research in advertising; three in the selling of advertising; and each of the following courses is offered in one institution: advertising practice, advertising laboratory, retail advertising, mail-order advertising, photo illustration.[32]

In 1927, eighteen of the twenty schools of journalism offered courses in advertising. Ten years later, thirty of the thirty-two schools of journalism offered courses in advertising.[33] The trend continued as more departments and schools of journalism or mass communications were established at colleges and universities across the country.

Colleges and Universities Offer Psychology Courses about Advertising: The First Researchers of Advertising

Several faculty members who taught courses in psychology in the late nineteenth century and early twentieth century also taught one or two courses that concerned advertising. These individuals conducted research about advertising as well.

Harlow Gale studied psychology at the University of Leipzig, in Germany. His mentor was Wilhelm Wundt, who founded experimental psychology. Gale not only learned from Wundt but was influenced by him.

After his return to the United States, Gale became a faculty member in the Department of Philosophy of the University of Minnesota. In addition to establishing a psychology laboratory, Gale taught courses in psychology, including a seminar in which students conducted several studies about the psychology of advertising.

In 1895 Gale sent a questionnaire to two hundred businesses in Minnesota to determine how they used advertising.[34] Gale's questionnaire asked participants to rank order ("order of merit") specific items.[35] His questionnaire may have been the first to employ this approach.

In one experiment relating to advertising, Gale had the male and female students enrolled in his seminar course observe entire advertisements to determine which elements attracted attention. Another experiment determined relevant and irrelevant items, including words and visuals, in advertisements. Another experiment pertained to "the attention value of position on the page."[36] Another experiment examined the attention value of colors. Gale also learned what his participants remembered from specific advertisements.[37] Another experiment pertained to an advertisement's power to influence or suggest.

Although Gale's samples were limited in size, his research was important. John Eighmey and Sela Sar wrote, "He was the first psychologist of advertising to see certain advertising appeals as signaling credibility based on reliance on a brand by many consumers, and to connect that appeal to the importance to consumers of interpersonal communication in the marketplace."[38] Gale discussed the results of several of his experiments in the article "On the Psychology of Advertising," which was published in *Psychological Studies* in July 1900. Then in 1903 Gale's position was terminated.

Walter Dill Scott attended Northwestern University, then McCormick Theological Seminary in Chicago, then the University of Leipzig. Like Gale, Scott learned about experimental psychology from Wilhelm Wundt.

Scott earned his doctorate at the latter institution and returned to Northwestern University in 1900. He taught courses in psychology and directed the newly founded psychology laboratory. In 1901 Thomas Balmer, who worked in advertising at Butterick, a publisher of magazines, and who was a member of the Agate Club of Chicago, an organization for professionals who worked in advertising, invited Scott to speak at a future meeting. George A. Coe, chair of the Department of Philosophy (a Department of Psychology did not exist at Northwestern at the time), encouraged Scott to accept Balmer's invitation.[39] Scott agreed and spoke about the psychology of involuntary attention as it applied to advertising. During the speech, Scott quoted Harlow Gale, specifically his research regarding color of ink and size of type and their relationship to attracting attention.[40] Members' reaction encouraged Scott to speak to the group several times. In addition, he was encouraged to elaborate on his speeches in articles for *Mahin's Magazine*, which was published by John Lee Mahin, the owner of an advertising agency in Chicago. Scott wrote twenty-six articles for the magazine; twelve of these articles became the basis for the book *The Theory of Advertising: A Simple Exposition of the Principles of Psychology in Their Relation to Successful Advertising*, which was published in 1903.[41]

In 1904 Scott offered the course "Advanced Experimental Psychology," which concerned the psychology of advertising. The course was given in the Department of Philosophy. Scott's advanced course was a laboratory course and was offered for several years.

Scott wrote *The Psychology of Advertising: A Simple Exposition of the Principles of Psychology in Their Relation to Successful Advertising*, which was published in 1908. The book concerned the psychological principles of advertising and was used in the course "Psychology of Business, Advertising and Salesmanship," which he taught the following year.

Now a full professor of psychology, Scott became a professor of advertising when the School of Commerce opened in 1909. He transferred the "Psychology of Business, Advertising and Salesmanship" course to the new school in 1910. Although he continued to teach courses in which advertising was addressed, he grew interested in the psychology of business and selling.

In 1914 he conducted a study about employment criteria for the National Association of Corporation Schools. This study encouraged him to study personnel selection and evaluation at companies. Eventually, Scott developed tests that were suitable for companies to use to measure their employees' qualities and abilities.

In 1916 Scott was granted a leave of absence to head the newly founded Bureau of Salesmanship Research at the Carnegie Institute of Technology. Scott and his staff developed an interviewer's scale suitable for the selection of sales personnel.[42] When the United States entered World War I, Scott was commissioned a colonel and became the director of the Committee on the Classification of Personnel in the Army, which developed rating scales that were used to classify personnel.

Scott returned to higher education after World War I. He formed the Scott Company for the purpose of providing psychologists to companies on a consulting basis. The psychologists helped companies with personnel matters. However, in 1920, when he became president of Northwestern University, he found little time for the company. In fact, in 1923, the company ceased to exist. Although he wrote with Robert Clothier *Personnel Management: Principles, Practices, and Point of View*, which was published in 1923, his duties to the university prevented him from researching and writing about psychology or advertising.

Scott retired from Northwestern University in 1939.

In 1909 Harry L. Hollingworth received his doctorate in psychology from Columbia University. Then he joined the faculty at Barnard College. In 1910 he offered an "Advertising Psychology" course for the Advertising Men's League of New York. This course eventually was transferred to New York University.

Like Gale, Hollingworth applied the "order of merit" approach to advertisements. His results influenced Edward K. Strong to conduct similar tests for his doctoral dissertation. Eventually, Strong's research, along with Hollingworth's, was presented in *Advertising and Selling: Principles of Appeal and Response*, which was published in 1913.[43]

Together with Harry Tipper, George B. Hotchkiss, and Frank A. Parsons, Hollingworth published *Advertising: Its Principles and Practice* in 1915. Hollingworth contributed "The Psychological Factors in Advertising" to the book, in which he listed twenty-nine appeals and their corresponding weights. This book was one of the first comprehensive texts about advertising. The authors revised the book in 1920, which they titled *The Principles of Advertising: a Textbook*.[44]

Hollingworth retired in 1946.

Edward K. Strong Jr. earned a bachelor's degree and a master's degree from the University of California–Berkeley. Then he attended Columbia University, where he studied psychology and worked as Harry L. Hollingworth's assistant. Influenced by Hollingworth, Strong studied advertising. He earned his doctorate in 1911, the year he married Margaret Hart.[45]

In 1914 he and his wife moved to Nashville, Tennessee, where he taught at George Peabody College and wrote about psychology for teachers. During World War I, he served on Walter Dill Scott's Committee on the Classification of Personnel in the Army, then as a personnel specialist at two military bases.

Strong became a faculty member at the Carnegie Institute of Technology after the war. In 1923 the Department of Applied Psychology at the Carnegie Institute of Technology was eliminated. Strong was offered a position at Stanford University. Although principally a professor of psychology, he taught courses in business administration and conducted research about Oriental Americans as well as about vocational interest measurement.

In 1925 he published *The Psychology of Selling and Advertising*. However, he is best remembered for his *Vocational Interests of Men and Women*, which was published in 1943. His first "Strong Vocational Interest Blank" was published in 1927.[46]

Daniel Starch earned his doctorate from the University of Iowa in 1906. He taught psychology at the University of Iowa and at Wellesley College before he joined the faculty at the University of Wisconsin in 1908.

Starch taught courses in educational psychology and later wrote a text about the subject. However, he grew interested in the psychology of advertising. In 1910, for instance, he wrote *Principles of Advertising: A Systematic Syllabus of the Fundamental Principles of Advertising* for a course he taught. Four years later, he wrote *Advertising: Its Principles, Practice, and Technique*, which, according to Neil Borden, "established him as a leader in the new field."[47]

Several years later, he was offered a position at the Harvard Business School, which he accepted. Starch taught courses in advertising and wrote *Principles of Advertising*, which was published in 1923. In addition, he conducted research employing the recognition method.

In 1924 he became the director of research for the American Association of Advertising Agencies. Two years later he established Daniel Starch & Staff. Once his business became successful, he left Harvard. His business became one of the most respected in the area of measuring advertising effectiveness, especially advertising appearing in magazines and newspapers.

Eventually, only a few programs in psychology continued to offer a course or two about advertising. Indeed, as more programs in journalism or business were established and these programs offered one or more courses in advertising, there was no need for programs in psychology to address the subject, unless it was in a "special topics" or seminar type of course.

Colleges and Universities Offer Advertising and Marketing

Owners and operators of businesses in the nineteenth century were not necessarily concerned about hiring individuals who had attended colleges and
universities. However, as Joseph S. Johnston Jr. and colleagues wrote,

> but fundamental changes in the pre–Civil War American economy, which
> accelerated rapidly after 1865, transformed business attitudes about formal
> education. Because of these changes, business study would soon outgrow the
> constraints of the cultural imagination and blend easily with the pragmatic,
> entrepreneurial, and individualistic character of American society. [48]

Private business schools, which offered courses in bookkeeping and eventually typing and shorthand, monopolized business education prior to 1890. [49]
Although these schools served a basic purpose, the curricula suffered because it focused on a few clerical skills, not business in general. Consequently, these schools failed to prepare individuals for positions of responsibility. [50]

According to Rakesh Khurana, "The first university business schools represented . . . an attempt to shift the traditional system of apprenticeship, with
its interest in character formation as well as in the transmission of knowledge
and skills, into an organizational context more amenable to the modern
age." [51]

James D. B. De Bow offered courses in political economy and commerce
at the University of Louisiana (now Tulane University) in New Orleans in
1849. De Bow helped establish a School of Commerce at the university in
1851. Unfortunately, primarily because the curriculum had very little appeal
among students, the program and school were abandoned in 1857. [52]

President Robert E. Lee of Washington College (now Washington and
Lee University) proposed a School of Commerce at Washington College in
1869, the year he proposed a School of Journalism. Lee wrote,

> In recommending a Commercial School, it is proposed not merely to give
> instruction in bookkeeping and the forms and details of business, but to teach
> the principles of commerce, economy, trade and mercantile law. Such a school
> may with great advantage be added to the schools of the college, as many
> students may, by its means, prepare themselves for business pursuits while
> obtaining such scientific and literary culture in the other schools as time and
> opportunity may allow. [53]

Unfortunately, Lee died a year later, while the School of Commerce and
Administration would not be established until decades later, in 1906.

The University of Illinois established a School of Commerce in 1870
from its Department of Commercial Science and Art, which was one of the
original departments when the university was chartered in 1867. The curricu-

lum was similar to the curriculum found in the typical private business school, which, of course, lacked rigor, particularly for a university. In 1880 the Board of Trustees voted to close the school.[54]

In 1881 the Wharton School of Finance and Economy (later Wharton School of Finance and Commerce) was established at the University of Pennsylvania, as a result of a financial gift of $100,000 from Joseph Wharton, a successful manufacturer and merchant in Philadelphia. However, the school struggled for two years primarily because the faculty had been educated in the liberal arts and did not necessarily believe that "practical" courses about commerce should be taught in a college or university.[55] These faculty members were replaced with faculty members who understood the subjects they were assigned to teach.

In 1898 the University of Chicago established a College of Commerce and Politics (later School of Commerce and Administration). In 1900 Dartmouth College established the Amos Tuck School of Administration and Finance, the first graduate school of management, and New York University established a School of Commerce, Accounts, and Finance. Charles Haskins was the founding dean.

The University of Illinois reestablished its School of Commerce in 1902. The School of Commerce became the College of Commerce and Business Administration in 1915. In 1908 Harvard University established a Graduate School of Business Administration. Edwin Frances Gay served as the first dean.

Between 1900 and 1913, twenty-five departments or schools of commerce or business were established at colleges and universities (see Table 10.2 for a sampling).

Tulane University established a College of Commerce and Business Administration in 1914. Morton A. Aldrich, a professor of economics, served as the first dean. In 1916 a College of Commerce and Journalism was established at the Ohio State University. James E. Hagerty served as the first dean. The following year, a School of Commerce and Finance was established at the University of Utah. Courses had been offered as early as 1896 in the Department of Economics and Sociology, however.

Between 1914 and 1918, thirty-seven programs were founded. Before the end of World War I, the typical school of commerce or business administration "was a school designed to equip its graduates with the tools of the trade necessary for immediate entrance on the job in the business world."[56] Some of these schools required few courses in liberal arts, science, and mathematics; as a result, faculty members in other academic disciplines criticized the "practical" types of courses being offered.

The American Association of Collegiate Schools of Business (now the Association to Advance Collegiate Schools of Business—AACSB) was organized in 1916 to promote and improve business education in colleges and

Table 10.2. Institution and Year Business or Commerce Program Established (a. Abandoned in 1857, reestablished in 1914; b. Abandoned, reestablished in 1906; c. Abandoned in 1880, reestablished in 1902; d. Abandoned in 1881, reestablished in 1907)

Institution	Year
University of Louisiana (Tulane University)	1849[a]
Washington College (Washington & Lee University)	1869[b]
University of Illinois	1870[c]
Baruch College (CUNY)	1871[d]
University of Pennsylvania	1881
University of Oregon	1884
University of Chicago	1898
University of California—Berkeley	1898
University of Wisconsin	1900
University of Vermont	1900
Dartmouth College	1900
New York University	1900
University of Michigan	1901
James Millikin University	1903
University of Colorado	1906
University of Cincinnati	1906
Northwestern University	1908
Oregon Agricultural College (Oregon State University)	1908
University of Pittsburgh	1908
University of Denver	1908
Harvard University	1908
Ohio University	1909
Lehigh University	1909
Olivet College	1910
Marquette University	1910
St. Louis University	1910
Boston University	1913
Columbia University	1916
University of Utah	1917
Indiana University	1920

universities. Several leading colleges and universities not only helped found the organization but became charter members before the first formal meeting, which was held in 1919.[57]

The City University of New York's Baruch College established a School of Business and Civic Administration in 1919. However, the college had offered a one-year course in commerce in 1871. This course was offered for 10 years. Beginning in 1907, the college offered courses in business. Although several courses concerning economics and business had been offered for years at Indiana University, a School of Commerce and Finance was not established until 1920. Establishment of business programs continued. By 1925, 183 colleges and universities offered instruction in one or more areas of commerce or business administration. Most of the thirty-four programs belonging to the AACSB required students to take work in accounting, business law, finance, marketing, and statistics.[58] Five years later, most of the large state-supported universities offered an undergraduate and/or graduate degree in commerce or business administration.

In 1902, at the University of Illinois, "advertising" was included in two courses—"Business Writing," or "Rhetoric 10," and "Domestic Commerce and Commercial Politics." Later, the latter course was titled "Mechanism and Technique of Domestic Commerce," or "Economics 38." John Lee Mahin lectured about advertising on the campus in 1905. However, the first course devoted exclusively to advertising was not offered until 1914. The course in advertising was transferred to the Department of Business Organization and Operation.[59]

The first full course in advertising offered by a collegiate school of business was offered by the School of Commerce, Accounts, and Finance of New York University in 1905. Visiting practitioners provided lectures about the practical aspects of advertising. The School of Commerce, Accounts, and Finance continued to offer the course, even though the course was criticized by the administration for being too practical.[60]

Although "Marketing of Products" was offered at the Wharton School of Finance and Commerce in 1904, a course in advertising was not offered until 1909. A few years later, two courses in advertising were offered, including "The Construction of Advertising Campaigns." Herbert W. Hess taught the courses. He wrote *Productive Advertising*, which was published in 1915 and which concerned the basic principles of advertising and the development of advertising campaigns.[61]

In 1908 the Department of Economics and Political Science of the University of Minnesota offered a course in advertising. In 1911 George B. Hotchkiss taught "Business Correspondence and Advertising Practice" in the Department of Business English of New York University. Boston University offered its first course in advertising in 1914.

In 1909 the Graduate School of Business Administration at Harvard University offered the course "Commercial Organization and Methods," which included advertising.[62] However, the first full course in advertising was not offered until 1916.

In 1915 George Burton Hotchkiss helped establish the Department of Advertising and Marketing at New York University. Courses that had been offered by the Advertising Men's League of New York City became the basis for the department.[63]

The same year the National Association of Teachers of Advertising was founded. Walter Dill Scott was instrumental in the organization's formation. This organization became the National Association of Teachers of Marketing and Advertising in 1924, then the National Association of Teachers of Marketing in 1933. This organization and the American Marketing Society, which was founded in 1930, merged to form the American Marketing Association in 1937.

Courses in marketing were not offered until 1902. According to H. H. Maynard, the first course, "The Distributive and Regulative Industries of the United States," was offered by the Department of Economics of the University of Michigan in 1902. The description of the course appeared in the university's catalog:

> This course which alternates with Course 34, will include a description of the various ways of marketing goods, of the classification grades, brands, employed, and of the wholesale and retail trade. Attention will also be given to those private organizations, not connected with money and banking, which guide and control the industrial process, such as trade associations, boards of trade, and chambers of commerce.[64]

However, Simon Litman claimed that the course "The Technique of Trade and Commerce," which he taught in 1902 at the University of California, was one of the first courses in marketing. Litman also claimed that a similar course was offered the same year at the University of Illinois.[65]

One of the first courses with "marketing" in its title was "The Marketing of Products," which was offered at the Wharton School of Commerce and Finance in 1904. The course emphasized advertising and publicity, as the following description from the university's catalog illustrates: "The methods now practiced in the organization and conduct of the selling branch of industrial and mercantile business. The principal subjects in the field are publicity, agency, advertising, forms and correspondence, credit and collections, and terms of sale."[66]

The Ohio State University offered courses in marketing as early as 1904; in 1907 it offered "Mercantile Institutions," a course that included advertising, as the description from the specific bulletin on Business Administration and Social Science illustrates:

> This course considers mercantile organization from two points of view: (1) The evolution of mercantile organizations in the United States and their relation to each other; the origin and development of the various mercantile institutions with special reference to the economic conditions which brought them into existence and perpetuated them. The various methods of marketing goods, and the functions of the various distributors, manufacturers, manufacturers' agents, brokers, jobbers, traveling salesmen, etc. Advertising, its psychological laws, its economic importance and the changes it has introduced in selling goods. The work of stock and produce exchanges. (2) The internal or administrative organization of mercantile concerns. A study of the divisions and subdivisions of mercantile concerns and the relation of the various departments to each other and to the whole. The systems in use of recording and preserving data.[67]

It should be noted that Robert Bartels claimed that this description was for "The Distribution of Products," a course that was offered in 1905. It was expanded into a two-term course—"Distributive and Regulative Institutions"—a term later. According to Bartels, the course's title was changed to "Mercantile Institutions" in 1906.[68]

Ralph Starr Butler developed "Sales, Purchase and Shipping Methods," a course in marketing, at the University of Wisconsin in 1910. This course became "Marketing Methods" in 1913.

As more schools of commerce or business administration opened, more courses in marketing were offered. These courses concerned (1) the functional approach—that is, the activities of the marketing process (buying and selling, transporting and storing, standardizing and grading, and advertising, among others), (2) the institutional approach—that is, the types of marketing institutions (wholesalers, agents, brokers, jobbers, and retailers, among others), and (3) the commodity approach—that is, the products (farming, forestry, mining, and manufacturing, among others).[69]

More courses in advertising were offered by universities as well. Indeed, as Harold E. Hardy reported, "as early as 1930, 66 per cent of all marketing schools offered . . . advertising"[70] In 1931, according to their study, James H. S. Bossard and J. Frederic Dewhurst reported that all of the forty-two member programs of the AACSB offered courses in distribution. "Marketing" was the most popular, followed by "Advertising" based on credit hours.[71] In 1950, 70.1 percent of all marketing programs offered advertising.[72]

According to Johnston and colleagues, "By the late 1950s and the early 1960s, undergraduate business study felt the sting of criticism from business and higher education leaders because of its overspecialization and vocationalism."[73]

In 1959, *The Education of American Businessmen: A Study of University-College Programs in Business Administration* was published; it was written by Frank C. Pierson and others and supported by the Carnegie Corporation.

At the time, courses as well as programs in advertising were found in schools of business and schools of journalism. Pierson and others' study examined the various disciplines, including marketing, offered by schools of business. The authors presented a suggested curriculum for undergraduates interested in studying business. Only one course was listed for marketing, and it was "Marketing Management." Not one course was listed for advertising.

The same year, Robert Gordon and James Howell published *Higher Education for Business*, which was supported by the Ford Foundation. The authors presented a "core" of courses for undergraduate business students. The authors believed that students should not be allowed to enroll in more than one or two electives in business after the "core." The authors listed one course in marketing and no courses in advertising.

Although several schools or colleges of business administration had changed their curricula before these studies were published, action regarding curricula was taken by the AACSB and subsequently by other schools or colleges of business administration after these studies had been read by academicians. For instance, by 1963 more than ten schools or colleges of business administration had discontinued their programs in advertising.

Some of these programs in advertising were adopted by schools of journalism and/or mass communications. According to Bill Ross and John Schweitzer, in 1963 seventy-seven schools had programs in advertising. The majority of these programs were located in departments or schools of journalism. The authors reported that in 1988 ninety-five schools offered programs in advertising. [74]

Today, out of the more than one hundred programs in advertising, only a few are located in schools or colleges of business administration. Most, if not all, of these few are in schools' or colleges' marketing departments.

FINAL THOUGHTS

In 1912, in his article "How the Colleges Are Teaching Advertising and Selling," Paul T. Cherington concluded that schools or colleges of commerce or business administration are the appropriate "homes" for advertising. [75] I agree with Cherington. Advertising's philosophy basically is the same as marketing's. Consequently, advertising programs should be in departments of marketing, which typically are in schools or colleges of commerce or business. However, as mentioned, most programs in advertising are in departments or schools of journalism. If an advertising program is in a department or school of journalism, the faculty responsible for advertising should attempt to have the program separated—that is, put in its own department (if it is large enough based on number of faculty and number of students) or in a department made up of advertising and public relations.

NOTES

1. Quentin J. Schultze, "'An Honorable Place': The Quest for Professional Advertising Education, 1900–1917," *Business History Review* 56, no. 1 (1982): 17.
2. Quentin J. Schultze, "The Quest for Professional Advertising Education Before 1917," document no. ED188177 (Washington, DC: Educational Resources Information Center, August 1980), 4.
3. Frank Gordon Coolsen, *The Development of Systematic Instruction in the Principles of Advertising*, MS thesis (Urbana: University of Illinois, 1942), 19.
4. Quentin J. Schultze, *Advertising, Science, and Professionalism, 1885–1917*, PhD dissertation (Urbana-Champaign: University of Illinois, 1978), 137–40; also Coolsen, *The Development of Systematic Instruction*, 19–26.
5. Schultze, *Advertising, Science, and Professionalism*, 144.
6. De Forest O'Dell, *The History of Journalism Education in the United States* (New York: Teachers College, 1935), 1.
7. O'Dell, *The History of Journalism Education*, 2.
8. O'Dell, *The History of Journalism Education*, 5.
9. Joseph A. Mirando, "The First College Journalism Students: Answering Robert E. Lee's Offer of a Higher Education," document no. ED402599 (Washington, DC: Educational Resources Information Center, 1995), 7–15; also O'Dell, *The History of Journalism Education*, 5–19.
10. Frederic Hudson, *Journalism in the United States* (New York: Harper and Brothers, 1873), 713.
11. O'Dell, *The History of Journalism Education*, 36.
12. O'Dell, *The History of Journalism Education*, 36.
13. Paul L. Dressel, *Liberal Education and Journalism* (New York: Teachers College, 1960), 21.
14. *The University of Pennsylvania Catalogue, 1893–94* (Philadelphia: The University of Pennsylvania, 1893), 111; also Vernon Nash, *Educating for Journalism*, EdD dissertation (New York: Teachers College, 1938), 14–15.
15. *University Daily Kansan*, May 18, 1934; O'Dell, *The History of Journalism Education*, 49.
16. O'Dell, *The History of Journalism Education*, 89.
17. O'Dell, *The History of Journalism Education*, 52.
18. O'Dell, *The History of Journalism Education*, 68.
19. Joseph Pulitzer, "The College of Journalism," *North American Review* 178 (May 1904): 641.
20. James Melvin Lee, *Instruction in Journalism in Institutions of Higher Learning*, Bulletin no. 21 (Washington, DC: U.S. Department of the Interior, Bureau of Education, 1918), 13; also O'Dell, *The History of Journalism Education*, 84.
21. Leon Whipple, "Journalism," *The Survey* 60 (June 1, 1928): 292; also Dressel, *Liberal Education and Journalism*, 24–25.
22. "The Journalists' Creed," *University of Missouri Bulletin* (July 1930), 2.
23. *University of Missouri Catalogue, 1908–1909*, 336; also Sara Lockwood Williams, *Twenty Years of Education for Journalism* (Columbia, MO: E. W. Stephens, 1929), 80.
24. John B. Powell, "A University Course in Advertising," *Judicious Advertising* 12 (May 1914): 76.
25. Coolsen, *The Development of Systematic Instruction*, 96.

26. "Editorial," *Journalism Bulletin* 4 (1927): 25; also Albert Alton Sutton, *Education for Journalism in the United States from Its Beginning to 1940* (Evanston, IL: Northwestern University Press, 1945), 16.

27. Sutton, *Education for Journalism in the United States*, 16.

28. Lee, *Instruction in Journalism*, 27; also Sutton, *Education for Journalism in the United States*, 17.

29. John B. Powell, "Advertising As It Is Being Taught in Schools and Colleges," *Printers' Ink* 90, no. 4 (January 28, 1915): 37; also *Printers' Ink* 90, no. 6 (February 11, 1915): 65.

30. Bruce O. Bliven, "Working to Make the Teaching of Advertising More Important," *Printers' Ink* 98, no. 3 (January 18, 1917): 58.

31. Daniel Starch, "Courses in Advertising," *Journal of Political Economy* 29, no. 5 (May 1921): 411.

32. Starch, "Courses in Advertising."

33. James L. C. Ford, *A Study of the Pre-war Curricula of Selected Schools of Journalism*, PhD dissertation (Minneapolis: University of Minnesota, 1947), 81.

34. John Eighmey and Sela Sar, "Harlow Gale and the Origins of the Psychology of Advertising," *Journal of Advertising* 36, no. 4 (2007): 149.

35. Eighmey and Sar, "Harlow Gale and the Origins," 150.

36. Eighmey and Sar, "Harlow Gale and the Origins," 153.

37. Eighmey and Sar, "Harlow Gale and the Origins," 154.

38. Eighmey and Sar, "Harlow Gale and the Origins," 158.

39. Edmund C. Lynch, "Walter Dill Scott: Pioneer Industrial Psychologist," *Business History Review* 42, no. 2 (1968): 151; also C. H. Sandage, "A Pioneer in Marketing: Walter Dill Scott," *Journal of Marketing* 25, no. 5 (July 1961): 74–75.

40. Lynch, "Walter Dill Scott," 151.

41. Lynch, "Walter Dill Scott," 152.

42. Lynch, "Walter Dill Scott," 158–59.

43. Coolsen, *The Development of Systematic Instruction*, 67–68.

44. Coolsen, *The Development of Systematic Instruction*, 73–74.

45. Jo-Ida C. Hansen, "Life Lines: Edward Kellog Strong, Jr.: First Author of the Strong Interest Inventory," *Journal of Counseling and Development* 66, no. 3 (November 1987): 120.

46. Hansen, "Life Lines," 120.

47. Neil H. Borden, "Daniel Starch," *Journal of Marketing* 21, no. 3 (January 1957): 266.

48. Thomas H. Wyman, "Foreword," *Educating Managers: Executive Effectiveness through Liberal Learning*, ed. Joseph S. Johnston Jr. and colleagues (San Francisco: Jossey-Bass, 1987), 126.

49. Benjamin R. Haynes and Harry P. Jackson, *A History of Business Education in the United States* (Cincinnati, OH: South-Western, 1935), 14.

50. Haynes and Jackson, *A History of Business Education*, 25.

51. Rakesh Khurana, *From Higher Aims to Hired Hands: The Social Transformation of American Business Schools and the Unfulfilled Promises of Management as a Profession* (Princeton, NJ: Princeton University Press, 2007), 105.

52. Haynes and Jackson, *A History of Business Education*, 84.

53. Frances Ruml, "The Formative Period of Higher Commercial Education in American Universities," *The Collegiate School of Business: Its Status at the Close of the First Quarter of the Twentieth Century*, ed. L. C. Marshall (Chicago: University of Chicago Press, 1928), 54.

54. Coolsen, *The Development of Systematic Instruction*, 100–101.

55. Ruml, "The Formative Period," 55.

56. Charles J. Kiernan, "The Rise of the Collegiate School of Business," *Thought Patterns: Toward a Philosophy of Business Education*, ed. Blaise J. Opulente (Jamaica, NY: St. John's University Press, 1960), 8:4.

57. Frank C. Pierson and colleagues, *The Education of American Businessmen: A Study of University-College Programs in Business Administration* (New York: McGraw-Hill, 1959), 51; also Khurana, *From Higher Aims to Hired Hands*, 144–46.

58. Pierson and colleagues, *The Education of American Businessmen*, 47.

59. Coolsen, *The Development of Systematic Instruction*, 111–12.

60. Coolsen, *The Development of Systematic Instruction*, 59–60.

61. Coolsen, *The Development of Systematic Instruction*, 107–8.

62. J. E. Hagerty, "Experiences of an Early Marketing Teacher," *Journal of Marketing* 1, no. 1 (July 1936): 21–22.

63. Coolsen, *The Development of Systematic Instruction*, 64.

64. H. H. Maynard, "Marketing Courses Prior to 1910," *Journal of Marketing* 5, no. 4 (April 1941): 383.

65. Simon Litman, "The Beginnings of Teaching Marketing in American Universities," *Journal of Marketing* 15, no. 2 (October 1950): 220.

66. Maynard, "Marketing Courses Prior to 1910," 383.

67. Hagerty, "Experiences of an Early Marketing Teacher," 21.

68. Robert Bartels, *The History of Marketing Thought*, 2nd ed. (Columbus, OH: Grid, 1976), 22–23.

69. Robert Bartels, *The Development of Marketing Thought* (Homewood, IL: Irwin, 1962), 159–64.

70. Harold E. Hardy, "Collegiate Marketing Education since 1930," *Journal of Marketing* 19, no. 4 (April 1955), 328–29.

71. James H. S. Bossard and J. Frederic Dewhurst, *University Education for Business: A Study of Existing Needs and Practices* (New York: Arno Press, 1973; originally, 1931), 412.

72. Hardy, "Collegiate Marketing Education since 1930," 329.

73. Joseph S. Johnston Jr. and colleagues, eds., *Educating Managers: Executive Effectiveness through Liberal Learning* (San Francisco: Jossey-Bass, 1987), 127.

74. Bill I. Ross and John Schweitzer, "Most Advertising Programs Find Home in Mass Communication," *Journalism Educator* 45, no. 1 (1990): 7.

75. Paul T. Cherington, "How the Colleges Are Teaching Advertising and Selling," *Printers' Ink* 80 (July 18, 1912): 54–64; also Schultze, "'An Honorable Place,'" 29.

Selected Bibliography

Adams, Bluford. *E Pluribus Barnum: The Great Showman and the Making of U.S. Popular Culture*. Minneapolis: University of Minnesota Press, 1997.

"A. D. Lasker Dies; Philanthropist, 71." *New York Times*, May 31, 1952.

"Advertising Loses Titan as Resor Dies." *Advertising Age* 33, no. 45 (November 5, 1962).

"Aesop Glim's Clinic." *Printers' Ink*, December 3, 1948.

Albion, Robert G. *The Rise of New York Port*. New York: Charles Scribner's Sons, 1939.

Applegate, Edd, ed. *The Ad Men and Women: A Biographical Dictionary of Advertising*. Westport, CT: Greenwood Press, 1994.

Atherton, Lewis E. "The Pioneer Merchant in Mid-America." *University of Missouri Studies* 14 (April 1939).

Atwan, Robert, Donald McQuade, and John W. Wright. *Edsels, Luckies, and Frigidaires: Advertising the American Way*. New York: Dell, 1979.

Barbour, C. A. "F. W. Ayer: An Appreciation." *Watchman Examiner*, March 22, 1923.

"Barnum and Advertising." *Printers' Ink*, July 14, 1910.

"Barnum on Top as Usual." *New York Times*, November 22, 1887.

Barnum, P. T. *Barnum's Own Story: The Autobiography of P. T. Barnum*. New York: Dover, 1961.

———. *Struggles and Triumphs or, Forty Years' Recollections of P. T. Barnum*. New York: Macmillan, 1930.

"Barnum's American Museum Burns." *New York Times*, July 14, 1865.

Bartels, Robert. *The Development of Marketing Thought*. Homewood, IL: Irwin, 1962.

———. *The History of Marketing Thought*, 2nd ed. Columbus, OH: Grid, 1976.

———. "Influences on the Development of Marketing Thought, 1900–1923." *Journal of Marketing* 16, no. 1 (July 1951).

Belding, Don. "End of an Era in Advertising." *Advertising Agency and Advertising and Selling*, July 1952.

Berchtold, William E. "Men Who Sell You." *New Outlook* 165, no. 1 (January 1935).

Bleyer, Willard G. *Main Currents in the History of American Journalism*. Boston: Houghton Mifflin, 1927.

Bliven, Bruce O. "Working to Make the Teaching of Advertising More Important." *Printers' Ink* 98, no. 3 (January 18, 1917).

Blum, John M., Edmund S. Morgan, Willie L. Rose, Arthur M. Schlesinger Jr., Kenneth M. Stampp, and C. Vann Woodward. *The National Experience: A History of the United States*. New York: Harcourt Brace Jovanovich, 1981.

Bok, Edward. "A Diabolical 'Patent-Medicine' Story." *The Ladies' Home Journal*, April 1905.

———. "The 'Patent-Medicine' Curse." *The Ladies' Home Journal*, May 1904.

———. "Why 'Patent Medicines' Are Dangerous." *The Ladies' Home Journal*, March 1905.

Borden, Neil H. "Daniel Starch." *Journal of Marketing* 21, no. 3 (January 1957).

Bossard, James H. S., and J. Frederic Dewhurst. *University Education for Business: A Study of Existing Needs and Practices*. New York: Arno Press, 1973; originally, 1931.

Bradsher, Earl L. *Mathew Carey: Editor, Author and Publisher—A Study in American Literary Development*. New York: AMS Press, 1966; originally, Columbia University Press, 1912.

Bridenbaugh, Carl A. *Cities in the Wilderness*. New York: Ronald Press, 1938.

Brigham, Clarence S. *Journals and Journeymen: A Contribution to the History of Early American Newspapers*. Philadelphia: University of Pennsylvania Press, 1950.

Brown, Thompson. "Hon. John Wanamaker: From Messenger-Boy to Merchant Prince—A Romance of Business." *Our Day* 17, no. 113 (September 1897).

Bryan, J., III. *The World's Greatest Showman: The Life of P. T. Barnum*. New York: Random House, 1956.

Buckley, Kerry W. "The Selling of a Psychologist: John Broadus Watson and the Application of Behavioral Techniques to Advertising." *Journal of the History of the Behavioral Sciences* 18 (July 1982).

"Burning of Barnum's Museum." *New York Times*, March 3, 1868.

Burns, Eric. *Infamous Scribblers: The Founding Fathers and the Rowdy Beginnings of American Journalism*. New York: Public Affairs, 2006.

Burton, Jean. *Lydia Pinkham Is Her Name*. New York: Farrar, Straus, 1949.

Bushman, Richard L., and Claudia L. Bushman. "The Early History of Cleanliness in America." *Journal of American History* 74, no. 4 (March 1988).

Carson, Gerald. *The Old Country Store*. New York: Oxford University Press, 1954.

———. "Sweet Extract of Hokum." *American Heritage* 22, no. 4 (1971).

Cherington, Paul T. "How the Colleges Are Teaching Advertising and Selling." *Printers' Ink* 80 (July 18, 1912).

Cist, Charles. *Sketches and Statistics of Cincinnati in 1859*. Cincinnati, OH: n. p., 1859.

Clark, Charles E. "The Newspapers of Provincial America." *Proceedings of the American Antiquarian Society*, vol. 100. Worcester, MA: American Antiquarian Society, 1990.

Cohen, David. *J. B. Watson: The Founder of Behaviorism: A Biography*. London: Routledge & Kegan Paul, 1979.

"Colonel Springs Again." *Tide*, April 14, 1950.

Cone, Fairfax M. *With All Its Faults*. Boston: Little Brown, 1969.

Converse, Paul D. "The Development of the Science of Marketing—An Exploratory Survey." *Journal of Marketing* 10, no. 1 (July 1945).

Cook, Elizabeth Christine. *Literary Influences in Colonial Newspapers 1704–1750*. New York: Columbia University Press, 1912.

Cook, James W. *The Arts of Deception: Playing with Fraud in the Age of Barnum*. Cambridge, MA: Harvard University Press, 2001.

———. *Remedies and Rackets: The Truth about Patent Medicines Today*, with an introduction by Oliver Field. New York: Norton, 1958.

Coolsen, Frank Gordon. *The Development of Systematic Instruction in the Principles of Advertising*. MS thesis. Urbana: University of Illinois, 1942.

———. "Pioneers in the Development of Advertising." *Journal of Marketing* 12, no. 1 (July 1947).

Copeland, David A. *Colonial American Newspapers: Character and Content*. Newark: University of Delaware Press, 1997.

Courtney, Alice E., and Thomas W. Whipple. *Sex Stereotyping in Advertising*. Lexington, MA: Lexington Books, 1983.

Croll, P. C. "John Wanamaker: Merchant and Philanthropist." *The Pennsylvania-German*, January 1908.

Cruikshank, Jeffrey L., and Arthur W. Schultz. *The Man Who Sold America: The Amazing (but True) Story of Albert D. Lasker and the Creation of the Advertising Century*. Boston: Harvard Business Review Press, 2010.

Davis, Burke. *War Bird: The Life and Times of Elliott White Springs*. Chapel Hill: The University of North Carolina Press, 1987.

Dennett, Andrea Stulman. *Weird and Wonderful: The Dime Museum in America*. New York: New York University Press, 1997.

Depew, Chauncey M., ed. *One Hundred Years of American Commerce . . . a History of American Commerce by One Hundred Americans: 1795–1895*. New York: Greenwood Press, 1968; originally, D. O. Haynes, 1895.

Dill, William A. *Growth of Newspapers in the United States*. Lawrence: Department of Journalism, University of Kansas, 1928.

Dressel, Paul L. *Liberal Education and Journalism*. New York: Teachers College, 1960.

Dyer, Davis, Frederick Dalzell, and Rowena Olegario. *Rising Tide: Lessons from 165 Years of Brand Building at Procter & Gamble*. Boston: Harvard Business School Press, 2004.

"Editorial." *Journalism Bulletin* 4 (1927).

Editors of *Advertising Age*. *How It Was in Advertising: 1776–1976*. Chicago: Crain Books, 1976.

———. *Procter & Gamble: The House That Ivory Built*. Lincolnwood, IL: NTC Business Books, 1988.

Egolf, Karen. "Resor, Helen Lansdowne: 1886–1964, U.S. Advertising Pioneer." *The Advertising Age Encyclopedia of Advertising*, vol. 3 (P-Z), ed. John McDonough and the Museum of Broadcast Communication and Karen Egolf. New York: Fitzroy Dearborn, 2003.

Eighmey, John, and Sela Sar. "Harlow Gale and the Origins of the Psychology of Advertising." *Journal of Advertising* 36, no. 4 (Winter 2007).

Ellis, William T. "John Wanamaker Gave Sunday to Church and Sunday School." *North American*, December 30, 1922.

Emery, Michael, and Edwin Emery. *The Press and America: An Interpretive History of the Mass Media*. Englewood Cliffs, NJ: Prentice Hall, 1988.

Ershkowitz, Herbert. *John Wanamaker: Philadelphia Merchant*. Conshohocken, PA: Combined, 1999.

Ferry, John William. *A History of the Department Store*. New York: Macmillan, 1960.

Folkerts, Jean, and Dwight L. Teeter Jr. *Voices of a Nation: A History of Media in the United States*. New York: Macmillan, 1989.

Ford, James L. C. *A Study of the Pre-war Curricula of Selected Schools of Journalism*. PhD dissertation. Minneapolis: University of Minnesota, 1947.

Fox, Stephen. *The Mirror Makers: A History of American Advertising and Its Creators*. New York: William Morrow, 1984.

Franklin, Benjamin. "Advice to a Young Tradesman, Written by an Old One. To My Friend A. B." *The Instructor; or, Young Man's Best Companion*, 9th ed., revised and corrected, ed. George Fisher. Philadelphia: B. Franklin and D. Hall, 1748.

Frasca, Ralph. *Benjamin Franklin's Printing Network: Disseminating Virtue in Early America*. Columbia: University of Missouri Press, 2006.

Gibbons, Herbert Adams. *John Wanamaker*. Port Washington, NY: Kennikat Press, 1971; originally, 1926.

Gleed, Charles S. "John Wanamaker." *The Cosmopolitan*, May 1902.

Glynn, Prudence. *Skin to Skin: Eroticism in Dress*. New York: Oxford University Press, 1982.

Goodrum, Charles, and Helen Dalrymple. *Advertising in America: The First 200 Years*. New York: Harry N. Abrams, 1990.

Gordon, John Steele. "Redeeming Time." *American Heritage*, December 1992.

"Great Conflagration." *New York Tribune*, July 14, 1865.

"A Great Loss to Barnum." *New York Times*, November 21, 1887.

Greeley, Horace, et al. *The Great Industries of the United States: Being an Historical Summary of the Origin, Growth and Perfection of the Chief Industrial Arts of this Country*. Hartford, CT: J. B. Burr and Hyde, 1872.

Gunther, John. *Taken at the Flood: The Story of Albert D. Lasker*. New York: Harper and Brothers, 1960.

Hagerty, J. E. "Experiences of an Early Marketing Teacher." *Journal of Marketing* 1, no. 1 (July 1936).

Haller, John S. *American Medicine in Transition: 1840–1910*. Urbana: University of Illinois Press, 1981.

Hansen, Jo-Ida C. "Life Lines: Edward Kellog Strong, Jr.: First Author of the Strong Interest Inventory." *Journal of Counseling and Development* 66, no. 3 (November 1987).

Hardy, Harold E. "Collegiate Marketing Education since 1930." *Journal of Marketing* 19, no. 4 (April 1955).

Harris, Neil. *Cultural Excursions: Marketing Appetites and Cultural Tastes in Modern America*. Chicago: University of Chicago Press, 1990.

Haynes, Benjamin R., and Harry P. Jackson. *A History of Business Education in the United States*. Cincinnati, OH: South-Western, 1935.

Herzberg, Oscar. "The Evolution of Patent Medicine Advertising." *Printers' Ink*, December 25, 1895.

Hildeburn, Charles R. *Sketches of Printers and Printing in Colonial New York*. New York: Dodd, Mead, 1895.

Hoffman, Ronald. "The Press in Mercantile Maryland: A Question of Utility." *Journalism Quarterly* 46, no. 3 (1969).

Holland, Donald R. "The Adman Nobody Knows: The Story of Volney Palmer, the Nation's First Agency Man." *Advertising Age* (April 23, 1973).

———. "Volney B. Palmer (1799–1864): The Nation's First Advertising Agency Man." *Journalism Monographs*, no. 44 (1976).

———. "Volney B. Palmer: The Nation's First Advertising Agency Man." *Pennsylvania Magazine of History and Biography* 98, no. 3 (July 1974).

Hopkins, Claude C. *My Life in Advertising*. New York: Harper and Brothers, 1927.

Hower, Ralph M. *The History of an Advertising Agency: N. W. Ayer and Son at Work, 1869–1949*. Cambridge, MA: Harvard University Press, 1949.

———. "Urban Retailing 100 Years Ago." *Bulletin of the Business Historical Society* 12 (December 1938).

Hubbard, Elbert. *Lydia E. Pinkham: Being a Sketch of Her Life and Times*. East Aurora, NY: Roycrofters, 1915.

Hudson, Frederic. *Journalism in the United States*. New York: Harper and Brothers, 1873.

Hugstad, Paul S. *The Business School in the 1980s: Liberalism versus Vocationalism*. New York: Praeger, 1983.

Hume, Ruth. "Selling the Swedish Nightingale: Jenny Lind and P. T. Barnum." *American Heritage*, October 1977.

"Indelible Mark on Advertising Left by Lasker, Agency Pioneer." *Advertising Age*, June 9, 1952.

"In First 100 Years, Thompson Spurs Rise of Magazines, Agency Concept, Ad Role in Sales Strategy." *Advertising Age* 35, no. 49 (December 7, 1964).

Ingham, John N. *Biographical Dictionary of American Business Leaders: Volume N–V*. Westport, CT: Greenwood Press, 1983.

Jackson, Donald Dale. "If Women Needed a Quick Pick-Me-Up, Lydia Provided One." *Smithsonian* 15 (July 1984).

Jacobs, Laurence Wile. "Stanley B. Resor: 1879–1962." *Pioneers in Marketing: A Collection of Twenty-Five Biographies of Men Who Contributed to the Growth of Marketing through Thought and Action*, ed. John S. Wright and Parks B. Dimsdale Jr. Atlanta: Publishing Services Division, School of Business Administration, Georgia State University, 1974.

James, Theodore, Jr. "World Went Mad When Mighty Jumbo Came to America." *Smithsonian*, May 1982.

Jensen, Merrill, ed. *Tracts of the American Revolution*. Indianapolis, IN: Bobbs-Merrill, 1967.

Johnson, Emory R., T. W. Van Metre, Grover G. Huebner, David Scott Hanchett, and Henry W. Farnam. *History of Domestic and Foreign Commerce of the United States*, vol. 1. Washington, DC: Carnegie Institution, 1915.

Jones, Fred Mitchell. "Retail Stores in the United States 1800–1860." *Journal of Marketing* 1, no. 2 (October 1936).

Jones, Robert W. *Journalism in the United States*. New York: E. P. Dutton, 1947.

"The Journalists' Creed." *University of Missouri Bulletin*, July 1930.

"J. Walter Thompson Company: Known Also in the Trade as 'Thompson,' as 'J. Walter,' and as 'JWT,' but by Whichever Name the Largest Advertising Agency in the World." *Fortune* 36 (November 1947).

Katz, Stanley Nider, ed. *A Brief Narrative of the Case and Trial of John Peter Zenger, Printer of the New-York Weekly Journal*, by James Alexander. Cambridge, MA: Belknap Press of Harvard University Press, 1972.

Khurana, Rakesh. *From Higher Aims to Hired Hands: The Social Transformation of American Business Schools and the Unfulfilled Promises of Management as a Profession.* Princeton, NJ: Princeton University Press, 2007.

Kiernan, Charles J. "The Rise of the Collegiate School of Business." *Thought Patterns: Toward a Philosophy of Business Education*, ed. Blaise J. Opulente, vol. 8. Jamaica, NY: St. John's University Press, 1960.

Klein, Maury. "John Wanamaker." *American History Illustrated* 15, no. 8 (December 1980).

Knowlton, Evelyn H. *Pepperell's Progress.* Cambridge, MA: Harvard University Press, 1948.

Kobre, Sidney. *The Development of the Colonial Newspaper.* Gloucester, MA: Peter Smith, 1960.

———. "The First American Newspaper: A Product of Environment." *Journalism Quarterly* 17, no. 4 (December 1940).

———. "The Revolutionary Colonial Press—A Social Interpretation." *Journalism Quarterly* 20, no. 3 (September 1943).

Kowall, Linda. "Original and Genuine, Unadulterated and Guaranteed!" *Pennsylvania Heritage* 15, no. 1 (1989).

Kreshel, Peggy J. "The 'Culture' of J. Walter Thompson, 1915–1925." *Public Relations Review* 16, no. 3 (1990).

———. "John B. Watson at J. Walter Thompson: The Legitimation of 'Science' in Advertising." *Journal of Advertising* 19, no. 2 (1990).

Kunhardt, Philip B., Jr., Philip B. Kunhardt, III, and Peter W. Kunhardt. *P. T. Barnum: America's Greatest Showman.* New York: Knopf, 1995.

Labaree, Leonard W., ed., and Whitfield J. Bell Jr., associate ed. *The Papers of Benjamin Franklin, Volume 3: January 1, 1745, through June 30, 1750.* New Haven, CT: Yale University Press, 1961.

Labaree, Leonard W., Ralph L. Ketcham, Helen C. Boatfield, and Helene H. Fineman, eds. *The Autobiography of Benjamin Franklin*, by Benjamin Franklin. New Haven, CT: Yale University Press, 1964.

Laird, Pamela Walker. *Advertising Progress: American Business and the Rise of Consumer Marketing.* Baltimore: The Johns Hopkins University Press, 1998.

———. "The Business of Progress: The Transformation of American Advertising, 1870–1920." *Business and Economic History* 22, no. 1 (1993).

Larrabee, C. B. "The Publisher Speaks: Bad Taste Leaves a Bad Taste." *Printers' Ink*, December 10, 1948.

Larson, Cedric A. "Highlights of Dr. John B. Watson's Career in Advertising." *Industrial Organizational Psychologist* 16, no. 3 (May 1979).

———. "Patent-Medicine Advertising and the Early American Press." *Journalism Quarterly* 14, no. 4 (December 1937).

Lasker, Albert D. *The Lasker Story . . . As He Told It.* Chicago: Advertising, 1963.

———. "The Personal Reminiscences of Albert Lasker." *American Heritage*, December 1954.

———. "Reminiscences." Columbia Oral History Collection (Columbia University, 1949–1950).

"The Late Fire." *New York Times*, July 15, 1865.

Leach, William. *Land of Desire: Merchants, Power, and the Rise of a New American Culture.* New York: Pantheon Books, 1993.

———. "Transformations in a Culture of Consumption: Women and Department Stores, 1890–1925." *Journal of American History* 71, no. 2 (September 1984).

Lears, Jackson. *Fables of Abundance: A Cultural History of Advertising in America.* New York: Basic Books, 1994.

Lee, Alfred M. *The Daily Newspaper in America: The Evolution of a Social Instrument*. New York: Macmillan, 1947.

Lee, James M. *History of American Journalism*. Garden City, NY: Garden City, 1917.

———. *Instruction in Journalism in Institutions of Higher Learning*. Bulletin no. 21. Washington, DC: U.S. Department of the Interior, Bureau of Education, 1918.

Lemay, J. A. Leo, and P. M. Zall, eds. *The Autobiography of Benjamin Franklin: A Genetic Text*. Knoxville: University of Tennessee Press, 1981.

Lief, Alfred. *"It Floats": The Story of Procter & Gamble*. New York: Rinehart, 1958.

Litman, Simon. "The Beginnings of Teaching Marketing in American Universities." *Journal of Marketing* 15, no. 2 (October 1950).

Loos, Rita E. "Who Was Lydia E. Pinkham?" *New England Journal of History* 52, no. 3 (1995).

Lynch, Edmund C. "Walter Dill Scott: Pioneer Industrial Psychologist." *Business History Review* 42, no. 2 (1968).

Marchand, Roland. *Advertising the American Dream: Making Way for Modernity, 1920–1940*. Berkeley: University of California Press, 1985.

Maynard, H. H. "Early Teachers of Marketing." *Journal of Marketing* 7, no. 2 (October 1942).

———. "Marketing Courses prior to 1910." *Journal of Marketing* 5, no. 4 (April 1941).

McMahon, Michael. "An American Courtship: Psychologists and Advertising Theory in the Progressive Era." *American Studies* 13 (Fall 1972).

McNamara, Brooks. *Step Right Up*. Garden City, NY: Doubleday, 1976.

Miller, Michael B. *The Bon Marche: Bourgeois Culture and the Department Store, 1869–1920*. Princeton, NJ: Princeton University Press, 1981.

Millman, Nancy F. "The Saga of P & G's Ivory Soap: Keeping a Brand Afloat 100 Years." *Advertising Age*, April 30, 1980; originally July 2, 1979.

Mirando, Joseph A. "The First College Journalism Students: Answering Robert E. Lee's Offer of a Higher Education." Document no. ED402599. Washington, DC: Educational Resources Information Center, 1995.

Mishra, Karen E. "J. Walter Thompson: Building Trust in Troubled Times." *Journal of Historical Research in Marketing* 1, no. 2 (2009).

Montgomery, Charlotte. "The Woman's Viewpoint." *Tide* (September 10, 1948).

Mott, Frank Luther. *American Journalism: A History: 1690–1960*, 3rd ed. New York: Macmillan, 1962.

———. *A History of American Magazines: 1741–1850*. New York: D. Appleton, 1930.

"Mrs. Lydia E. Pinkham's Vegetable Compound." *British Medical Journal*, July 1, 1911.

"The Museum Fire." *New York Times*, December 26, 1872.

Nash, Vernon. *Educating for Journalism*. EdD dissertation. New York: Teachers College, 1938.

Nepa, Francesco L. "Resor, Stanley Burnet." *American National Biography*, vol. 18. John A. Garraty and Mark C. Carnes, eds. New York: Oxford University Press, 1999.

"New York Fires." *New York Times*, December 25, 1872.

Nord, David Paul. *Communities of Journalism: A History of American Newspapers and Their Readers*. Urbana: University of Illinois Press, 2001.

Norris, James D. *Advertising and the Transformation of American Society, 1865–1920*. New York: Greenwood Press, 1990.

O'Dell, De Forest. *The History of Journalism Education in the United States*. New York: Teachers College, Columbia University, Bureau of Publications, 1935.

Parker, Peter J. "The Philadelphia Printer: A Study of an Eighteenth-Century Businessman." *Business History Review* 40, no. 1 (1966).

Payne, George Henry. *History of Journalism in the United States*. Westport, CT: Greenwood Press, 1970; originally, D. Appleton, 1920.

Pettengill, S. M. "Reminiscences of the Advertising Business." *Printers' Ink*, December 24, 1890.

Pierson, Frank C., et al. *The Education of American Businessmen: A Study of University-College Programs in Business Administration*. New York: McGraw-Hill, 1959.

"Playboy of the Textile World." *Fortune*, January 1950.

Plummer, Wilbur C. "Consumer Credit in Colonial Philadelphia." *Pennsylvania Magazine of History and Biography* 67 (October 1942).

Pope, Daniel. *The Making of Modern Advertising*. New York: Basic Books, 1983.

———. "Stanley Burnet Resor: 1879–1962." *Dictionary of American Biography, Supplement 7: 1961–1965*, ed. John A. Garraty. New York: Charles Scribner's Sons, 1981.

Powell, John B. "Advertising As It Is Being Taught in Schools and Colleges." *Printers' Ink* 90, no. 4 (January 28, 1915).

———. "A University Course in Advertising." *Judicious Advertising* 12 (May 1914).

Presbrey, Frank. *The History and Development of Advertising*. New York: Doubleday, 1929.

Pulitzer, Joseph. "The College of Journalism." *North American Review* 178 (May 1904).

"The Recent Fires." *New York Times*, December 29, 1872.

Reilly, Philip J. *Old Masters of Retailing*. New York: Fairchild, 1966.

Reiss, Benjamin. *The Showman and the Slave: Race, Death, and Memory in Barnum's America*. Cambridge, MA: Harvard University Press, 2001.

"Resor Retires after 53 Years at J. W. Thompson." *Advertising Age* 32, no. 9 (February 27, 1961).

Rice, Edwin Wilbur. "Mr. Wanamaker as I Knew Him." *Sunday-School World* (March 1923).

Richardson, Lyon N. *A History of Early American Magazines 1741–1789*. New York: Octagon Books, 1966; originally, Thomas Nelson and Sons, 1931.

Root, Harvey W. *The Unknown Barnum*. New York: Harper and Brothers, 1927.

Rosenberg, Chaim M. *Goods for Sale: Products and Advertising in the Massachusetts Industrial Age*. Amherst: University of Massachusetts Press, 2007.

Ross, Bill I., and John Schweitzer. "Most Advertising Programs Find Home in Mass Communication." *Journalism Educator* 45, no. 1 (1990).

Rotzoll, Kim B., and Arnold M. Barban. "Advertising Education." *Current Issues and Research in Advertising*, vol. 2. Ann Arbor: University of Michigan Press, 1984.

Rowell, George P. *Forty Years an Advertising Agent: 1865–1905*. New York: Printers' Ink, 1906.

Rowsome, Frank, Jr. *They Laughed When I Sat Down: An Informal History of Advertising in Words and Pictures*. New York: McGraw-Hill, 1959.

Ruml, Frances. "The Formative Period of Higher Commercial Education in American Universities." *The Collegiate School of Business: Its Status at the Close of the First Quarter of the Twentieth Century*, ed. L. C. Marshall. Chicago: University of Chicago Press, 1928.

Sandage, C. H. "A Philosophy of Advertising Education." *Journalism Quarterly* 32, no. 2 (1955).

———. "A Pioneer in Marketing: Walter Dill Scott." *Journal of Marketing* 25, no. 5 (1961).

Sangster, Margaret E. "John Wanamaker at Eighty: A Personal Interview." *Christian Herald*, June 26, 1918.

Schisgall, Oscar. *Eyes on Tomorrow: The Evolution of Procter & Gamble*. Chicago: J. G. Ferguson, 1981.

Schultze, Quentin J. *Advertising, Science, and Professionalism 1885–1917*. PhD dissertation. Urbana-Champaign: University of Illinois, 1978.

———. "'An Honorable Place': The Quest for Professional Advertising Education, 1900–1917." *Business History Review* 56, no. 1 (1982).

———. "The Quest for Professional Advertising Education before 1917." Document no. ED188177. Washington, DC: Educational Resources Information Center, 1980.

Selinger, Iris Cohen. "Master Builder of Brands; for a Century and a Quarter, N. W. Ayer Has Resolutely Gone about the Business of Shaping the Images of Its Roster of Blue-Chip Clients." *Advertising Age* 65, no. 14 (April 9, 1980).

Shaw, Steven J. "Colonial Newspaper Advertising: A Step toward Freedom of the Press." *Business History Review* 33 (Autumn 1959).

Sivulka, Juliann. *Soap, Sex, and Cigarettes: A Cultural History of American Advertising*, 2nd ed. Boston: Wadsworth, Cengage Learning, 2012.

———. *Stronger Than Dirt: A Cultural History of Advertising Personal Hygiene in America, 1875 to 1940*. Amherst, NY: Humanity Books, 2001.

Sloan, Wm. David, and Julie Hedgepeth Williams. *The Early American Press, 1690–1782*, History of American Journalism 1. Westport, CT: Greenwood Press, 1994.

Smith, Jeffery A. *Printers and Press Freedom: The Ideology of Early American Journalism.* New York: Oxford University Press, 1988.

Smith, Roland B. "After Hours: Publicity Isn't Advertising." *Printers' Ink*, December 17, 1948.

Smyth, Albert H. *The Philadelphia Magazines and Their Contributors 1741–1850.* Freeport, NY: Books for Libraries Press, 1970; originally, 1892.

Sobel, Robert, and David B. Sicilia. *The Entrepreneurs: An American Adventure.* Boston: Houghton Mifflin, 1986.

"Springmaid." *Tide* (July 16, 1948).

Springs, Elliott White. *Clothes Make the Man.* New York: J. J. Little and Ives, 1949.

Stage, Sarah. *Female Complaints: Lydia Pinkham and the Business of Women's Medicine.* New York: W. W. Norton, 1979.

Starch, Daniel. "Courses in Advertising." *Journal of Political Economy* 29, no. 5 (May 1921).

Steele, Valerie. *Fashion and Eroticism: Ideals of Feminine Beauty from the Victorian Era to the Jazz Age.* New York: Oxford University Press, 1985.

The Story of the Springs Cotton Mills: 1888–1963. Fort Mill, SC: Springs Mills, 1963.

Sullivan, Mark. "Did Mr. Bok Tell the Truth?" *The Ladies' Home Journal*, January 1906.

———. *The Education of an American.* New York: Doubleday, Doran, 1938.

Sutton, Albert Alton. *Education for Journalism in the United States From Its Beginning to 1940.* Evanston, IL: Northwestern University Press, 1945.

Sutton, Denise H. *Globalizing Ideal Beauty: How Female Copywriters of the J. Walter Thompson Advertising Agency Redefined Beauty for the Twentieth Century.* New York: Palgrave Macmillan, 2009.

Swasy, Alecia. *Soap Opera: The Inside Story of Procter & Gamble.* New York: Times Books, 1993.

Tarbell, Ida M. *The Nationalization of Business 1878–1898.* New York: Macmillan, 1936.

Taylor, George Rogers. *The Transportation Revolution, 1815–1860.* New York: Holt, Rinehart and Winston, 1951.

Taylor, James D. "Elliott White Springs—Maverick Ad Leader." *Journal of Advertising* 11, no. 2 (1982).

Tebbel, John, and Mary Ellen Zuckerman. *The Magazine in America 1741–1990.* New York: Oxford University Press, 1991.

Teeter, Dwight L., Jr. "John Dunlap: The Political Economy of a Printer's Success." *Journalism Quarterly* 52 (Spring 1975).

"Textile Tempest." *Time*, July 26, 1948.

Thomas, Charles M. "The Publication of Newspapers during the American Revolution." *Journalism Quarterly* 9, no. 4 (December 1932).

Thomas, Isaiah. *The History of Printing in America, with a Biography of Printers in Two Volumes.* New York: Burt Franklin, n.d.; originally, 1874.

"Tide Leadership Survey." *Tide*, August 27, 1948.

Trytten, John M. "Sex in Advertising: The Easy Way Out!" *Sales Management*, May 28, 1973.

Tungate, Mark. *Ad Land: A Global History of Advertising.* London: Kogan Page, 2007.

Turner, E. S. *The Shocking History of Advertising.* New York: E. P. Dutton, 1953.

Vinikas, Vincent. *Soft Soap, Hard Sell: American Hygiene in an Age of Advertisement.* Ames: Iowa State University Press, 1992.

Wallace, Irving. *The Fabulous Showman: The Life and Times of P. T. Barnum.* New York: Knopf, 1959.

Ware, W. Porter, and Thaddeus C. Lockard Jr. *P. T. Barnum Presents Jenny Lind.* Baton Rouge: Louisiana State University Press, 1980.

Washburn, Robert Collyer. *Life and Times of Lydia Pinkham.* New York: G. P. Putnam's Sons, 1931.

———. "Lydia Pinkham." *The American Mercury* 22, no. 86 (February 1931).

Weld, L. D. H. "Early Experience in Teaching Courses in Marketing." *Journal of Marketing* 5, no. 1 (April 1941).

Werner, M. R. *Barnum.* New York: Harcourt, Brace, 1923.

Whaley, Lauren. "The Plan 75 Years in the Making." *Planet JH Weekly*, May 7, 2004.

Whipple, Leon. "Journalism." *The Survey 60*, June 1, 1928.

Wicke, Jennifer. *Advertising Fictions: Literature, Advertisement, and Social Reading*. New York: Columbia University Press, 1988.

Williams, Sara Lockwood. *Twenty Years of Education for Journalism*. Columbia, MO: E. W. Stephens, 1929.

Wood, James Playsted. *Magazines in the United States*, 3rd ed. New York: Ronald Press, 1971.

———. "A Pioneer in Marketing: Stanley Resor." *Journal of Marketing* 25, no. 6 (1961).

———. *The Story of Advertising*. New York: Ronald Press, 1958.

Wright, Louis B. *The Cultural Life of the American Colonies 1607–1763*. New York: Harper and Brothers, 1957.

Wyman, Thomas H. Foreword. *Educating Managers: Executive Effectiveness through Liberal Learning*, ed. Joseph S. Johnston Jr. and colleagues. San Francisco: Jossey-Bass, 1987.

Yaeger, Dan. "The Lady Who Helped Ladies." *Yankee* 53, no. 9 (1989).

Young, James Harvey. *The Toadstool Millionaires: A Social History of Patent Medicines in America before Federal Regulation*. Princeton, NJ: Princeton University Press, 1961.

Index

About the Author

Edd Applegate has taught undergraduate and graduate courses in advertising and mass communications at Middle Tennessee State University and other universities and colleges. Prior to teaching, he worked in public relations for a state educational organization, for which he wrote numerous articles that were published in various newspapers.

Applegate has written several books, including *Journalism in the United States: Concepts and Issues* (2011), *The Advocacy Journalists: A Biographical Dictionary of Writers and Editors* (2009), *Muckrakers: A Biographical Dictionary of Writers and Editors* (2008), and *Strategic Copywriting: How to Create Effective Advertising* (2004), to mention a few. He coauthored with Art Johnsen *Cases in Advertising and Marketing Management: Real Situations for Tomorrow's Managers* (2006). He contributed to and edited *The Ad Men and Women: A Biographical Dictionary of Advertising* (1994).

He has contributed numerous chapters and entries to other books and encyclopedias. His scholarly research and reviews of books have appeared in *American Journalism*, *ASJMC INSIGHTS*, *CHOICE*, *Resources in Education*, *Feedback*, *JACA: Journal of the Association for Communication Administration*, *Journal of Advertising Education*, *Journalism and Mass Communication Educator*, *Journalism and Mass Communication Quarterly*, *Journalism History*, *Journalism Studies*, and *Public Relations Quarterly*, among other academic journals. Other scholarly research has been presented at academic conferences and published in various proceedings, including those published by the American Academy of Advertising, the International Academy of Business Disciplines, and the Marketing Management Association.

Applegate has received grants and fellowships from the Freedom Forum Media Studies Center, the Gannett Foundation, the Missouri Commission on Humanities, the National Endowment for the Humanities, the American Association of Advertising Agencies, the American Press Institute, the Donald and Geraldine Hedberg Foundation, the Direct Marketing Educational Foundation, and other organizations.

He received his doctorate from Oklahoma State University. He has continued his formal education at Pennsylvania State University and Vanderbilt University, among other universities.

Applegate helped develop numerous articles and create hundreds of advertisements for several college and university publications. He has helped more than twenty-five clients in middle Tennessee improve their communications and advertising.

Lightning Source UK Ltd.
Milton Keynes UK
UKHW021356250422
402024UK00015B/195